THE HERITAGE OF THE
REFORMATION

THE
HERITAGE OF THE
REFORMATION

ESSAYS COMMEMORATING
THE CENTENNIAL
OF EDEN THEOLOGICAL SEMINARY

Edited By

ELMER J. F. ARNDT

RICHARD R. SMITH

NEW YORK   1950

Copyright, 1950, By

RICHARD R. SMITH PUBLISHER, INC.

120 East 39th Street, New York 16, N. Y.

TYPOGRAPHY BY BROWN BROTHERS LINOTYPERS

PRINTED IN THE UNITED STATES OF AMERICA

BY THE FERRIS PRINTING COMPANY

TO THE ALUMNI

OF

EDEN THEOLOGICAL SEMINARY

CONTENTS

INTRODUCTION 9

THE RECURRING PROTESTANT SPIRIT 14
By Allen G. Wehrli

THE LIVING WORD IN THE SCRIPTURES 35
By Herbert H. Wernecke

BIBLICAL MOTIFS IN REFORMATION THE-
OLOGY 59
By Allen O. Miller

JESUS THE CHRIST, OUR LORD 81
By Samuel D. Press

SACRAMENTAL FELLOWSHIP 101
By Elmer J. F. Arndt

PROCLAIMING THE WORD 125
By Frederick W. Schroeder

LITURGICAL FREEDOM AND LITURGICAL
REFORM 143
By Purd E. Deitz

THE NEW REFORMATION AND PRAYER 167
By John Biegeleisen

EDUCATION, CHRISTIAN EDUCATION, AND
THE REFORMATION 187
By Harold A. Pflug

EVANGELICAL AND PROTESTANT ETHICS 211
By H. Richard Niebuhr

THE ECUMENICAL REALITY OF THE CHURCH 230
By Carl E. Schneider

THE RELEVANCE OF REFORMATION DOC-
TRINE IN OUR DAY 249
By Reinhold Niebuhr

INTRODUCTION

WHEN the preparation of a volume of essays to mark the Centennial of Eden Theological Seminary was urged by the alumni, the theme for the book practically suggested itself. The founders of the seminary brought with them the heritage of the continental Reformation and a conviction of the fundamental unity of the Lutheran and Reformed traditions. Their commitment to Evangelical Christianity in an irenic and what we now call an ecumenical spirit provided the direction which has characterized the seminary through its century of work. Thus the concentration in these essays on the heritage associated with the names of Luther, Zwingli, and Calvin is an expression of historical connection; it does not imply a lack of appreciation of those movements associated with other names on the continent of Europe and in Britain which also have so richly contributed to the Protestant heritage; nor does it involve a disregard of the Christian movement before the Protestant Reformation.

The characteristic spirit of the school, with which the authors are in various ways associated, determined the manner of treatment exemplified in these essays. They express in various ways a great appreciation of the Reformation. The Reformers, in their several ways, presented and proclaimed the evangelical character of Christianity. They cut through the encrustations of historical accretions to the gospel of the free and sovereign grace of God in Christ given to faith. They subjected the liturgy, doctrine, institutions, and life of the church to the New Testament. The Reformation is, indeed, a historical movement, internally com-

plex, intricately related to other movements—intellectual, cultural, social, and political—contemporaneous with it. Like other
movements in human life, it is historically conditioned. But it
was and is something more than a historical event. It was a
movement of the Spirit summoning men to yield themselves
without reservation to Christ the Lord and Savior and to subject
the whole of life to his lordship.

The sixteenth century Reformation needs to be understood in
the total context of God's acts in human history. History, like
nature, is a sphere in which God acts. In it he manifests his freedom, his initiative, his judgment, his redemptive purpose, and
his lordship. He calls men and nations to serve him; but he
does not become dependent on their service; he provides means
of grace; but he does not divest himself of his personal action.
In the Protestant Reformation that same grace and judgment,
which have always characterized the action of God, are manifested. As he manifested his freedom in his dealings with Israel
of old and interpreted his action through his prophets, so again
in the Reformation, in dealing with the church in western
Europe, he manifested his freedom.

Such an understanding of the sixteenth century Reformation
obviously has important implications for Protestantism itself. If
Protestant churchmen perceive clearly the element of pretension
in the claims of the Roman Catholic Church, they need to be
alert also to the temptations of prideful pretension and false
security within the Protestant churches. The recovery of the
gospel and the reform of worship and life, which together constituted the sixteenth century Reformation, is not a possession
undergirding a claim to superiority but a heritage to be appropriated in living obedience to the present demands of the Lord
of life. The responsibility confronting Protestant churches is not
met by the repetition of formulations of the sixteenth century or

by the exclusive preoccupation with its controversies. The dynamic of the Reformation, not the historically conditioned deposit of the dynamic, is the vital heritage; and the present task is to give expression to that dynamic in coming to grips with the issues and responsibilities of contemporary occasions. Certainly this does not mean disregard of the past or contempt for the Reformers' work. It does mean fidelity to the spirit of the Reformation in the freedom with which Christ set us free. It means that the same Spirit of God, who spake through the prophets and who ever works in the church effecting reformations, demands of us the living appropriation of the past in confrontation with the present, not the preservation of a dead past—no matter how perfect the process of preservation. "The letter killeth, but the spirit maketh alive."

Such an understanding of our twentieth century relation to the sixteenth century Reformation is equally removed from the evaluation of it as a misfortune to which all the ills of contemporary society in the West are to be traced and from the other extreme which is mainly preoccupied with reiterations of its crystallizations. Rather does it point the way to a much more difficult, but necessary, attitude and task: the continuous subjection of our liturgies, doctrines, institutions, and life to the judgment of the New Testament and the constant rededication of the church to the service of its living Lord. The historical impact and the teaching of the Reformation are certainly important; yet it is in the first instance a movement of the Spirit which summons men to yield themselves to Christ and subject the whole of life to his lordship. It is not a legacy automatically received by natural descent.

The Reformation was a movement which was inspired and empowered by a fresh apprehension of Evangelical Christianity: the message preached with passionate conviction that "God was in Christ reconciling the world unto himself," that God, the Holy One, is gracious. Christianity is the message of God's action in Christ for man's redemption; it is not a philosophy, though it has furnished much to philosophy; it is not a system of theology, though systems of theology have been elaborated to express its meaning and develop its implications; it is not an institution, though it has given rise to institutions which more or less ambiguously reflect and embody it. It has been and is a message with astonishing power to transform ancient cultures, to inspire new cultures, to reform the life of the churches, to cause upheavals which broke the existing unity because it was too small for its fullness, and to inaugurate and vitalize movements for more inclusive unity. The movement for a more inclusive unity in our own generation draws its deepest inspiration from the prophetic character of the Evangelical Christianity which the medieval unity could not include. The unity sought is a twofold one: on the one hand, it expresses itself against the practices of racial, class, and national discrimination and segregation; for justice and human rights in the social order; and for a world order in which force is subordinated to law; on the other hand, it expresses itself in the ecumenical movement looking toward the recognition in actuality as well as in spirit of the unity of Christians in Christ with all that involves for doctrine, worship, and institutional order.

It is such a dynamic understanding of the sixteenth century Reformation which gives to the following essays such unity as they possess. It is the unity, not of a common theme or agreement in detail, but of orientation or perspective. It is a unity which provides amply for individual variation as well as community of purpose. Perhaps it is best expressed in the Pauline phrase, "the unity of the Spirit," which embraces variety of functions and diversity of gifts and which stresses both the source of such unity as we now have and the wider unity for which he hope. *Veni, creator spiritus!*

* * * * *

Thanks are due to Miss Phyllis Widicus for her competent and conscientious work in making the typescript. Not only did Miss Widicus type the final draft of the essays but also, in most instances, typed preliminary drafts from handwritten manuscripts.

E. J. F. A.

THE RECURRING PROTESTANT SPIRIT

Allen G. Wehrli

IN large sections of the Protestant world it has become customary to speak of *the* Reformation as if there had been but one. And once observed and considered, this is a phenomenon that one contemplates with increasing distress, because it has some very definite and unfortunate implications. For in its more overt forms this fixation demands with insistence that all theological doctrines conform somehow to the pattern set in the sixteenth century and that all rites and ceremonies as well as the foundation of ecclesiastical orders be in harmony with the institutions created by the heroes of the Protestant Reformation. It is probably seldom realized, even among the faithful, that attitudes of this kind magnify the events of the sixteenth century above those of any other, including the first. It is furthermore patent that exclusive preoccupation with the results ecclesiastical issuing from the vital church life of the sixteenth century has bequeathed to all subsequent Protestantism a tenacious atmosphere of controversy, in which the very names of Zwingli, Luther, and Calvin suggest that there is something permanently irreconcilable even among the Protestant elements within the larger body of Christ.

The foregoing observations, however, by no means imply that the Protestant Reformation of the sixteenth century was unimportant. Nor are we tempted thereby to minimize in any way its outstanding spiritual achievements. We grant without reservation its liberating force in matters of religious faith and its vitalizing power in the realm of human devotion. In fact it is difficult to over-emphasize the impulse it loosed in the direction of inward freedom, or to over-stress the new sense of God's nearness and accessibility which it ushered in. Yet these things which are the chief glory of the Protestant Reformation are in no sense the peculiar creation of the sixteenth century. At best and essentially they are recaptured treasures, spiritual gifts given in the long ago but long since lost to an *ecclesia* whose faith had cooled into doctrine, whose piety had petrified into rite, and whose every spiritual ministry had been surrendered to a hierarchy. Thus the chief values and the stirring events of the Protestant Reformation point back to similar values but to different events, in other centuries and in other ages. Specifically the great Reformers, one and all, look back to other days and other ages in order to replenish the equipment with which they were asked to face life and its realities. With peculiar diligence they studied the Scriptures, particularly the New Testament, in order to discover the essential spirit and the true nature of the early New Testament Church. Accordingly, it is the events of the first century which give shape largely to those which took place in the sixteenth.

The unique religious character, therefore, of the sixteenth century lies not in the fact that it was the sixteenth, as differentiated from every other. Nor does its chief claim to fame reside in the formulations of truth and the patterns of practice and organization which arose within it. Neither does its importance rest upon the peculiar church institutions which were born while it lasted. The fact that again, with vigor and discernment, it laid hold upon truths and values which transcend the centuries gives to it its unique character.

In our time, there are upon us both the necessity and the hope of an ecumenical church. It goes without saying that that necessity cannot be met nor can the hope be realized so long as our common faith continues as the helpless prisoner of multifarious varieties of doctrinal formulation. Even so, our definitely diverse forms of worship, however and whenever authenticated, will continue to militate against the creation of a universal fellowship of believers. Under such circumstances it will not do for each constituent Protestant group, in conference and discussion, to contribute nothing more than a restatement and a re-emphasis of its traditional heritage. Nor will it be sufficient to go back to *the* Reformation. For in both cases our horizons will be too largely filled with historical forms—old enough to be tyrannical in their demands and yet not sufficiently universal to promote brotherhood effectively. If then we cast our vision over a broader area, back to vital periods in Christian and Israelite history, we shall increase our chances of laying hold upon what is imperishable in *the* Reformation, while at the same time we shall be extricating ourselves from the more temporary cast of its historically conditioned forms.

RECURRENT CHARACTERISTICS

This broader period more or less arbitrarily chosen begins in the eighth and seventh centuries before Christ with the events that eventuated in the Deuteronomic Reform. In various significant ways the Deuteronomic Reformation of the seventh century before Christ affords parallels to the situation, the problems, and the achievements of the Protestant Reformation of the sixteenth century. In addition to the two reformations thus mentioned, and beween them chronologically, there are two other vital periods in the annals of the Judeo-Christian tradition which should come under review at the same time. The first of these is the brief but all-important period of the ministry of Jesus of Nazareth. The second, not long afterwards, is the precarious age in which St. Paul's struggle with the Judean Christians took place. In a basic sense these periods also may be termed periods of reformation. For in spite of differences between them, all four of these uniquely vital periods exhibit characteristics which offer parallel situations and therefore contribute to our understanding of the nature of religious reformation per se.

When, therefore, these four recurring instances of the reformation experience are contemplated together we may note that every reformation worthy of the name is rooted first of all in a profound sense of dissatisfaction with the existing or contemporary religious institution. In the Deuteronomic Reformation this dissatisfaction is exemplified by the eighth and seventh century prophets' denunciation of the sanctuaries, the sacrificial system, and the priesthood of Israel's official religion, which brought about the reformation itself. In a similar way the life and teachings of Jesus brought him into conflict with the official custodians of the Torah of his day. After a time this dissatisfaction drew from him sharp criticism of the leading groups and the controlling minds. It brought him into conflict with the Pharisees whose teachings he branded as misrepresentations of the truth. Very definitely he criticized the abuse to which the temple had been subjected. And primarily he called into question the validity of religious results and values which were accepted by his official contemporaries as standard.

As for St. Paul, we find him but a short generation later vigorously opposing the leaders of the young Christian Church to whom the direction of its affairs and the definition of its functions and activities had meanwhile fallen. To him Peter and the other Judean leaders who controlled the institution and directed its life were falling short of what the gospel of Jesus Christ required. In the case of the Protestant Reformers, we find that it was men such as Zwingli, Luther, and Calvin who, in a sense, brought to conclusion and focus a process of criticism which had long been directed against the official Catholic Church of their time. In this instance it was notably the hierarchy against which their strictures were directed. They placed the chief blame for the perversion of the faith and the corruption of the Church upon the official priesthood. This protest culminated necessarily in an attack upon the papacy of Rome.

In all four of these situations profound dissatisfaction concerns itself with two things. For one, the existing church is criticized for what it neglects to proclaim and to nurture in the life of its people and in the world. Secondly, it is accused of emphases that are one-sided, and therefore distorted, and of activities that are inadequate, hence largely inconsequential. Both of these conditions result in a caricature of the virtue and piety which the institution normally claims to be fostering.

Thus the prophets found Israel's official religion neglecting to proclaim the righteousness of their God, omitting to emphasize the concern of man for his neighbor as well as ignoring widespread immorality among the people. And matching these delinquencies, on the positive side, was the corrupt worship at the sanctuaries where joy in the Lord had been utterly distorted into gluttonous and lustful revelry; while the priests all but promoted sin in order to swell church income from penalties at fixed rates.

On this point, the situation in the case of Jesus seems to be particularly clear. With vividness he charged those who opposed him with leaving undone the weightier matters of the law, such as justice, mercy, and faith, in favor of more trivial matters such as the tithing of mint, anise, and cummin. In similar vein, he all but scourged those whose excessive zeal for peripheral matters imposed the same observance of inconsequential externals on the proselyte for whose conversion they were prepared to compass land and sea; and he accused them simultaneously of making of such a convert twofold more a son of hell than themselves. Thus official neglect and standard distortion are vividly mingled together.

St. Paul's charges against his Judaizing opponents are no less serious. They were emerging as custodians of the faith which had been committed to the fellowship. As such their activities constituted the process by which the new faith was being molded into doctrine and by which the forms of devotion were being cast. And concerning them he was eloquently certain that the mold they were casting for the glorious gospel of Jesus Christ was too small, that the thing most distinctive was being left out or neglected, that the grace of God which is essentially free was being cast aside in favor of an ancient compliance with the regulations of the Torah. Doctrinally then, as well as practically, they were omitting essentials and creating, perhaps unwittingly yet actually, the caricature of the very thing that they had set out to mold. For St. Paul those whom he criticized were really attempting to contain him whom the heaven of heavens cannot contain.

For the Reformers of the sixteenth century the pattern of their criticism is basically similar, although the application of the reforming principle finds expression in different ways. Faith in God, said their critique of the church, is almost totally absent from the things which the church attempts to produce. Direct reliance upon him in life's vicissitudes, yes, even the foundation-truth that God is available to any and all of those who seek him, is completely obscured. The natural corollary of such neglect and omission, they continued to charge, is the fateful substitution of the church for the Scriptures and of the hierarchy for the Deity.

From all of this one is perhaps justified in concluding that the process of reducing the faith to tenets and doctrines, that the shaping of forms for the expression of religious piety, and that the distribution of function as among classes of believers are always fraught with danger and are periodically in need of reform. Without such self-criticism one is tempted to say that any church, and every faith, will fall victim to its own processes of definition and organization and will finally succumb to the temptation of making itself more important than God.

Portrait of the Reformer

Turning now to the individuals who emerge as the leaders of reform movements and to a consideration of the persons in whom the basic striving for correction of evils is embodied, we are moved to assert that every reformer, worthy of the name, is essentially someone from within the tradition who has been awakened to the serious inadequacies of his established religion or church and has become sensitive to its unfortunate official fruits. Almost without exception he is one who has become aware, or has received a revelation of the intrinsic character, the original nature, and content of the faith of which the institution claims the custody. Second, he claims and proclaims its continuing validity and availability and he accuses the church of his time of neglecting its treasures in favor of compromise with existing powers and lesser concerns. Third, he is essentially a spirit divinely stirred to effort and activity which he is personally unable to evade or shirk. Fourth, his spirit is catching and presently he has become, without originally wanting to, the living center of a group which on its fringes swells or shrinks according to its fate at the hands of men.

Through the centuries the prophets of Israel uniformly assert that to them has come a new awareness, a disconcerting awareness, a fresh revelation of the eternal Jehovah. None of them,

with the possible exception of the Second Isaiah, ever claims to
have received a *new* revelation. Always they assert that what
they have seen, that what Jehovah has now showed them anew,
was always available. Their assumption invariably is that the
treasures they proclaim have now been rediscovered, that the
faith newly apprehended is an ancient thing, which has suffered
neglect at the hands of those whose obligation it had been to preserve it and to promulgate it in season and out of season. They
are eminently conscious that they themselves are not tinkering
with the faith. Instead they are convinced that they are criticiz-
ing those who have, in one way or another, succeeded in moving
it away from its true base. Their task, as they see it, is to re-
construct what has been distorted, to restore what has been lost,
to embody in contemporary form what is vital and abiding,
to teach the content and to live the essence of the *ancient*
faith.

Even in the case of Jesus, whose surpassing uniqueness is
beyond dispute, we have one who disclaims every intention of
having come to destroy the law and the prophets. Although he
vividly contrasts what he himself teaches with that which they
of old time have said, he nevertheless insists that he had come
to fulfill the law, not to destroy it. He too preached a new
awareness of the eternal God and came as the intimate embodiment of the gospel of salvation inherent in the nature of the
Father from the beginning. He too proclaimed the original
nature of the ancient faith now constricted in rigid, temporary
forms. He revived its essential content and pointed forward to
its hitherto unrealized implications. Far from annihilating what
had been in matters of religion, he literally "filled full" the
faith, to the point of bursting, with what God had intended
from the beginning. What we have come to call new in him
was based definitely and securely upon that which was already

come. Even as of the prophets it can be especially said of Jesus that he arose within the tradition. Furthermore, it seems to be evident that he remained within the tradition, confining his activities, limiting his preaching and teaching, concentrating his efforts almost entirely upon those who were Jews like himself. He claimed to have been sent primarily to seek the lost sheep of the House of Israel. His contacts with Tyre and Sidon, for example, and his presence within the Decapolis were exceptional occurrences. A mission to the Gentiles, as far as Jesus himself was concerned, seemed never to have been a part of his program.

As we come to a consideration of the person of St. Paul there are some apparent variations from the usual pattern. Yet in spite of his long and vehement adherence to the particularisms of the Judaistic faith, he is nevertheless a critic of the young Christian Church who criticizes from within the ranks. It is essentially as a *Christian* that he finds fault with the newly emerged Christian Church. Unlike the prophets, unlike Jesus, and unlike the Protestant Reformers—all of whom together castigated evils of century-long standing, all of whom tugged at and tussled with rigidly entrenched ecclesiastical institutions, time-honored and demonstrably authoritative—St. Paul found himself face to face with similar things in less ancient form. In fact, the inadequacies within the young Christian Church to which he could point and the doctrines and practices concerning which he had become so apprehensive were still in the process of formation. The Church was too young as yet to have attained anything like final form for its doctrines or rigid regulations with regard to its practices. In a sense it was still in the stage of early formative development although that process had gone an alarmingly great distance in the direction of narrow rigidity for one so sensitive to basic essentials as was St. Paul.

Yet fundamentally, one is compelled to say, he was fighting the same *kind* of enemies that the other reformers fought. For them their respective churches had "arrived" whereas, for him his church was threatening quickly to do the identical thing. Thus the apparent differences in the pattern of St. Paul's experience from those of the others discussed are merely differences of condition and circumstance rather than differences in nature and essence. Fundamentally he is fighting the same battle they fought, he is interested in the same kind of values that fascinated their interest and compelled their devotion. In this connection it must also be pointed out that in spite of his great reputation as an innovator, as one whose creative genius made of Christianity a potentially world-wide fellowship, St. Paul was nevertheless in a wholesome sense a traditionalist. For invariably he first brought his gospel of Christ crucified, risen and ascended, to the Jewish communities within the larger Gentile world. Thus always his mission was begun, in every new community that he could reach, although the inevitable logic of the universal Christian Gospel consistently drove him beyond the bounds of any sectarian community.

As for the persons of such men as Zwingli, Luther, and Calvin it can readily be demonstrated, and frequently has been, that their original aims and efforts were concerned with the reformation of *the* church to which they belonged. It is a matter of record that no one of them had set out, to begin with, to establish another separate church. That, as a result of their reformatory labors, new and separate ecclesiastical institutions resulted was in no sense due to a conscious founding activity. They can be said to have been motivated solely by an overwhelming desire to cleanse and purify the Church of Jesus Christ on earth. And it is perhaps not too much to add that they were personally distressed when their efforts failed to accomplish this result.

As for the second point in our analysis of individual reformers, it is legitimate to claim that all of them had hopes for
"their" church, however corrupt it had come to be. In it they
worked with consummate devotion and within it they hoped
to continue to live. What distressed every one of them was the
compromises that had been made with the powers of this
world, with potentates domestic as well as foreign, and the
growing preoccupation of the church with matters increasingly
petty and with concerns more and more external.

Concerning the third point, it can be said of all of the ancient
prophets that they were gripped by the living spirit of God and
under its compulsion any one of them could have said what
Amos actually put into words, namely: "The Lord hath spoken,
who can but prophecy?" For Jesus, oneness with the Father
was a constant condition so that His will and the Father's were
always and forever identical. St. Paul, claimed and driven by
the same divine impulsion, was moved to exclaim: "Woe is me
if I preach not the gospel." While for the sixteenth century the
words of Martin Luther: "I can do no other," are indicative of
the experience that was a common possession of all the eminent
Reformers.

In the fourth place, it seems to be a historical inevitability
that individuals thus inflamed by the spirit of God become
centers of a fellowship, formed in each case, around the individual to whom the new spiritual charge had come. With
reference to Israel's prophets, the evidence is but fragmentary;
yet the fact that Isaiah is known to have had disciples and the
further fact that the impetus of the prophetic movement continued to live and to grow seems clearly to indicate that Israel's
spiritual giants never stood really alone. With regard to Jesus
and St. Paul, the evidence is abundant and direct that around
them significant groups were formed which could be counted

upon to keep alive and to propagate the vision and the work of the central personality. That, finally, the Protestant Reformers had followers is only too evident. That these were imbued with essentially the same spirit which animated the respective central personality is also abundantly observable. Furthermore, it is clear that in all of these cases the number of adherents that may cluster about the gigantic central figures seems to be utterly unimportant. And the influence exerted by the company, large or small, is completely out of proportion to whatever the numbers involved may be. For each of the several discipleships there is also an accompanying and fluctuating fringe. Regardless of how potent a spiritual enterprise may really be, there always attach to it varying grades of more or less faithful adherents. And the numbers swell or diminish, respectively, according to the price which loyalty entails.

THE PRIORITY OF THE POSITIVE

In reformations positive affirmation generally seems to antedate actual protest. Yet actual protest inevitably comes later as a result of official resistance to the vitalized restatement of that part of the religious heritage which contradicts contemporary practice and its resultant teaching. Criticism from outside any organization can do little directly toward the improvement of that organization. At best it can help to inform and to impress the sensitive spirits within a fellowship with the need for a reformation and the direction in which it ought to go. But genuine reform and creative betterment in the shape of honest protest almost always occurs within the institution or the fellowship itself. In each of the situations under review that condition obtains.

It was from within that Israel's prophets, goaded by the imperfections of their religion and appalled by its evident abuses, undertook to re-form their church. And at least to the extent that they announced Jehovah as coming, or as about to do something in the earth, their initial activity was always positive. The great ones among them never gave themselves to programs for partial improvement, their interest was never commanded by slight revisions upward, and they were not given to mere amelioration of evil. With unmistakable clarity they called for total regeneration and for a wholehearted return to obedience to the entire will of God. That type of procedure must be rated as positive and as basically creative even though their initial predictions more often than not sounded like the very crack of doom and usually called for destruction, by God himself, of a sinful kingdom, or of a people become godless. Subsequently, however, and inevitably, their activity came to aim directly at the constituted authorities of the established national religion, not because the prophet's preaching was negative, but rather because the authorities inevitably opposed any reforms that were so evidently drastic and total. Thus actual attack is in reality produced, at least partially, by official resistance on the part of controlling powers.

The early part of the ministry of Jesus is, as far as we can see, practically devoid of conflict with officialdom. Here too, and eminently so, the teaching of the Master took the form of positive affirmation. By precept and in practice Jesus taught and demonstrated that God the Father is good; that he is just, always and everywhere; that he cares for the sinner, and even seeks him out; that no repentant soul who turns to him will be turned away. Through the great teacher it became clearly evident also that no man could earn his salvation no matter what the extent of his so-called merits might be. Yet all men, however undeserving, could come to the Father to receive his forgiveness and to enjoy his salvation. Such preaching and teaching did not at once meet with official protest. But, when people responded and began to believe and started to act on the basis of their belief, then the new teacher was looked at askance and subsequently persecuted because his preaching disagreed with and disavowed the current interpretation of the church of his time. Therefore, without benefit of direct attack on his part, Jesus was branded by the opposition as the enemy of religion and as one who misled the people. Generally, then, it is in response to attack upon himself and upon his teachings that Jesus rebukes and denounces his detractors. Thus only when he and his disciples are directly set upon by the Pharisees and Scribes does he accuse their tradition of nullifying the very law of God. Here again, then, the pattern is the same. Protest against the established religion, whose functioning was hopelessly mechanical, followed upon a ministry of teaching which had been positive, creative, and purifying. Once more the reformer's direct action is in the nature of counter-attack against the institutions that resist reform and remaking.

In much the same way St. Paul's early career is taken up with the positive proclamation of the gospel of Jesus Christ. After the initial embarrassment, incident to his own period of violent antagonism to the Christian fellowship, he is evidently accepted by the brethren and permitted to work under the blessing of the fellowship, untrammelled by any other authority than that of his own direct commission. As with the others, so in St. Paul's experience, conflict with the church as such comes later. After he has worked, subsequent to his preaching, and not until Gentiles have been converted and included in the churches which he established, does the occasion for the conflict arise. Only when his judgment concerning those worthy of inclusion in the congregations is challenged, when right-wing committees from the Jewish branch of the church in "correct" Jerusalem visited his congregations and presumed to reject such among the flock as he had accepted, only then does he rebel with vigor against the emerging order within the church. With him the question of whether Jewish law should determine eligibility for membership in the Christian church was not an academic one. As a vital issue within Christendom it arose after the fact; it became vital only when it was put to the practical test. St. Paul's stand against the venerable Peter and his opposition to the Jerusalem church was not a matter of dialectic preference with him. It had become an issue destined to determine the official doctrine of the Christian religion. And it arose at a time when the young church was in danger of slipping back to something which in the previous generation had been successfully eliminated. Thus, again, only when the very nature of the Christian religion was in danger, did St. Paul do battle against the official authorities within the church.

Turning once more to the chief individuals of the Protestant Reformation we find very largely the same sequence of events. They too reaffirmed the content, defined, and brought forth the essential nature of Christian teaching and life because they were convinced that these things had been long neglected and practically eliminated from the on-going life of the Church. With them too, the initial drive and the sole purpose of their early efforts was a creative one—to restore within the church those things spiritual that belonged. As in the other instances cited, their overt attack upon the Roman Church came subsequently, after that church had challenged their claims and opposed their efforts. In one way or another their contest with the hierarchy, their feud with the pope, was in the nature of counter-attack and that feud, by and by, became a part of their reformatory efforts. From the beginning there was no thought in their mind of schism within the church.

EFFECTS OF REFORMATION

By and large the results spiritual, following upon any genuine reformatory activity, are similar. The results historical, however, are sometimes vastly different. On the historical level principally two types of outcome ensue. The struggle produced by the reform movement in a group may resolve itself within the church. In that case somehow the storm is weathered. The crisis passes and, in one way or another, factions previously hostile slowly find their natural way toward peace. Failing that, the result may be schism. This can be due to a variety of factors. It may be that the issues at the base of the struggle are too profound to admit of peaceful resolution. It may also be that the human factor, the intransigence of the principal leaders of opposing forces, prevent the contending factions from finding their way back to common ground. Whatever the reason, in this case the result is division.

Sometimes separation comes comparatively quickly. In other instances the road to complete division is long. Still, whether the struggle resolves itself within the fellowship or whether it results in division is of secondary importance spiritually, since the essential value of any significant reform lies in the circumstance that the dead bones of the classic faith are once more infused with life. This salutary effect is achieved to a great degree whenever a church can weather a reformation without ensuing division. But even when the storm is not weathered, after separation has resulted, spiritual renewal is nevertheless achieved. Such a result would be assumed for the protesting, reforming group. And the assumption would have substantial validity. But it would have substance also in the remaining group. Although officially opposed to the attempted reform and successfully withstanding its enactment within the whole fellowship, the religiously orthodox party to the struggle nevertheless shares directly and even unwittingly, at least to a limited extent, in the spiritual renewal issuing from the struggle itself and from the intimate contact it had with the opposing forces.

As an illustration of a struggle solved from within the institution the Deuteronomic Reform is a good one. For when resolved "within" the existing institution, reform is achieved together with a restoration of harmony within the fellowship and the sense of oneness is rescued. That sort of outcome eventuated officially under King Josiah in the year 621 B.C. It meant that the long struggle of the classic prophets of Israel in the interests of a spiritualized religion had finally borne some official fruit. With the event Israel's national religion made room for the moral vigor and the religious vitality of the prophetic message. And these things gave to Israel's church a new relevancy, a new religious quality, and a much higher level of spirituality than had ever been attained by any religion anywhere up to that time. But something else also happened. Views, as between prophet and priest, were jostled into balance. Compromise ensued. The sacrificial system though purified was retained. But the popular sanctuaries save one were abolished. In effect both law and gospel were legitimatized in one religion. The official faith had, or could now have, both inwardness and visibility.

The reform of St. Paul will serve us as another example of a struggle resolved within the fellowship. Here, too, harmony was achieved in the sense of oneness restored. However, less compromise was resorted to in the resolution of the struggle between St. Paul and the Jerusalem church. Apparently St. Paul's position was more clearly victorious over the Judaizers' opposition than was that of the prophets in the case of the Deuteronomic Reform. Yet subsequent tradition hailed the leaders from both sides of the conflict with equal acclaim. More specifically, the book of Acts, coming very obviously after the peace, commemorates both of the principals, Peter as well as Paul. Their zeal for the faith and their respective missionary activities are presented in parallel, one as well as the other, and both of them are equally honored as heroes of the new faith with no hint of their earlier opposition recorded. On the whole one is inclined to be partial to any group that can resolve its struggle within the fellowship. Nevertheless, even that desirable outcome is fraught with its own peculiar dangers. For it can and does happen that once the controversy is overcome, the joy in the peace resulting often brings with it early spiritual slumber and consequent vulnerability. And the church that had been previously stirred to its depths by an enforced stock-taking of its essential character once more tends to lose its moral alertness.

On the other hand, when the reforming protest within a church has resulted in schism and separation has taken place, where afterward there are two or more churches where originally there had been but one, spiritual renewal to a greater, *and* to a lesser degree respectively is nevertheless realized in both parts. Historically, one is confronted with the stubborn fact of an earlier united fellowship torn asunder, and with overtones of genuine regret accompanying the phenomenon. Also one is forced to reckon with the prospect of long-continued belligerence between the new churches. Naturally in this situation one must admit that a sharpening of particular views and the formation of specifically pointed doctrines will follow. The dangers in this instance are not compromise. One need have no fear that the beliefs of either group will lose their cutting edge. There will be no adaptation of the practices in the one group to those of the other, nor is it likely that there will be anything resembling accommodation between their respective teachings. The dangers in the divided situation lie in another direction altogether. The progressive sharpening of views whetted by a continuing atmosphere of controversy will bring on an inevitable over-emphasis on particularistic teaching. The newly emerged reform group is prone to throw itself with vigor into the formulation of its newly emerging or evolving doctrines, and these are apt to become extremely particularistic and will likely assume exaggerated prominence over and above all other valid teaching. On the other side the older branch will stiffen its insistence upon the things that it has left, emphasizing with avid polemics the possession of spiritual treasures to be found nowhere else.

The life and death, the teaching and the example of Jesus of Nazareth resulted eventually in the separation of his especial followers from the faith into which he himself was born and in which he had lived. His frank and definite efforts at renewal of the life of the church of his time resulted, perhaps inevitably, in the separation of his group from the prevailing faith. But the process of separation was slow. And the growth of antagonisms between the two groups was progressively cumulative; yet they have been possessed of a special persistence and have reached a high degree of acrimoniousness. In the doctrines regarding the Messiah, for example, we are confronted with a historical phenomenon that has perpetuated and fed the controversy between the two groups throughout the centuries. This particular controversy has helped a bit to keep alive man's interest in the vital subject of eschatology. But for the most part it serves as one of the best illustrations of the consummate evil that comes as a result of schism in the church.

Perhaps our best illustration of all that is involved, both good and bad, in a spiritual struggle resulting in division is the Protestant Reformation of the sixteenth century. From it every item in the over-all reformation pattern can be copiously illustrated. That, first of all, renewal of the spiritual life of mankind was vitally stimulated by it is one of the most obvious facts of history. The further fact that the Roman Church profited particularly in a spiritual way from contact with its rival religion is especially evident in those countries where the contestants actually faced each other. On the other side, however, the fact of the fellowship torn asunder is equally impressive in this connection. Not only has there resulted a division between Catholicism and Protestantism. Particularly distressing is the fact that Protestantism itself has developed some branches whose irreconcilability has persisted with great vehemence over a number of centuries. The dangers inherent in separation have yielded especially bitter fruits in the area of church doctrine. The progressive development of particularism has gone on apace into the present era. It would seem, for example, that Lutherans and Calvinists have grown increasingly adept at becoming even more Lutheran and more Calvinist respectively as the years go by.

On the whole we are forced to conclude that, whether the reformation experience is resolved within the fellowship thus without division, or whether it results in division, reformation experiences are necessary. This is true despite the fact that either way the outcome is likely to be both good *and* bad. For in either case (because the general human climate, which unagitated tends inevitably to unspiritualize *any* institution that has "found rest" or become indigenous in the world) *every* church becomes ripe periodically for the reformation experience induced by some God-awakened prophetic soul or souls. Whether we will or no, human institutions (and the church is classifiable at least partially in that category) will go stale. And in that static state spirituality vanishes, moral energy grows progressively weaker, and the institution bereft of these things has nothing left but its tradition and its pageantry. Spiritual alertness to the encroachment of evil inevitably tends to disappear altogether leaving the church vulnerable to those subtle corruptions which have again and again marred its life. Finally and basically, it is the failure to watch and pray which causes the religious institution, as well as the individual, to succumb to temptation. Thereupon its recurring falls, even as that of Adam, consist in its unwary enjoyment of its own paradise coupled with inevitable disobedience to some definite command of its God.

THE LIVING WORD IN THE SCRIPTURES

HERBERT H. WERNECKE

WHILE the report comes to us again and again that the Bible is the best seller, few of us fail to realize that, though it may not be the least read book as we remember its use in churches, church schools, and countless homes, it does not have the authority and influence today it once had, nor that which it should have.

In dealing with the Puritan period, J. R. Green in his *Short History of the English People* concluded, "England became the people of one book and that book was the Bible." Out of the England so characterized came both the Puritans and the Pilgrim fathers, influential for wholesome progress in the course of the centuries far out of proportion to their numbers. It is significant that a recent Parliamentary committee in Britain reported: "As the practice of reading the Bible, regularly and religiously, at home has decreased, by so much has the nation deliberately impoverished itself." [1]

It is encouraging to see the renewed attention given to the Bible, attested by such statements as that of Georgia Harkness when she says frankly, "I have rediscovered the Bible." [2] She gives expression to the loss or neglect of it, on the one hand, and to its new meaning and significance for her now. While many causes combine to explain this changed situation, this essay concerns itself particularly with the significant part the Bible played in the Protestant Reformation and the changing

---

[1] J. Paterson, "The Living Word," *Religion in Life*, XVII (1948), 2, p. 259.
[2] "A Spiritual Pilgrimage," *The Christian Century*, LVI (1939), 11, p. 348.

views of the Bible since, which have tended towards its disuse
for a considerable time and, lately, towards a healthier understanding of its fundamental importance. This account will involve a recognition of the views held by the Reformers and the
transition from the older view of an inerrant and verbally inspired Bible to the current existential view that the Word of
God is somehow written in, and yet to be distinguished from,
the words of the Bible. Viewpoints have varied all the way
from a merely human Bible of the rationalists and the verbally
inspired Bible of the fundamentalists to an appreciation of the
contribution made by the critical study of the Bible to a clearer
understanding of it as God's authoritative message to mankind.

THE NEW PLACE OF THE SCRIPTURES IN THE REFORMATION

For many, the main achievement of the Protestant Reformation was the substitution of the Bible for the church as the final
authority in religion. At times that opinion is clothed in the
words, "to the infallibility of the Church, the Reformers and
later Protestants opposed the infallibility of the Scriptures."
Chillingworth, in *The Religion of Protestants, A Safe Way to
Salvation,* makes the significant statement that "the Bible alone
is the religion of Protestants." Such statements contain considerable truth. That is why they have persisted. Yet they are
at the same time examples of the over-simplification of the
popularizer of knowledge which neglects to include quite essential explanations and amplifications of such terse summaries.

For the sake of better understanding it will be well, first of
all, to clarify such key-words as protestantism, authority, and
Bible. Protestant is in no sense antithetical to Catholic; it is
opposed to the catholicism of Rome. Every intelligent Protestant
confesses, "I believe in . . . the holy Catholic Church." Neither
is the term primarily negative, for *protestari* means "to profess,

bear witness, declare openly." It is this meaning that is clearly reflected in the significant use of it at the Diet of Speyer (1529): "We must protest in matters which concern God's honor, and the salvation and eternal life of our souls; every one must stand and give account before God for himself, and no one can excuse himself by the action or decision of another, whether less or more." Here is an open declaration of definite truths of a *positive,* even revolutionary, character.

The question of authority is so central for understanding the nature and meaning of human life in general that it is well to note the three senses in which the word is commonly used. "There is the final authority in which right and power are united; there is the educative authority which has right so far as its truth has been assimilated, but no power; and there is the authority of power, hardly to be found in complete isolation from right, but not primarily dependent upon it." [3] The first meaning (right and power united) is of primary importance in this essay, for it describes the final claim and hold which the Bible, as the authoritative Word of God, has upon us.

Just what is meant by the Word of God, likewise, is so determinative that it is necessary briefly to elucidate the term. The older view held that the Bible *is* the Word of God whereas lately it has been claimed that the Bible *contains* the Word of God. The significance of the distinction will be more evident if the four main senses in which the term Word of God is used are discriminated.

The primary meaning of the Word of God in the biblical writings is the revelation given to prophets and apostles. Hence the prophets declare repeatedly, "Thus saith the Lord." Similarly, apostolic history is written in terms that glorify the Word

[3] H. Cunliffe-Jones, *The Authority of the Biblical Revelation* (London, 1947), p. 13.

of God, and the apostolic preaching is explicitly distinguished from human words. So Paul writes to the Thessalonians: "And for this cause we also thank God without ceasing, that when you received from us the word of the message, even the word of God, ye accepted it not as the word of men, but as it is in truth, the word of God, which also worketh in you that believe." [4] In this sense it seems to be synonymous with the word "gospel" as indicated in Mark 1:14 and Luke 5:1 respectively: "Now after that John was delivered up; Jesus came into Galilee, preaching the gospel of God" and "Now it came to pass, while the multitude pressed upon him and heard the word of God, that he was standing by the lake of Gennesaret. . . ."

The second meaning of the phrase, Word of God, is the incarnation of the Eternal Word in and through Jesus Christ our Lord, most explicitly expressed in the Prolog to the Fourth Gospel. In this sense Edwin Hoskyns could write: "The Gospel is, as the earlier evangelists had declared, the Word of God. And Jesus is Himself the Gospel, *is* the Word of God." [5]

A third use of the Word of God appears in the meaning of this gospel as made known in preaching. The Twelve appointed seven deacons by the choice of the main body of the disciples to look after administration, and said of themselves, "But we will continue steadfastly in prayer and in the ministry of the word." [6] So also Barnabas and Paul "proclaimed the *word of God* in the synagogs of the Jews." [7] While it is difficult to discern the precise meaning of the phrase, "the word of God" in Hebrews 4:12 "For the word of God is living and sharper than any two-edged sword . . . ," it definitely seems to apply both to the gospel and to the declaration of that gospel in preaching. Chris-

[4] I Thess. 2:13.
[5] *The Fourth Gospel* (London, 1940), I, 163.
[6] Acts 13:15.
[7] Acts 13:5.

tian preaching seeks to make divine revelation a contemporary fact bringing us to decision and to progressive recognition of the meaning and implication of the gospel.

The fourth meaning of the term Word of God is the Scripture text. While, as noted above, the word of God is the revelation given to prophets and apostles, we only come to a true understanding of that revelation through the text of the Bible. The two are inseparable. While the Bible is the earthen vessel through which the treasure of the gospel comes to us, only through it or in it do we have our knowledge of the revelation which is the content of Christian preaching.

It is essential that we keep these four meanings clearly in mind as we seek to understand the significant place the Bible came to occupy in the time of the Reformation and since the sixteenth century.

While scholars have differed as to the primary principle of the Reformation—some finding it in the doctrine of justification by faith, others in the assertion of the priesthood of all believers or the right of private judgment and others again in the claim that the Holy Scriptures are the infallible rule of faith and practice—the one fundamental conviction that pervades the entire movement is the direct and immediate relation of every Christian soul to God, and of God to every Christian.

Luther was not disturbed by intellectual difficulties concerning doctrines or statements of doctrine but rather by an overwhelming anxiety to find peace with God. While his superiors regarded him as a young saint, he describes his own spiritual condition thus: "I felt that I had long lost Christ and his baptism. I was the most miserable man on earth; day and night there was only wailing and despair, and no one could restrain me." [8] After some two years of anguished failure to find peace

[8] *Luther's Works,* Erlangen ed., XXXI, 278, 279.

of soul in the religious practices of his time, it dawned upon him that, according to the Scriptures, the righteousness of God is not the righteousness by which a righteous God justifies us through faith. Of this faith Luther says,

There are two kinds of believing: first, a believing about God which means that I believe that what is said of God is true. This faith is rather a form of knowledge than a faith. There is, secondly, a believing in God which means that I put my trust in Him, give myself up to thinking that I can have dealings with Him, and believe without any doubt that He will be and do to me according to the things said of Him. Such faith, which throws itself upon God, whether in life or in death, alone makes a Christian man.[9]

In this instance, Luther's experience is typical of the new life that issued forth in the Reformation. The form of it varied according to background and personality; but Reformers and pre-Reformers alike proclaimed the great truth that had been so largely neglected throughout the entire period of medieval theology. In order to know God, man must be in direct living touch with God himself; that the truly Christian man must cling directly and with a living faith to the God who speaks to him in Christ, saying, "I am thy salvation."

When this fundamental religious experience had made Luther realize that the Father who has revealed himself in his Son is accessible to every humble, penitent and faithful seeker after God, he was led to announce the spiritual priesthood of all believers. "It is faith that incorporates the believer in Christ, and in this way the soul through faith alone, without works, is from the Word of God, justified, sanctified, endued with truth, peace, liberty, and filled full with every good thing, and is truly

[9] *Luther's Works* (Erlangen ed.) XXII, 15. Cf. XLVII. 5: "If thou holdest faith to be simply a thought concerning God, then that thought is as little able to give eternal life as ever a monkish cowl could give it."

made the child of God. Faith brings the soul and the word together, and the soul is acted upon by the word, as iron exposed to fire glows like fire because of its union with the fire." [10]

From this conception of faith as *personal trust* in a *personal Savior* who had manifested in his life and work the fatherly mercy of God, the Reformers came to view the Word of God as a personal and not as a dogmatic revelation. On the divine side there was God pouring out his love in Christ the Incarnate Word; on the human side there was the appropriation of this love by faith. The chief function of Scripture, therefore, was to present Jesus Christ to us as personal Savior. It is God speaking to man as his personal God. In medieval theology saving faith and Scripture had been primarily intellectual and propositional; with the Reformers they are always first of all experimental and personal. This personal relationship to the Scriptures caused the Reformers to translate the Bible into the languages of the people in order to place it into the hands of every man. Luther remarked that a boy of nine with the Bible could know more about divine truth than the pope without it.

In describing the authoritative character of Scripture the Reformers insisted that its recognition was awakened by the testimony of the Holy Spirit. Just as God himself makes us know and feel the sense of pardon in an inward experience by a faith which is God's work, so that same Spirit enables the believer to recognize that God is speaking to us authoritatively in and through the words of Scripture.

What they meant by the authority and infallibility of Scripture can only be seen by noting their teaching about the relation between Scripture and the Word of God. Though differing in details, their general conception is essentially the same. The distinction between the Word of God and the Scriptures is more

[10] T. M. Lindsay, *A History of the Reformation* (New York, 1911), I, 441.

than the difference between the Word of God and the Word of God written. "If the use of metaphor be allowed, the Word of God is to the Scripture as the soul is to the body." [11] Lindsay summarizes the position of the great Reformers on this point as follows:

Luther says that the word of God may be described in the phrase of St. Paul, "the Gospel of God, which He promised afore by his Prophets in the Holy Scriptures, concerning His son, who was born of the seed of David according to the flesh, who was declared to be the Son of God with power, according to the spirit of holiness, by the resurrection of the dead." Calvin calls it "the spiritual teaching, the gate, as it were, by which we enter into His heavenly kingdom," "a mirror in which faith beholds God," and "that wherein He utters unto us His mercy in Christ, and assureth us of His love toward us." The Scots Confession calls it the revelation of the Promise "quhilk (which) as it was repeated and made mair clear from time to time; so was it embraced with joy, and maist constantlie received of all the faithful." And Zwingli declares it to be essentially "that our Lord Jesus Christ, the very Son of God, has revealed to us the will of the Heavenly Father, and, with His innocence, has redeemed us from death." (*Zurich Articles of 1523,* i, ii.) "It is the sum of God's commands, threatenings and promises, addressed to our faith, and above all the gospel offer of Christ to us. This word of God need not take the form of direct exhortation; it may be recognized in the simple histories of men or of nations, recorded in the Scripture." [12]

Zwingli, with the clearer dogmatic insight which he always showed, felt the need of a statement about the theological place of Scripture very early, and declared in the *First Helvetic Confession* that "canonic Scripture, the word of God, given by the Holy Spirit and set forth to the world by the prophets and apostles, the most perfect and ancient of all philosophies, alone contains perfectly all piety and the whole rule of life." [13]

[11] *Ibid.,* I, 462.
[12] *Ibid.,* I, 462 f.
[13] *Ibid.,* I, 467, footnote.

The Zurich reformer expresses himself in the same vein in a sermon dated September 6th, 1522, in which he emphasizes that only the Holy Spirit is requisite to make the Word intelligible; no church, no council, much more, no pope is needed.

From these statements it is evident that the Reformers uniformly believed that the Scripture *is* the Word of God, not understanding the copula as expressing logical identity but some such relation as can be more exactly rendered by *presents, conveys, records,* all of which words are used in the writings of Reformers or in the creeds of the Reformation churches. The authoritative character and infallibility belong really and primarily to the Word of God and only secondarily to the Scriptures. Scripture shares these attributes only as it is a vehicle of the Word of God.

Infallibility and divine authority belong, then, to the sphere of faith and of the witness of the Spirit and therefore to that personal manifestation of God and of his will toward us in every part of Scripture. But this manifestation is given in a course of events which are a part of history, a record which therefore also has its human side. Thus the Scriptures are a divine-human record. The supernatural is encased in human forms of expression. To apprehend the former, faith illumined by the Holy Spirit is necessary; to discover when the books which record the Word of God were written, or by whom, or in what style or how often they were edited or re-edited is a matter of diligent and patient historical research. Therefore, speaking about Genesis, Luther could ask, "What though Moses never wrote it?" [14] He could call the Psalter "the Bible within the Bible" and could rank highest in the New Testament the Gospel of John, First John, the Pauline Epistles and First Peter.

In this direct approach to the Scriptures, letting each man "hold to what his spirit yields him" (Luther), the leading

[14] *Luther's Works,* Erlangen ed., LVII. 35.

Protestant Reformers agreed. In Calvin's *Institutes* we find repeated emphasis on the *testimonium Spiritus Sancti internum.* Zwingli studied and expounded the Scriptures without feeling the need of any authority external to the Bible. Though more largely influenced by Humanism than any of the others, there is no indication that he had any doubt about the final authority of Scripture as the basis of doctrine; rather he relied completely upon individual interpretation to elucidate its meaning without the help of any other authority. In fact, he gave a prominence, unusual even among the Reformers, to the pulpit as the center of Christian worship and to the exposition of the Word of God as the central feature of divine service. So thoroughly did he expound the Scriptures at Zurich that he has been called the first scientific interpreter of Holy Writ.

To the Reformers the Bible was definitely not an external infallible authority. They regarded the Bible as "a new home for a new life within which they could have intimate fellowship with God Himself—not merely knowledge about God, but communion with him: (while) medieval thologians looked at the Bible as a sort of spiritual law book, a storehouse of divinely communicated knowledge of doctrinal truths and rules for moral conduct—and nothing more." [15]

THE LOSS OF REFORMATION INSIGHTS

The later Protestants, however, failed to hold this enlightened attitude towards the Bible which the original Reformers had so clearly stated, so valiantly defended, and so constantly applied. Their successors came to attribute to the Bible an authority no less absolute and mechanical than that which had been ascribed to it in the medieval Church so that it came to be regarded by many as a verbally inspired, infallible law book, which could

[15] T. M. Lindsay, *op. cit.,* I, 455.

provide authoritative decisions on every point of human life and conduct. The height of mechanical inspiration, including the vowel points of the Masoretic text, is enunciated in greatest detail in the *Second Helvetic Confession.*

The Reformers with trained mind and balanced judgment were able to hold a balance between the authority of the written word and the integrity of the individual soul. But the majority of people, when they began to read the Bible for themselves, simply carried over from their former views a conception of the Scriptures that provided them with authoritative decisions on every point. Quite ludicrous were some of the practices adopted in the attempt to obey biblical injunctions literally, proving everything by the citation of texts wrested from their context. "When the puritans objected to square caps when men's heads were round, Laud did not answer by an appeal to common sense. He proved from the Bible that heads were square, for does not Leviticus 19:27 read: 'Ye shall not round the corners of your heads.' And at a much later day, when bibliolaters objected to the use of chloroform in childbirth because God had said man should be born in pain, J. Y. Simpson found his retort—and perhaps it was the best for his critics—in that the Bible said that when God removed Adam's rib in order to make Eve, He caused a deep sleep to fall upon him, which showed that He approved of anaesthesia." [16] That the Scriptures, in spite of such misconceptions, continued to nourish a vigorous devotional life, often through an extensive use of allegorical interpretation, is a convincing testimony to the unique quality of the events and truths contained therein.

Since the suspicion of critical scholarship continues to be with us and it is still thought by many that the right of private judgment destroys all authority in the Scriptures, leading

[16] C. W. Dugmore, *The Interpretation of the Bible* (London, 1944), p. 66.

through deism, sectarianism and Socinianism to license, confusion, and chaos where every man believes and does "what seems right in his own eyes," we assert that this would follow only if the Bible were regarded as an infallible book in precisely the same sense as the medieval Church was regarded as infallible. If we believe that God speaks directly to all, and that the Holy Spirit illumines all, so that all are taught of God, then there is harmony between God's external revelation to all men in Christ Jesus seen in the Bible, and that inner response of the Spirit by which the soul receives and apprehends the revelation. In other words, the right of private judgment is not the right of private fancy, the right to think as we please; it is rather the right, even the duty, to listen when God speaks to us, to receive for ourselves at God's hand the testimony of his Holy Spirit, the Spirit of truth.

This confusion, or the feeling of the lack of authority in any other conception of the Bible than that of verbal inspiration, has upset the faith of many who, confronted by the findings of a critical approach to the Bible, have concluded that the Bible is but a book among books. While this conclusion is quite natural for the partially informed, there is a sense in which the critical approach with its truer understanding of the nature of the Scriptures and the light it has thrown upon date, authorship, method of composition, purpose and inter-relationship of the various documents, has placed our faith on surer foundations.

In Pietism at its best there was present both a reverence for Scripture and a critical spirit. Of great significance is its declaration that religion is something altogether personal, and directly related to that, its unswerving return to the Bible and the application of Scripture truths. Even though it erred at times in the direction of unbridled subjectivism by ignoring the influences of the facts and conditions of history and by a fanatic apocalypticism, it is to its everlasting credit that the New Testament text of its most illustrious exegete, Johann Albrecht Bengel (1687–1752), with its Apparatus Criticus became the starting-point for modern textual criticism of the New Testament.

Unfortunately, this wholesome balance referred to above was not long maintained because other causes influenced the course of biblical criticism in the centuries following the Reformation in a quite different direction. Most important of all perhaps was the spirit of Humanism fostered by the Renaissance. While theologians could not go the whole way in accepting the doctrine that man was the measure of all things, they could not remain unaffected by it, so that quite naturally more attention was directed to the motives and methods of the human agents by whom the biblical books were written. Rationalism was insinuating doubts as to the credibility of the miracle narratives in the Bible. Natural science, armed with the prestige of great accomplishments (Wiggam's "Decalog of Science" in the twenties), not only conflicted with the traditional interpretation of the creation narrative in Genesis but was hailed by many as the savior which made superfluous any idea of special revelation.

All these factors combined and interacted to bring about the movement of biblical criticism. The great critics were, as a rule, genuinely convinced that they were rendering a greatly needed service to true religion. They tried to establish the most correct text and then sought to interpret it against the background of its historical setting. The fact that the course of biblical criticism is strewn with the wreckage of abandoned theories no more condemns it than the history of rejected scientific hypotheses condemns science. The critics' job was to determine the factual material out of which a theology was to be constructed. If the evidence showed that there had been a misconception as to the

manner of God's revelation, then theology had to be revised to
allow for the newly established data, thus replacing a defective
theology by a better.

Had this been the spirit and the method more generally,
biblical criticism would not have had the reputation of destructive criticism which it so frequently has had and, at times, de-
served. This negative influence was due to two clearly discernible tendencies—the humanistic and rationalistic inclinations of
many critics which became a fixed bias distorting interpretation,
and the over-absorption in details that made biblical criticism
an end in itself instead of a means to an end.

The legitimate reluctance to accept the supernatural so long
as a natural explanation was possible, became an unquestioned
axiom. Critics became intoxicated with the discovery that biblical writers were, after all, but fallible human beings, and not
passive instruments played upon by the Holy Spirit. Seeing
more clearly the human side of the divine-human book, they
created the expectation that everything could be explained from
the purely human angle. In effect, God was pushed aside.
Though the word "revelation" continued to be used, it soon
came to be a pious term for the human process of discovery,
different from philosopher or poet or scientist in degree rather
than quality. So the claim of the uniqueness of the biblical revelation gradually faded and, in not a few cases, disappeared
entirely, resulting in an avowed humanism to those whose
minds thought logically.

Inter-related with this development is, of course, the influence
of rationalism, of the theory of evolution from natural science
as assuring inevitable progress for mankind as well as the conclusions of the comparative religion theory exponents that the
most that can be claimed is that Christianity is the best that has
been achieved up to date. It was recognized as the supreme

religion but its claim of finality could no longer be accepted. Obviously the Scriptures, though still in some sense the word of God, were regarded as a not entirely harmonious collection of the words of a number of more or less gifted men, thus detracting immensely from the authority the Bible had exercised from the first century to the sixteenth.

The second very serious weakness of the higher critical approach, the over-absorption in details, led to a diluting, at times the obliteration of the theological content. When engaged in the demonstration that Document A could not have been written by B if he also compiled X, the critics became fascinated by the mere thrill of the game, forgetting the ultimate purpose of their very essential research. The *Theologe* became *Philologe* and was assisted by professional *Philologen* with little or no pretensions to theology. All this may be justifiable provided the goal is reached, but very frequently the biblical student never arrived at theology. Even today the tendency remains to all too large an extent that there is an interest in criticism for its own sake or it is viewed as a cross to be borne because of its tendency towards religious aridity, and even the study of theology and thorough Bible study are considered to be two different things, at times even quite unrelated.

This radical difference in attitude toward the Bible has been rather significantly summarized in a chapter heading, "The Failure of Liberalism To Interpret the Bible as the Word of God." [17] An example of this is seen in the uncritical acceptance of the doctrines of the universal reign of natural law and of biological evolution. The most that Harnack could say was, "We are firmly convinced that what happens in space and time is subject to the general laws of motion, and that in this sense, as an interruption of the order of nature, there can be no such

[17] Dugmore, *op. cit.*, pp. 92 ff.

things as 'miracles.'" [18] Similarly, Bousset, best known as the author of *Kyrios Christos,* concludes, "Only a bold step forward will save us. If the science of history demands that the seals be broken and the special revelation be surrendered, then we must seriously consider the idea of a universal revelation." [19] For him the revelation that came to the prophets was simply their *conviction* concerning the meaning, nature and aims of life.

The general effect of the labours of criticism had been to disintegrate the Bible, to break it up into a number of parts with little or no real connection between them. There was an inclination to drive a wedge between the Gospels and the Epistles, and to deepen this into an antithesis between "the religion of Jesus" and "the faith of Paul." Further, "the quest of the historical Jesus" led to a separating of the Synoptics from the Fourth Gospel and a disparagement of the "historical" value of the latter. Above all, there was a tendency to dig a deep gulf between the Old Testament and the New Testament and to represent the Old Testament as of minor significance for the faith of Christ, or even as completely negligible. Harnack resuscitated Marcion's demand for the removal of the Old Testament from the Canon of Christian Scriptures; and some eclectics have advocated its replacement by the sacred books of the world-religions. Even when critics of a more conservative disposition proclaimed the abiding value of the Old Testament, the underlying assumption was that the labours of criticism had destroyed the authority of the Old Testament; and they gave the impression of seeking salvage among the ruins.[20]

While there were and are varying degrees of liberalism, and we owe a real debt to pioneering souls who braved the criticism of blazing new trails, yet the verdict of the last century, and

[18] *What Is Christianity?* (2nd ed., New York), pp. 28 f.
[19] *What Is Religion?* (New York, 1907), p. 213.
[20] Ed. by F. W. Camfield, *Reformation Old and New, A Tribute to Karl Barth* (London, 1947), p. 152.

more specifically, the last few decades is that the postulates of
natural science were too largely allowed to become the dogmas
of theology. God's revelation of himself gave way to man's
thoughts about God. God's mighty acts gave place to man's
evolving civilization. The attempt to compromise, or accommo-
date to nineteenth century science, led to reducing the Gospel
to a message about God, the essence of which was found in a
few simple beliefs held with great tenacity and promulgated
with great force by Jesus. T. W. Manson reminds us forcibly
and solemnly:

And, let it never be forgotten, all was done with the very best
intentions, in the firm belief that Liberalism was on the side of
progress, and that the purification and strengthening of the Christian
religion was now in full swing. The truth, now coming clearly to
light, is that Christianity was being gently and gradually transformed
into humanism—and humanism when it is full grown brings forth
totalitarianism. In the light of the present day it is most instructive to
look back forty years and see the naive way in which Bousset, at the
end of his book *What Is Religion?* declares that Christianity must
be the religion of the progressive nations, and that the typical figures
in a progressive nation are Goethe and Bismarck. A strange trinity—
Jesus, Goethe, and Bismarck—to preside over the future destiny of
the race. We may well suspect the premises that lead to such odd
conclusions.[21]

Over against these approaches that tended towards under-
mining the authority of the Bible, is the more constructive one
of the Form Critics. Without accepting their extreme positions,[22] the aims and results of this approach deserve careful
attention. This group has investigated the formation of the

---

[21] Quoted by Dugmore, *op. cit.*, pp. 102 f.
[22] Bultman, *Jesus* (Berlin, no date), p. 12, "Denn freilich bin ich der Meinung,
dasz wir vom Leben und von der Persoenlichkeit Jesu so gut wie nichts mehr wissen
koennen. . . ."

Gospel tradition in the pre-literary stage. Their findings indicate not an untheological nucleus but exactly the reverse. As far back as they can go, they trace a continual process of theological interpretation permeating the tradition. Theology is no late accretion but is at the very heart of the Gospel in its earliest announcement as well as in its earliest recorded form. The angel's brief word to the shepherds, "Unto you is born this day in the city of David, a Savior, who is Christ the Lord" is laden with theological implications.

THEOLOGICAL INTERPRETATION

All in all, however, the destructive critical approach was predominant in Europe and America when "God let loose Karl Barth." Wellhausen died in 1918; Karl Barth's Commentary on Romans made its first appearance in 1919. These occurrences strangely constitute a turning point which marks a remarkable transformation in the approach to the Bible. G. Hendry, in an essay written as a tribute to Karl Barth on his sixtieth birthday (1947), compares the change to the experience of Christian in *Pilgrim's Progress,* when having rested a while in the pleasant arbor "about the midway to the top of the Hill Difficulty, he felt in his bosom for the Roll, that he might read therein and be comforted, but he felt and found it not;" whereupon he resolved to go back and search "if haply he might find his Roll that had been his comfort so many times on his Journey."

During the first two decades of this century, biblical study was still dominated by the critical interest—the sifting of the text, analysis of the documents, the illumination of the historical and cultural background. But increasingly it was felt that all was not well—"Christian missed his Roll." Significantly this loss was felt, not by the scholar but by the pastor, who, face to face with the hungry people, became acutely aware that the rations issued by critical scholarship had increasingly become a miserable inadequate *ersatz* diet. This was the historical start-ing-point of the so-called "theology of crisis" and ever since that Karl Barth's theocentric emphasis has been a wholesome cor-rective to the humanistic tendencies prominent in liberal circles, particularly as noted above. Whereas the general endeavor had been to seek what light could be shed upon the Bible through critical research, today there is a growing concern to ask what light the Bible has to shed upon us, what its authentic message is, a desire to recover the theological interpretation of the Bible as the Word of God. So clear is this new tendency that we read repeatedly of the rediscovery of the Bible—an over-statement, of course, since the Bible has never been completely lost.

Karl Barth describes the Bible as "the book of the words of men which bear witness to the Word of God and which there-fore are the Word of God." While we must distinguish between the Bible and the Word of God to which it bears witness, we cannot separate them. According to this noted theologian, the Bible becomes the Word of God for us when it overpowers us and gains the mastery over us, i.e., when it creates faith in us. When the Word of God creates faith in us, it is God's own work, his miracle, his in-Spiriting. It is not in our power to make it happen. At the best we can pray for it.

It is authenticated to us as the Word of God by the testimony of the Holy Spirit. The problem of the Bible as the Word of God is posed and can be posed only within the church. It is the church's confession of faith in the Bible as the Word of God which raises the problem and it therefore cannot be discon-nected from the testimony of the church. It dare not be severed from its context.

The Bible is given into our hands as a single volume, and this not by accident, but as the outward sign of the church's confession of faith, as expressed in the canon, that the various writings contained in this volume bear a single and united testimony to the Word of God. The canon imposes upon us the task of endeavoring to understand the Bible as a unity in the diversity of its component parts.

This approach has resulted in a clear recognition that the Bible instead of being man's search for God is rather God's search for man. It has also called us back to the realization that the Old and the New Testaments form a unity. It has brought about a more accurate understanding that revelation is given primarily through events rather than through propositions, though "it cannot be enough to say that in revelation we meet the divine self, for if this meeting is pure immediacy which does not provide us with truths about God, it would remain incommunicable and unable to provide the reasoning heart with principles of understanding." [23] The late Archbishop Temple's conception of the Scripture, as consisting of great divine acts of judgment of redemption interpreted for us by men called and qualified by God to interpret his ways, puts the emphasis at the right point. That these recent pioneers like Barth speak at times in unguarded terms which they later modify or even retract is to be expected, for they are at the best but words of men. So some neo-orthodox theologians can in one breath say that criticism has left the Scriptures a "heap of ruins" and in the next breath affirm that through this "heap of ruins" we encounter Christ. While the apparent dualism of some neo-orthodox theologians, who practically deny any point of contact between God and man and glory in irrationality, is difficult to accept, the thoroughly theological approach indicated above is a greatly needed contribution.

A word needs to be said regarding the growing conviction

[23] H. R. Niebuhr, *The Meaning of Revelation* (New York, 1941), pp. 175–176.

in Protestantism that a greater authority should be ascribed to the church than the Reformers allowed, especially since it is so directly related to the authority of the Scriptures. The assertion is frequently made that the Bible is in a double sense the product of the church, the books having been written and the canon determined by the religious community. The Church, it is claimed, was normative for the New Testament, and the reversal of this historic position is not only untenable, but has proved the source of controversy, division and confusion.

But is it true that the Bible is the product of the church? Certainly we must recognize the partly conscious and the partly unconscious influence of the community upon the individual writers, even their conscious dependence upon the community for certain facts and interpretations. It is also true that parts of the Bible do not rise above the general level of religion in the day of their writing. But the eighth century prophets, far from merely reflecting the level of religion in their religious community, appear rather "as the towering summits of a mountainous landscape." [24] The same can be said of Paul and the other New Testament authors. While the writing of the Bible was quite naturally influenced by the church, it was *produced,* not by the religious community as a whole, but rather by "holy men of God who spoke as they were moved by the Holy Spirit," and it is in this distinctive fact that their unique authority resides.

As to the second claim, namely, that the church determined the canon, there can be no doubt. The history of its formation is the record of the gradual crystallization of the mind of the church as to what should constitute its normative Scriptures. Not so much by formal decision was it established but rather by the movement of the mind of the church as a whole which

[24] C. H. Dodd, *The Authority of the Bible* (New York, 1929), p. 138.

recognized in the books selected the authentic expression of apostolic Christianity. The books whose apostolic authorship was, or is, doubtful and disputed, were received into the canon because they were recognized to be the kind of books which the apostles or their disciples could have written, bearing genuine witness to the apostolic faith. The elimination of the Apocrypha by the Reformers indicates that the church does and should— even must—adjudicate upon the canon.

Two things must be remembered. "When the church receives the Scripture and seals it with her suffrage, she does not authenticate a thing otherwise dubious or controvertible; but knowing it to be the truth of her God, performs a duty of piety, by treating it with immediate veneration." [25] At the same time it is clearly evident that, because of the testimony of the church to it, men are "moved and induced . . . to an high, reverent esteem for the Holy Scripture." [26]

Not only is the church's decision in determining the canon a matter of historical record, but it is also implied in the Protestant view of the authority of the Bible. To recognize certain Scriptures (as distinguished from other literature) as normative is, in fact, to affirm a canon. The Reformers quite rightly were concerned not merely that everybody should have a Bible but that the people should have *the* Bible.

Because the Reformers did not clarify this sufficiently, post-Reformation scholastics found the criterion of canonicity in the fact of inspiration *antecedently* established rather than in the collective testimony of the Spirit in the Church. Instead of recognizing that the inspiration and the authority of Scripture are simultaneously validated through the inner operation of the

[25] Calvin, *Institutes of the Christian Religion*, trans. by John Allen (6th Am. ed., Philadelphia, 1928), I, 7, 2.
[26] *Westminster Confession of Faith* in Schaff, *Creeds of Christendom*, III, 602 f.

Spirit, they first affirmed the fact of inspiration and then deduced therefrom the Bible's authority. Thus the Bible became "an external and objective standard, possessing independent value of its own quite apart from its effect upon the mind and heart of the reader." [27] The result is the "paper pope" with its correlate, the doctrine of verbal inspiration, since a purely external standard must be inerrant. Over against this, evangelical Protestantism may well affirm on the Church's authority, guided by the Holy Spirit who is present in both Church and Word and in its authoritative Scripture, its public canon, over against all mystical and rationalizing tendencies. The Spirit of God guided not only the writing of the text and its transmission but likewise the selection of the canon.

It is clear then that *ecclesia reformata semper reformanda* (a church once reformed ought always to be reformed). The Reformation did not create a static attitude towards the Bible but rather caught glimpses of new truths which the succeeding centuries supplemented and at times prevented. Beyond those insights, the Lord had and has "yet more light and truth to break forth out of His holy Word." Through the abandonment of the theory of verbal inspiration, a change as far-reaching in its implications as the displacement of the old Ptolemaic astronomy by the Copernican was for the scientific world, a great multitude of evangelical Protestants, unwilling to give up the Bible and unable to accept verbal inspiration, find themselves in a theological no-man's land. To the extent, however, that the gains of the intensive historical study of the Bible are taken up into a theological understanding of it as a revelation of the living God, to that degree we may look forward to a new authoritative influence of the Bible. The Bible continues to be the effective means of setting man face to face with Christ.

[27] A. C. McGiffert, *Protestant Thought Before Kant* (New York, 1911), p. 146.

While the quality of our Christian insight and our Christian life do not vary directly with the amount and clarity of our biblical knowledge, the way to the Gospel is familiarity with the language and thought of the Bible. And this familiarity can come to us only by responding to the revelation of the Bible. The use of the Bible will be more fruitful as we relate it to our condition and need, making it "existential," a personal confrontation with the living God. It is less a matter of intellectual apprehension of abstract truth than a doing of the truth.[28] While it is possible to have a living faith in Christ even with an extremely meager knowledge of the Scriptures, since the history of the interpretation clearly shows that the church has maintained its essential witness in a remarkable manner at times with a very limited and bizarre understanding of the Bible, at the same time it is true that the continued vitality of the Church's life, the richness of its experience, the transforming power of its witnessing is directly related to its continual reappropriation of the meaning of the Biblical message.

Truly, "man liveth not by bread alone but by every *word* that proceedeth out of the mouth of God."

[28] Cf. I John 1:6 and John 7:17.

BIBLICAL MOTIFS IN REFORMATION THEOLOGY

Allen O. Miller

EVERY heritage has its peculiarities. Sometimes its peculiarities reflect a narrowness of mind and a shallowness of
spirit which make the devotees of the heritage merely peculiar
or eccentric. Less often, perhaps, but much more significantly,
they indicate distinctiveness, in a sense that lends distinction to
its character. The Reformation heritage had its peculiarities,
and some that no doubt make it appear peculiar. There are
others, however, that mark it as the distinctive bearer of the
essential features of the Hebrew-Christian biblical motif in
human history. The distinctive genius of this heritage is its
kind of theological orientation.

Christian theology has both a broad and inclusive and a
specific and definitive character. Broadly speaking it includes
all Christian doctrines. Specifically it means "the doctrine of
God." As a scientific discipline, however, the proper "object"
of Christian theology is always God. This is evidenced by the
fact that, in the affirmations of Christian faith, God is always
the "subject." Our discussion of theology in the Reformation
heritage is therefore concerned specifically with the doctrine
of God.

Reformation theology at its best is a dynamic reality like the
God whose revelation it aims to interpret. No formulation of it
may claim finality. The theology of the Reformation was conceived in the response of faith to the divine self-disclosure as
recorded in the Scriptures. It was carried in the womb of

59

Augustinianism, and came to birth in the spiritual labor pangs
of the sixteenth century Reformers. Like all interpretative
effort, which aims to make explicit for thought the truth which
lies implicit in experience, Reformation theology aims to communicate with clarity the truth which the faithful apprehend
in the experience of being justified by grace, through faith in
Jesus Christ.

Reformation theology is faith seeking understanding. From
its conception, however, this type of Christian theology has had
to fight off attempts from without and tendencies within to
make it a static and formal discipline. In theology, reason,
which, by the very nature of man, is the basic tool of all scientific endeavor—descriptive, discursive or interpretative—must
always be handmaiden to faith in her marriage with truth.
Rationalism, the over-zealousness of reason in the service of
truth, forgets that reason's first duty is to faith, thus cutting the
spinal nerve of Reformation Theology. Any scholasticism, for
example, whether Roman or Protestant, which confuses belief
as intellectual assent to church doctrine with faith in the living
God, is the inevitable foe of the biblical motif in theology. When
a potentially inductive approach to theology, expressed in the
Augustinian formula "faith seeking knowledge" (*fides
quaerens intellectum*),[1] is transformed into a theologically de-
ductive approach, as in Anselm's "I believe in order to understand" (*credo ut intelligam*), where belief means intellectual
assent (*assensus*),[2] it is not surprising that Luther should have
bent over backward, in his derogation of reason, not only to

[1] This formula, used by Anselm as the sub-title for the *Proslogium* has its source
in Augustine's teaching that (a) "Faith precedes, the intellect follows." Sermo
CXVIII: 1 (Ben.); (b) "A certain faith is the starting-point of knowledge." *De
Trinitate*, IX, I, 1; (c) "Faith seeks, understanding finds; whence the prophet says
'unless ye believe, ye shall not understand' (Isaiah 7:9)." *De Trinitate*, XV, II, 2.

[2] The Roman Catholic conception of faith as *assensus* is already explicit in
Augustine *Enchiridion* VII: "Faith believes . . . the Creed."

establish the primary of faith, but also to place the locus of faith in the heart.

But Luther's "faith alone" (*sola fide*) points, in still another way, to what in medieval Roman Scholasticism he took to be a perversion of the gospel of grace by rationalism. Here again Augustinianism is the framework within which both Luther and his scholastic opponents operated. Augustine, having declared that the grace of God (the Word become flesh) is the one feature of Christianity which he had not found in Neo-Platonic philosophy, attempted to synthesize the gracious love of God toward man (biblical *agape*) with the aquisitive, self-motivated love of man (platonic *eros*), thereby to direct the latter toward the former. For this Christian love of man toward God, Augustine used the term charity (*caritas*).[3] Following this emphasis, Aquinas interpreted faith in Romans 3:24–25 as faith perfected by charity (*fides caritate formata*),[4] declaring that it is ultimately not by faith alone but by what he called the formal righteousness of *caritas,* forming and adorning the soul, that man is justified and brought into fellowship with God. When, therefore, Luther insisted upon *sola fide,* we must understand that he was basically at odds with the whole *caritas* conception.

In the stead of this charity, we place faith, and we say, that faith apprehendeth Jesus Christ, who is the form which adorneth and

---

[3] "Scripture enjoins nothing except charity, and condemns nothing except lust, and in that way fashions the lives of men . . . I mean by *charity* that affection of the mind which aims at the enjoyment of God for His own sake, and the enjoyment of one's self and one's neighbour in subordination to God; by lust I mean that affection of the mind which aims at enjoying one's self and one's neighbour, and other corporeal things, without reference to God." *De Doctrina Christiana,* III, X, 15, 16. For a detailed study of the synthesis and separation of the biblical and Greek love-motifs in Christian thought, see Anders Nygren's *Agape and Eros,* Parts I and II, trans. by A. G. Hebert and Philip S. Watson (New York, 1932 and 1939).

[4] "Charity is said to be the form of faith, in so far as the work of faith is perfected and formed by charity." *Summa Theologica,* trans. by Dominican Fathers (London, n. d.) II–II, iv, iii.

furnisheth faith . . . Christian faith is not an idle quality or empty husk in the heart, which may be in deadly sin until charity come and quicken it; but if it be true faith, is a sure trust and confidence in the heart . . . so that Christ is the object of faith, yea rather even in faith Christ himself is present.[5]

It puts the antithesis in more proper light to define Luther's position regarding salvation as "not by charity, not by works of merit, but by faith alone, by grace alone."

In the period since the sixteenth century, however, Roman scholasticism has not been the only form of rationalism against which Reformation theology has had to maintain the dynamic character of the gospel of grace. There has also been the Enlightenment, heir to the humanist Renaissance, in which it was claimed that reason should be set free, for service to truth, from any obligation to faith at all. More dangerous than both of these, because it threatens the vitality of the Reformation heritage from within, is the recurrent dogmatism of its own orthodoxy i.e., Protestant scholasticism.

It is in the midst of this multi-front conflict that theology in the Reformation heritage comes clearly to recognize that its distinctiveness lies in what is basic to its character as a revelation theology, as a covenant theology, and as a trinitarian theology.

REFORMATION THEOLOGY AS REVELATION THEOLOGY

To affirm that God is himself the source of all our human knowledge of him is to declare that revelation is the foundation of all sound theology. The English word revelation, like its Greek equivalent *apokalypsis,* implies the unveiling or uncovering of that which has been hidden. Thus Luther can speak of God as at once the hidden God (*deus absconditus*) and the re-

---

[5] *A Commentary on St. Paul's Epistle to the Galatians* (Philadelphia, 1875), p. 235. Discussion on Gal. 2:16.

vealed God (*deus revelatus*). The precise meaning which the concept of revelation has for the Reformation heritage arises out of the biblical context in which God discloses himself to the people of Israel as a transcendent and living Person. Thus the phrase 'Word of God' has come to have special significance in the light of the fact that a person regularly communicates with other persons in language. A word is always a projection of a person in person-to-person encounter. The Word of God is the language of God to man in divine-human encounter.[6] As such, it is the medium of expression of the will of God.

Theology in the Reformation heritage is a theology of the Word of God in a dual sense: biblical, as the record of the Word of God; confessional, as response to the Gospel of the Word of God. The two are complementary in the same manner that a dialog requires two persons to be complete. Revelation is incomplete without response. Response is imposible without revelation.

The locus of authority regarding the Word of God for the heirs of the Reformation is the Scriptures of the Old and New Testaments. Nevertheless, the Bible is clearly, in the first instance, the words of men. It is a product of history and of men who are a part of that history. It is a record of the religio-political events of the descendants of Abraham. Yet the record points beyond itself to him to whose Word it continually bears witness. The Word of God and the Bible are indissolubly tied together. Yet they are not identical. Nor is it quite correct to say that the Word of God is in the Bible, for although the Word *is to be found* in reading the Bible, the Word is more than the sum of all these words of men. The Bible as the prime witness

---

[6] The "divine-human encounter," as the conceptual framework for biblical, revelation theology, was suggested by the title in English translation of Emil Brunner's *Wahrheit als Begegnung* (Zurich, 1938); trans. by Amandus W. Loos (Philadelphia, 1943).

to Israel's dynamic encounter with God is the human record of the Word of God.

Therefore, the biblical character of Reformation theology is not to be mistaken for that biblicism which has arisen in the period of her own orthodoxy. Biblicism is a perversion of the personal character of the Word of God, as witnessed in the Scriptures, into a mechanically received verbal literalism, and a perversion of the dynamic character of the will of God into a cold and formal legalism. It is of great significance to one who stands in the Reformation heritage that a century of biblical criticism has restored first of all our appreciation for the historical character of the divine-human relationship recorded in the Scripture, and within the historical the intensely personal character of the divine-human encounter. The continuing contributions of Biblical criticism in distinguishing the Word of God from the words of men, through which *the* Word has been proclaimed and recorded within the Bible, are a necessary part of the working tools of a Reformation theology.

The biblical story, however, as the *record* of the Revelation of God's will through His Word is only one-half of the meaning of our initial declaration that Reformation theology is revelation theology. The other half is the *response* which the revelation elicits from those in whom faith is begotten. Reformation theology rests not only upon the biblical witness to the Word of God but also upon the confessional response to the Gospel of the Word of God. Philip Schaff affirms this polarity of revelation and response in theology in the opening sentence of volume II of his *Creeds of Christendom*: "The Bible is the Word of God to man; the creed is man's answer to God."

Significantly the normative confessional response to the divine Word is, like the witness, to be found in the Scriptures. Indeed the biblical confessions are the very best examples of the confessional element in Reformation theology. In the first place they

complete the dialog of actual person-to-person encounter. Grace
calls forth faith and faith responds in grateful commitment.
Secondly, the nature of the response clarifies the nature of the
Word which brings the response. "For with the heart man
believeth unto righteousness; and with the mouth confession is
made unto salvation." [7] Indeed, it was in such a confessional
mood that Luther's principle of discrimination of the Word of
God within the Scriptures, as that which is related to Christ and
our justification, was affirmed: "Scriptures must be understood,
not against, but in favor of, Christ, and must either be related to
him or not be regarded as true Scripture." [8] Even more specifically confessional is his argument in *A Treatise on Christian
Liberty*:

> You ask, "What then is this Word of God, and how shall it be
> used, since there are so many words of God?" In faith alone is the
> saving and efficacious use of the Word of God, Romans X, "If thou
> confess with thy mouth that Jesus is Lord, and believe with thy heart
> that God hath raised him up from the dead, thou shalt be saved." [9]

Biblical confession comes in two dimensions: confession of
sin and confession of faith.[10] It is evident, however, that the two
dimensions are actually aspects of one response. For example,
in the Old Testament Solomon prays at the dedication of the
temple:

> When thy people Israel are smitten down before the enemy because
> they have sinned against thee, if they turn again (repent) unto thee,
> and *confess* thy name, and pray . . . then hear thou in heaven, and
> forgive the sin of thy people Israel. . . .[11]

[7] Rom. 10:10.
[8] Thesis 41 on Rom. 3:28. W. A. 39, I 47.
[9] *Works of Martin Luther,* trans. by W. A. Lambert (Philadelphia, 1916), II, 315.
[10] Cf. Lev. 5:5, Ps. 32:5, Neh. 9:2, Dan. 9:20, Matt. 10:32, John 9:22, Rom.
10:9-10; Phil. 2:11.
[11] I Kings 8:33-34a.

Again, Isaiah's response to the vision of Yahweh in the temple is first, "Woe is me! for I am undone; because I am a man of unclean lips, . . ." and then "Here am I, send me." [12] The same antiphony is found in the New Testament *kerygma*: "If we *confess* our sins, he is faithful and just, and will forgive and cleanse us from all unrighteousness . . . Whoever *confesses* that Jesus is the son of God, God abides in him, and he in God." [13]

If, as is the clear intent of the New Testament, confession is meant to accentuate the positive, the most important evidence is that which reports the first-hand confession of those for whom Jesus Christ is the unique revelation of God, the Word of God in most intimate personal encounter.[14] It was out of such primitive confessions of faith that the early and medieval church developed the rules of faith and the creedal formulae of all Christian theology, and in their wake the Reformation heritage produced catechisms and confessional symbols.

In fashion similar to the relation which was discovered to exist between the Scriptures and the Word, an observation must be made concerning the relation of confessional standards to confessions of faith. In the confessional symbols there is an understandable tendency for the second personal form of address of the confession "Thou art the Christ," to give way to

[12] Isa. 6:5–8.

[13] I John 1:9 and 4:15.

[14] There are four such reports:

1) The affirmation of Nathanael at his call by Jesus: "Thou art the Son of God, Thou art King of Israel!" (John 1:49)

2) The confession of Peter at the retreat with Jesus and his disciples at Caesarea Philippi: "Thous art the Christ, the Son of the living God!" (Matt. 16:16)

3) The witness of Thomas the doubter to the Risen Jesus: "My Lord and My God!" (John 20:28)

4) The question of Saul consequent upon the vision of Jesus on the way to Damascus: "Who art thou Lord?"; and Saul's answer to his own question offered a few days later in the synagogue in Damascus, "He is the Son of God." (Acts 9:5, 20)

an impersonal declaration, e.g., "The churches, with common consent among us, do teach that the decree of the Nicene Synod . . . is true, and without doubt *to be believed*." [15] The confessional character of Reformation theology, however, is not to be mistaken for that perversion of its foundation, which is commonly called confessionalism,[16] by which is meant rigid adherence to a particular doctrinal standard or profession of belief as a test of faith. Confessional symbols are testimonies of faith, but when used as tests of faith are divisive and deadly, resulting all too frequently in arbitrary patterns of inclusion and exclusion. Thereby they belie the fact that undergirding, and ultimately transcending, all the variant and competing professions, Lutheran, Reformed and others, there is a common confession of faith in "the God and Father of our Lord Jesus Christ," and in "Jesus Christ as Lord and Savior."

The recovery of the personal dimension in the Gospel of forgiveness and reconciliation, upon repentance and faith in each new generation, is the *sine qua non* of avoiding the abyss which yawns on both sides of Reformation theology. On the one side there is the rationalistic humanism of proud self-sufficiency, in which no confession rises to man's lips, and on the other the rationalistic dogmatism of confessionalism in which faith has been sterlized and supplanted by intellectual belief. The extent to which the ecumenical movement represents such a vital spirit, as this demands, will determine its hopefulness as the bearer of a new reformation in our time.

Taken together, in their dynamic form, these two comple-

---

[15] The Augsburg Confession, I, I. (Italics ours).

[16] "Systematic theology can be confessional only in so far as the confessional element is of assistance in understanding and perceiving that which is essentially Christian. . . . The work of systematic theology involves, therefore, with reference to confessionalism a continual self-examination, far removed from all naive confessional self-sufficiency." Gustaf Aulén, *The Faith of the Christian Church,* trans. by Eric H. Wahlstrom and G. Everett Arden (Philadelphia, 1948), p. 18.

mentary aspects of the divine-human encounter as personal dialog between God and man, the biblical witness and the confessional response, constitute the two pillars of a theology of the Word of God.

REFORMATION THEOLOGY AS COVENANT THEOLOGY

To speak of Reformation Theology as covenant theology is to bring the two components of revelation and response, in encounter, together within one dynamic context. "All real living is meeting," of *I* and *Thou,* says Martin Buber.[17] The real meetings of life, however, are fundamentally not clandestine but have plan and purpose and belong to a context. Even the chance happening of "boy meets girl" is not without a social frame of reference. Meaningful person-to-person addresses always occur as a part of a context, either potential or actual: children encounter each other within the family, in school, or in the community; workers at their jobs; neighbors at the community store. To be sure our human egocentricity tends to make us seek familiar contexts for meeting and thereby to exclude ourselves and others, on merely artificial lines of color or class or nationality, from some of the most fruitful "real life" experiences. The solution of our problem, of course, is not to escape from our being bound to these smaller contexts of personal encounter. It is to recognize the interrelation of smaller within more and more inclusive contexts.

Reformation theology must always remind itself and those to whom it would communicate the Word of God that the divine-human person-to-person encounter is not without con-

[17] *I and Thou,* trans. by Ronald Gregor Smith (Edinburgh, 1937), p. 11. In the *I-Thou* category Buber includes all personal relationships, man to man and God to man. This is not to say that the latter is to be judged by the character of the former. Rather, for Buber, the *Thou* which meets man through grace gives him the norm for the pattern of relationship which takes place when he says *Thou* to another man.

text. The biblical idea of covenant gives it its context, and at the same time a basis for the resolution of the problem of contextual exclusiveness. The divine-human covenant is universal in scope and intense in its demands for loyalty. Like all interpersonal agreements it pre-supposes the moral freedom, good faith, and responsibility of both parties. It consists of mutually declared rights and duties, promises and demands. The divine-human covenant is unique in that, without breaching any of the conditions listed above, God always takes the initiative in its institution, and makes of it an indestructible relationship.[18] Its devotees in historic Israel broke their part of the bargain repeatedly, according to their own admission, yet never questioned the goodness of God's motive in its initiation, nor his faithfulness in its sustentation.[19] They misrepresented his declarations: "I am Yahweh, your God, and ye shall be my people!"[20] indicating by their actions that they thought that their being chosen involved exclusive rights and privileges, but they never doubted that God's covenant-love both explained the present and guaranteed the future.[21]

The Scripture abounds in records of historical covenants of this kind. According to Christian belief, however, biblical history bears especial significance. It records not merely the history of the Hebrew people; it is *the way in which God wills to act upon all mankind in every moment.* Faith sees in the Scriptures a universal pattern of covenant relationship, in which there are included two interdependent but unequally valid forms of encounter, known as the old and new covenants. This eschatological form of interpretation of biblical history is native to Reformation theology and is one of its claims to distinction.

[18] Amos 2:9 ff.
[19] Mic. 3:9–11.
[20] Jer. 7:21–26.
[21] Hos. 11:1 ff. Cf. Isa. 1:2, 5:1.

Eschatology has a double usage in theological discourse, one general and one specific. Specifically it deals with last things, the final judgment and redemption, etc. It aims to interpret the Eternal as the goal of that which is revealed in the context of the temporal and historical. More generally, echatology is the framework of all revelation theology, in which the events of the temporal and historical are regularly interpreted in the perspective of eternity and as the effects of divine initiative. It is in this more general sense that Reformation theology treats the biblical covenants eschatologically.

Eschatology is the theological counterpart of what in philosophical discourse is called the philosophy of history. Eschatology is the Christian philosophy of history. No philosophy has found such profound significance in history as does Christian theology. Greek idealism, modern Hegelian rationalism, Hindu mysticism all adjudge history as the negation of Eternity. History is becoming, not being; illusory (*maya*), not real. History is cyclical, only the image of eternal sphericity. Naturalisms— evolutionary, dialectical, and atomistic—agree in adjudging historic existence as ultimate, purposeful in terms of itself, but declare it to be of no *eternal* significance.

In Christian theology history has become the instrument of God. The temporal is the context of the activity of the Eternal. Against the background of the divine Kingdom, time and history have eternal significance. Time and history are not in themselves eternal, but man who inhabits them is declared to be made for eternity. The divine revelation made manifest in the divine-human encounters of history, especially in the Incarnation, assures man at once of the eternal significance of his temporal existence and of the transhistorical goal which gives meaning to his historical decisions.

According to this manner of interpretation there is a basic

motif which is at work in the biblical covenants—the principle
of promise and fulfilment. Its operation between the old and
new covenants is sometimes referred to as the relation of law
and gospel. A more careful investigation will indicate, however, that the promise-fulfilment motif of God's will operates
within as well as between covenants. For example, the old
covenant is not merely law, but a cycle of law and prophecy;
and the new covenant of the gospel involves both Christ and
the Church. Thus in prophecy there is at once the fulfilment
of an older covenant code and a promise of a new covenant.[22]
And Jesus Christ, in whom the prophetic promise of the reconciliation of man to God was fulfilled, is similarly the promise of
the full redemption of man from sin into a new fellowship with
God through his sacramental Body, the Church. It is, moreover,
within this four-part pattern of law, prophecy, Christ and the
Church that the universal activity of God, as Creator-Sustainer,
Judge-Redeemer, Reconciler and Recreator, becomes evident,
and to which the four-fold sequence of the Christian life cor-
responds: creation, fall, reconciliation and recreation.

Furthermore, throughout the eschatological sequence from
creation to recreation, the encounter between God and man is
made manifest in two correlate modes of divine activity: the
Word of address, and the gift of the Spirit.[23] Yahweh, the
author of covenants, not only makes the demands, he gives the
power to meet the demands; he not only makes promises, but
the promises are such that their fulfilment is ultimately contingent upon his own nature, he holds men accountable for
their failures in the agreement, but he suffers, in his own heart,
the judgment which accompanies their hope of redemption.

[22] Jer. 31:31–34. Cf. Exod. 20:22 ff.
[23] For example, Gen. 1:1–3, "In the beginning God created . . . and the Spirit
of God moved. . . . and God said . . ."

The Word as divinely addressed is always accompanied by the Spirit as divinely given. The Word as addressed expresses the existential irreducibility of God and man, the gift of the Spirit, their continuous functional correlativity in the divine plan. The proclamation of the Word, by its very nature, depends ultimately for its effect, as confrontation, upon the power of the spiritual gift which accompanies it.

Reformation theology, by virtue of its eschatological interpretation of the biblical covenants may make its greatest contribution to our troubled times in terms of the doctrine of the Church, as at once the Body of Christ and the *koionia* of the Holy Spirit.[24] Moreover, it is at this point that the ecumenical temper of the Church in our generation may discover that its composition is vital and dynamic because it reunites two motifs which partisan forces within Protestantism have mutually neglected. The ecumenical Church brings together the promise inherent in the Word, as proclaimed by the more orthodox Lutheran and Reformed traditions, with the fulfilment of the promise in the empowering activity of the Spirit, as experienced by the more radical sects of the Reformation heritage, such as Anabaptist, Mennonite, Quaker.

REFORMATION THEOLOGY AS TRINITARIAN THEOLOGY

Within the context of what God has done in covenant-encounter, i.e., in the eschatological framework of the two modes of the divine address and the divine gift, we may venture to affirm something about what God is. Theology in the Reformation heritage, because it accepts revelation as its fundamental category, i.e., is basically biblical and confessional, and because it acknowledges the eschatological context of the divine-human encounter, has, in what it affirms about God, an accent which is

[24] I Cor. 12.

very easily lost in association with philosophical thought patterns. Nonetheless, on peril of not speaking to the conditions of men in other cultures and settings than those in which its dogmatics are accepted on assent, theological thought must always endeavor to express the biblical witness to God in terminology which, while in no wise sterilizing the dynamic, personal language of the Bible, will stand up under conceptual analysis.

Two concerns engage the attention of Reformation theology regarding the nature of God: his essential nature and his eternal modes of existence. The first leads to an affirmation of the polar unity of the essential nature of God; the second leads to a declaration of the triunity of his existence.

The essential unity of God is one of the pillars of all Hebrew-Christian theology. From the *Shema Israel* of Deuteronomy 6:4 to the creedal formulation of the Council of Nicaea, there is a continuous emphasis upon monotheism. Withal, it would appear that the nature of the revelation which such formulae attempt to express has tended to vary the character of the monotheistic emphasis, by placing the accent from one time to another upon two different kinds of unity: internal homogeneity and external singleness. The *Shema* says: "Yahweh our God is one Yahweh." The accent is upon internal homogeneity. It does not say, without interpretation, "one God." It affirms divine unity internally, and only implies the denial, externally, of other gods. Nicene theology, on the other hand, affirms both the singleness of the one God and the homogeneity of the divine essence (*homoousion*), but insists upon a new pattern of internal distinction within the unity (*una substantia, tres personae*).

For Christian theology the problem is no longer to distinguish between unity as internal and external. The problem is rather, as Leonard Hodgson puts it, to distinguish between simple and complex unity.[25] The "God" of Nicene theology is not a simple mathematical unity, and need not be so either to represent the biblical revelation or to be an actual unity. Unity may be and is, in theological expression, a complex unity of the type of a living organism. An organism is a complex whole, composed of various elements unified in a single life history, in which there is mutual or reciprocal dependence of the whole and its constituent parts, and whose elements can only play their part in that life if they are different and complementary to each other. Theology in the Reformation tradition finds the concepts of organic unity a useful device in what it says about the nature of God.

The biblical words for God are numerous and do not all have the same etymological emphasis. The main ones, however, when taken together, suggest a polar unity in his essential nature. Polarity is a type of organic unity, which expresses two-ness of different or even opposite elements in a tension, and in which the two are united functionally without loss of identity. Specifically, the Hebrew words *elohim* (god) and *adonai* (lord) are polar within the broader unity of the name Yahweh (Jehovah). This is evidenced by the fact that, when in later times the sacred name was no longer used, either of the other words could be substituted for it in a context where the other one was already used. Moreover, behind this practical fact there appears a polarity of meaning between the words themselves: *adonai,* generally used as an address of reverence or of personal respect, when applied to deity expresses "worship": and *elohim,* derived from the root meaning strong or powerful, when used for deity means "the Almighty."

To say that Yahweh is supremely worshipful and supremely

---

[25] *The Doctrine of the Trinity* (New York, 1944), pp. 89–96. Hodgson suggests a tri-personality or social unity conception of trinity. We follow Karl Barth and others in attempting to distinguish *personae* and *hypostases* in line with classical denotation, as 'modes of existence' rather than as 'centers of consciousness.'

powerful is to express in a polar unity the essence of what the *Shema,* the story of Moses at the bush, Isaiah in the temple and countless confessional references declare to be his essence. In spiritual terminology it is to affirm that God is at once holiness and love, i.e., holy love. Holiness, expressing the divine motif of worshipfulness, accents the existential irreducibility of the person of God to human character. Love, expressing the motif of divine motivation to action, revealed in its fullest in covenant activity, accents the functional correlation of God and man in encounter. The two words, as a definition of the essential nature of God, must never be allowed to compete with each other for the supremacy in our thinking; for when they do, holiness without love becomes unduly austere, and love without holiness becomes sentimental and spineless.

Other words, often attributed to the deity in pairs, indicate, it would appear, specific expressions of holy love, or love-holiness, as the universal character of the divine essence. For example: "the power of God and the wisdom of God" are by Paul attributed to Christ.[26] They are also attributed to the creator—creature encounter in the Psalms and in Proverbs. In the prophetic literature the mercy of God and the righteousness of God are brought into productive relation.[27] The use by Jesus of fatherhood and kingship in correlate yet distinctive application to God expresses the same duality in the unity of love-holiness.

If the recently suggested interpretation of Exodus 3:14, "I CAUSE TO BE THAT WHICH COMES TO BE," be correct,[28] it is apparent that the restoration of the name YAHWEH by the modern translators of the Old Testament may have much more significance

---

[26] I Cor. 1:24.
[27] Cf. Hos., Amos and Mic. 6:6–8.
[28] R. B. Y. Scott, article "Jehovah" in *An Encyclopedia of Religion,* Vergilius Ferm (New York, 1945), suggests: "He who causes to be what happens" or "He causes to be what exists."

for Christian theology than merely to preserve historical accuracy. A word which is produced out of the causative form of the root meaning *to be*, and implying 'The Eternal Source of all,' is not one which Reformation theologians should permit to be covered up under the less striking substitute—Lord. Here is expressed in one word the essence of both *adonai* and *elohim*, and what is more important a word with an emphasis synonymous with *ruach* (spirit), often used in conjunction with it or with other deity-words to express *energetic source of power and action*.

The unity, therefore, of the divine essence, of which holy love is the inner polar definition, is the Eternal Spirit who is called Yahweh. In dealing with the modes of revelation of deity, we have already observed the prominent role that the motive power of the Spirit plays in convenant-encounter. We have now to declare that that *Spirit,* whose gift of himself is a mode of revelation along with the proclamation of the Word of promise, is the source of the covenant-encounter through which he continues to disclose his innermost essence—holy love.

It is by no means unessential that a theology in the Reformation heritage declares the triunity of God. The triunity of God is the most inclusive affirmation about God that the understanding-seeking faith can produce. By that token, it is the area in which greatest honest variation of interpretation has persisted through the centuries.

Christian theology may produce variations in the doctrine of the trinity, but there is a solid core of trinitarian religion from which to set out. (1) The earliest form of confessional response to the Word of revelation was in solid agreement in affirming the saviourhood and redemptive work of Jesus Christ. (2) The primitive church was well aware of what we declared in connection with the discussion of the modes of revelation in covenant-encounter, that the gift of the Spirit in the new covenant is the fruition of the Incarnation of the Word. The abiding presence and indwelling of the Counsellor assured those who were reconciled by the grace of Christ, that participation in the fellowship in the Spirit, in which he was conceived, was their continuing privilege. (3) But both Word as proclamation and Spirit as gift have their source in the Eternal, whom Jesus called Father and of whom Hebrews thought Yahweh when they said *adonai* (lord). The simple distinction between God over us, God with us, and God indwelling in us, which expresses the three-fold form of the activity of the Spirit in the encounters of the biblical covenants is not an over-simplification of the religious trinity of Christian confession.

At this juncture it is much easier to explain how a doctrine of the triune God becomes inevitable for Christian theology than it is to explain the doctrine. The mystery of the triune modes of God's existence remains a mystery after our best efforts. To say, however, that the bringing together of the Yahweh monotheism of the *Shema* and the empirical facts and confessional evidence concerning the two modes of divine self-disclosure (the address of the Word and the gift of the Spirit) as they operated in the New Covenant, is inevitably to suggest a trinity. It becomes triunity only when faith expresses the conviction that "what God is in revelation, He is antecedently in Himself." [29] The modes of revelation of God's essence become the bridge to a declaration concerning the eternal modes of God's existence.

Furthermore, it is the Pauline benediction at the end of II Corinthians (13:14) which gives the clue to the manner in which the modes of revelation in history may be transmuted, in

[29] K. Barth, *Doctrine of the Word of God,* trans. by G. T. Thomson (New York, 1936), p. 533.

avoidance of Sabellius' heresy, into eternal modes of existence. The attribution of special functions and characteristics to the three *personae* of the triune God has always been practiced by worthy theologians, including the Fathers and the Reformers,[30] but always with the understanding that, in the final analysis, such special functions and characteristics (with the exception of the relational character which distinguishes the several *personae* from each other) are shared in by the whole trinity. The apostolic benediction is superior to all other expressions of this effort, we suggest, because it maintains the essence throughout in the key attributive concept, varying it functionally in accord with the internal character of all dynamic, volitional, personal activity: The *love* of God (the Eternal Father in the Trinity) is the will, the source of the covenant-encounter, the energy of salvation; the *grace* of our Lord Jesus Christ (the Eternal Son in the Trinity) is the act, the Word of revelation, the work of salvation; the *fellowship* of the Holy Spirit (the Eternal Spirit in the Trinity) is the motive, the gift of the Spirit, the power of salvation.[31]

Grace is love at work; and fellowship is love empowering; love is gracious and powerful. Will, act, and motive; source, word, and gift; energy, work, and power; love, grace, and fellowship—these are all analogical to Father, Son and Holy Spirit; and, applying as they do functionally and dynamically to the inner character of personal life, they seem clearly to

[30] "There is in God a certain distinction or economy, which makes no change in the unity of the essence." Tertullian, quoted by John Calvin, *Institutes of the Christian Religion,* trans. by John Allen (6th Am. ed., Philadelphia, 1928), I, xiii, 6.

[31] It is reassuring, after having attempted such an interpretation, to find the following, in John Calvin's *Institutes,* I, xiii, 18, "I doubt the propriety of borrowing similitudes from human things, to express the force of this distinction . . . Yet it is not right to be silent on the distinction which we find expressed in the Scriptures; which is this—that to the Father is attributed the principle of action, the fountain and source of all things; to the Son, wisdom, counsel, and the arrangement of all operations; and the power and efficacy of the action is assigned to the Spirit."

express as well as human limitations will permit the triunity of God's eternal existence as one Holy Spirit of Love.

These analogies, moreover, help to clarify the problem of the relation of the *personae* of the Triune God to each other. Reformation theology has always followed the Nicene formula in its western interpretation which, although denying subordination of Son and Spirit in the affirmation of *homo-ousion*, declares the Son to be begotten of the Father and incarnate by the Holy Spirit, whereas the Spirit proceeds from the Father and the Son. By these analogies, *the Son* is begotten of the Father as the act is begotten of the will to act, and is incarnate of the Spirit as the act embodies the motive, *or* as work is begotten of energy and as work embodies power. *The Spirit* proceeds from the Father and the Son in the same fashion that motive power for action proceeds both from the will to act and from actual work accomplished. *The Father* is the ultimate source of both the Son and the Spirit as the will to act in the source both of the act and of the motive power for action, and as energy is the source of both work and power.

In spiritual terms, the saving grace of Jesus Christ is begotten of the love of the Father and is embodied in the fellowship of the Church. The fellowship in which we participate proceeds both from the will of the Father and from the work of our Lord Jesus Christ. The love of God is the dynamic source of both the reconciling work of Jesus Christ and the recreating fellowship of the Spirit in the Church.

We have deliberately taken our position within the Reformation heritage, neither denying that there are other interpretations of Christian theology nor admitting that Reformation theology is just one among others. To be sure, all theology is fallible because it is a product of human understanding, and Reformation theologians are no less fallible than others. If there is any reason for the appearance and continued existence of this heritage in human history, however, it lies in the fidelity with which it aims to represent the biblical motif in Christian thought. Insofar as Reformation theology is true to its own purpose it is an effort to examine and to understand the best-attested affirmations of Christian faith about God and his activity.

One of the prime *desiderata* of our time is the achievement of an ecumenical Christian theology to express the convictions which belong to the ecumenical movement. It is our judgment that Reformation theology can best abet that end, neither by claiming to be an ecumenical theology nor by trying to become one, but by witnessing to those basic features of the *ecumenical Christian faith*, which places the Christian life in the context of the divine-human covenant-encounter, and which finds the meaning of all life in the self-disclosure of the divine love through the confrontation of his Word in Jesus Christ and the gift of his Spirit in the fellowship of the Church.

JESUS THE CHRIST, OUR LORD

Samuel D. Press

THE recovery of the Christian message in its purity from its authentic sources is the great achievement of the Reformers of the sixteenth century. By recentering the faith of the Christian fellowship in the sole lordship of Jesus Christ over the Church and the world they became the prophetic organs for the restoration of the Church, issuing in the birth of Protestantism. They not only came to see the central place of Christ in biblical revelation, but through personal experience they also received a deepened understanding of the *sola gratia* and the *sola fides* in the gospel. The new insight into the all-encompassing redemptive work of God in Christ led them to the recognition that Jesus is the sole mediator of our salvation, the one and only Head of the Church. Christ does indeed elect to carry on the work of his Church on earth through human servants chosen from the fellowship of forgiven sinners, but none of them can ever substitute for him. Christ has no vicar on earth, and his Church needs none because the living Christ is always present in its midst. He is its Lord.

Simultaneously the Reformers came to have both a clearer understanding of the purely spiritual character of Christ's Kingdom and also of the work of his Church on earth. Jesus' reply to Pilate, "My Kingdom is not of this world" [1] and his answer, "It is not for you to know times or seasons, which the Father has set within his own authority," [2] to the disciples'

[1] John 18:36–37.
[2] Acts 1:6–8.

question whether he would then restore the kingdom make it crystal clear why the Church can have no other head than its spiritual head, the risen Christ who alone has conquered the world. These words also make it clear why it dare not follow any leadership purporting to take the place of Christ, whether it be pope or bishop or any other ecclesiastical executive. His true servants know that they can do no more than lead men to Christ, for he alone is the way, the truth and the life.

What makes the proclamation of the gospel from the pulpit effective is that the hearers hear and see no one but Jesus alone. Likewise the sacraments become real with a living meaningfulness only by his presence in the midst of us. Apart from him they sink to the level of mere ritual or, what is worse, to a mechanical and quasi-magical process. In him lie both the glory and the strength of the Church. Without him the Church cannot carry out its unchanging mission to demonstrate to the world the spirit and the power of the eternal Word which conquers the world, heals the nations, relieves our sin-ridden society from its woes, and saves humanity from the doom of perdition.

To have Christ in its midst is the distinctiveness of the Church. Not its acquired possessions or the achievements of its own works, but the spiritual riches that are his gift constitute its imperishable, inexhaustible wealth. The Church's supreme prerogative, a prerogative intended for all men, is to serve him, of whose service the Gelasian Sacramentary says: *Cui servire regnare est.* To serve him is to reign because his service is perfect freedom. In the spiritual sphere of divine truth and righteousness all is freedom, for there grace reigns supreme.

To this eternal world of pure freedom in God, Christ is the door. He is the way to God because he is the truth; in him is the life of God. He alone has the power to make our life in every part, in all of its relationships a divine worship, a worship in spirit and truth, a constant growing in grace, in goodness, an ever deepening adoration before the throne of the Almighty, and an honoring of God as God in the obedience of faith and in the selfless service of love to his children on earth.

Herein lies the core of the lordship of Jesus Christ: he came on earth to hallow in the souls of men the Great Name, the Name of the Holy God who alone is good. The master purpose of Jesus' life was to establish over the whole world the kingship of him who reigns in the sovereignty of absolute freedom. His messianic mission as the Christ was to set the divine authority of overpowering goodness against the self-assertive will of man in revolt.[3] Therefore he gave himself to the holy ministry of the forgiving love of God who in simultaneously condemning and conquering sin seeks to win back man the sinner to the obedience of faith. Thus the man Jesus of Nazareth became the first-born of a new creation, the head of a new humanity forming a brotherhood of sons of the Father in heaven. In the words of Pascal:

Jesus Christ, without riches, and without any external exhibition of knowledge, is in His own order of holiness. He did not invent; He did not reign. But He was humble, patient, holy, holy to God, terrible to devils, without any sin. Oh! in what great pomp, and in what wonderful splendor, He is come to the eyes of the heart, which perceive wisdom.[4]

THE DIVINE DELIVERER

Neither the sages of the Orient nor the learned and the artists of the Occident had a cure for sin and its cancerous evils ending in dreaded death to the soul of man. The vaunted empire-builders in history, hailed as heroes in the sphere of military conquest, have brought much woe but not peace on earth.

[3] Cf. Rom. 12:14–21.
[4] *Pensées*, Fragment 792. Trans. by W. F. Trotter (New York, 1941).

Towering well nigh to the zenith of intellectual attainments with all the inventive master minds in the field of technology, man lacks the means of staying and overcoming moral deterioration, social disintegration, and economic impoverishment in human society. But with Christ's coming into our world there arose over humanity the "sun of righteousness with healing in its wings" [5] for all the woes of the children of time. His appearance is, therefore, the transcending event in human history.

He, who is the center of history, came not out of our race but into our humanity from above. Yet the tie that binds him to us and us to him is the most intimate of our existence. It is the one in which we recognize the organic solidarity of humanity. For it was through him that all which has been created came into being, and without him came nothing that has come to be. [6] The divine and the human, the Creator and man made in his image, are neither opposites nor mutually exclusive. In fact, God's relation to us constitutes the very essence of our humanity. Our relation to God based upon his relation to us is the unique datum of our being. Therefore we belong to Christ, who belongs to God, as we belong to no one else. Jesus Christ is the key to human existence. He is the sun in the realm of our spirit.

His claim on us stands not only in the creative beginning of life but also encompasses our life in its entirety. When man fell away from his Creator, becoming the prodigal son who left his Father's house with the words, "Give me my share of the property," then it was God who reached out to fallen man, found him in misery at the end of his road, and in his mercy redeemed him by reconciling him to himself in the Crucified.

The story of God's saving activity in Jesus the Christ is the theme of all the apostolical witnesses; it is the *kerygma* of the

[5] Mal. 4:2.
[6] John 1:3.

first Christian community. All the prophetic organs of ancient biblical revelation point to this event: God's advent on earth in Jesus Christ. So central to our Christian faith is the Christological question, "Who do men say that the Son of Man is?" that the struggle to understand Jesus as the Christ, the Son of God and the Lord over life and death, has engaged the Church through the centuries and continues to do so in every new generation. In its profoundest theological meaning the Christological question is the religious question which confronts every man. Therefore, the true answer to the Christological question comes home to us not in an intellectual formula commanding universal assent, but in a personal decision of faith.

The locus of religious insight, the organ for divine revelation, according to Scriptures, is in the heart, i.e., in the depth of self where man comes face to face with God alone, realizes himself as known by the all-knowing Lord of life, and makes the existential decisions which determine his life in its wholeness. We can not grasp the meaning of the divine lordship of Christ until we learn to know him as our Savior and come to believe in him as the Son of God. All the men of the New Testament confess him to be the Son of God as the One in whom God is fully revealed to us in his grace and power. In the Christ, God meets us as our Deliverer who breaks the chains of captivity in which we are held by sin and puts an end forever to the dominion of death, the iron ring around our existence.[7]

To have the Christian faith, then, means to know for a certainty that Jesus Christ reigns as King over humanity, that through him God has indeed taken the affairs of the world of sinners into his hands. Through Jesus God has spoken his final word in judgment and mercy over our race. Outwardly the stream of history flowed on as usual. Yet during the short span

[7] Cf. Heb. 2:14–15 and I. Cor. 15:55.

of years which encompasses the life and the messianic ministry of Jesus on earth the most momentous event in the spiritual history of man occurred. It marks the end of the Adamitic era and the beginning of the Christian era. Here was the man in whose life the kingly reign of God became a reality on earth.

In the man Jesus of Nazareth the ancient promise of a Deliverer—according to later prophecy in the person of a scion of the House of David—finds its true spiritual interpretation. In him Old Testament prophecy is confirmed by historical fulfilment. "Jesus of Nazareth King of the Jews" (as Pontius Pilate denominated him in the short legend inscribed above his head on the cross) is the man whom God gave to the world to be our King.

This strange man on his cross whose life on earth lived in an unbroken relation of loyalty to his Father in heaven stands out as the one purely white spot on the dark background of our sinful race in revolt against God. Him whom the world of sinners rejected God chose to be our Savior and Lord. In the words of Luther: "God will not and can not be known otherwise than through that despised man Jesus." That life in its content is tremendously and transcendingly more luminous than what all of our Christological doctrines so earnestly endeavor to say. The story of Jesus of Nazareth from his entrance into the world until the day he was taken up into heaven can be understood only as a soteriological datum. What to our unregenerate mind seems sheer foolishness is, to the eyes of faith, a lesson in the wisdom of God, "because the foolishness of God is wiser than men and the weakness of God is stronger than men." [8] As the New Testament men tell it, the life of Jesus is the story of a true man in whom dwelt the fulness of the Godhead.

Jesus saw in his messianic calling not the dignity of an office

[8] I Cor. 1:25.

but a holy commission laid on him as the Son of God. He knew it to be the royal prerogative of the Son of Man to bestow the sovereign grace of his Father upon a lost world, to offer to prodigal man God's forgiveness. He exercised this function not by the proclamation of a lordly edict or by arrogating to himself supernatural powers. Rather he gave his life in personal service on behalf of his brothers to the worship of God. He actualized his Father's holy will among them. He fulfilled all the demands of divine righteousness on the moral plane of man's life in history. He sanctified himself for us that we might be sanctified in truth.

The man Jesus of Nazareth, who stood before John the Baptist on the banks of the Jordan, came to be baptized by John in order to fulfill all righteousness. He did not begin his messianic ministry by heralding himself as Israel's promised king who would turn the tide of world affairs. In John's baptism, he saw the divinely ordained way, the way of righteousness, for the bringing in of the kingly reign of God which was to make an end of sin and to establish everlasting righteousness by making reconciliation for iniquity.[9] Voluntarily he joined the rank and file of sinners who obeyed the call to the way of righteousness.

Jesus, the man of Nazareth, was the humblest man that had ever come before this messenger of God on the banks of the Jordan who preached repentance to all comers without respect to person. But this practised discerner of spirits, with the instinct of the true prophet of God, recognized in the man Jesus the spirit of holiness which distinguished him from all the thousands who had come out to him. *"Er reucht den Geist,"* says Luther. Overwhelmed by the moral majesty of this candidate for baptism, this stern, unbendable man of God who "never

[9] Cf. Dan. 9:3–24 and Matt. 21:25–32.

feared the face of any man," broke down before Jesus and confessed himself a sinner in need of baptism from him who was sent to baptize with the Holy Spirit and fire. This man, Jesus of Nazareth, who made the cause of sinners, their guilt, and their need of righteousness his cause, the voice from heaven declared to be the Holy One, the beloved Son, sent by the Father to be the Savior of his people.

Day after day, morning and evening, a lamb was sacrificed in the temple at Jerusalem to cover the sins of the nation. But all these religious offerings could not transform the people, as the Baptist came to see. All of their religious doings were powerless to stay the downward course of the nation in moral depravity to ruin. In Jesus, the sinless man upon whom he had seen the Holy Spirit descend from heaven, John the Baptist recognized the One awaited through the ages by all who looked for the redemption of Israel. Here at long last was the Lamb of God come to take away the sin of the world at the cost of his own blood.

The meaning of the life of Jesus, as our Savior and Lord has been unravelled for us in the light of the events of Calvary and Easter Morn. For the life of Jesus is not the achievement of divine sonship but the unfolding of his divine sonship in the fulfilment of the will of God for our salvation. The portrait of Jesus depicted in the New Testament is neither that of a superman conqueror in his own might nor that of one outfitted with a supernatural equipment. The Jesus whom his contemporary followers describe for us was a simple, true man of God who lived his life completely under revelation. His one consuming interest in life was to do the will of him whom he loved with his whole heart and to accomplish the new deed of God which he knew to be his divine mission: to redeem the wayward children of God in the world.

To learn to know the will of his Father, Jesus depended on the Word—on every word that came to him from the mouth of God, in ancient and ever-new revelation. Holy Scriptures were for him living messages of an ever-present God.[10] He reminds us that "God worketh still" in order that we also might see his presence in gospel history and in the events of our personal lives so as to receive his guidance which leads us in the way of holiness. By living in the Word and by whole nights spent in prayer, Jesus gained assurance for himself of the course his Father led him step by step. Through his unfaltering obedience to, and by his implicit trust in, his holy Father, Jesus walked in accordance with the Spirit of holiness.[11]

Only a sinless One could become the Christ who delivers us from our sin.[12] Such a One could not stem from our race of sinners. He who mediates for God can only be one who comes to us from God; he comes among us as the One who reflects the glory of God; he is the only One that can reveal the Father fully in the souls of men. That is what his disciples experienced in Jesus, the eternal Son of God, who came into our flesh and blood to reveal himself as our true brother. He put on humanity with all its consequences.

The great miracle of the incarnation is that God poured out his glory into a human life. This tremendous divine action in history reveals God, the Holy One, as seeking to establish fellowship with man the sinner by transforming him into the likeness of the Son of his love. This divine purpose is manifest throughout the whole Old Testament from the calling of Abraham to the precious promise given through Malachi. It is the throbbing pulse of the history of salvation.

---

[10] Exod. 40:34–38 and John 5:17.
[11] Cf. I Pet. 1:16, Matt. 5:48, Mark 10:18.
[12] Luke 5:8, 7:6–7.

The man, Jesus of Nazareth, whom God gave us to be our Savior, our King, and our Lord, first became our brother. The author of the epistle to the Hebrews expresses a profound insight into the purpose of the incarnation of the Son of God in stating: "Wherefore when he cometh into the world, he saith, . . . a body didst thou prepare for me . . . Then said I, Lo, I am come . . . to do thy will, O God." And the author adds: "By which will we have been sanctified through the offering of the body of Jesus Christ once for all." [13] Though the royal lordship of Jesus the Christ comes eminently to the foreground with his resurrection, in that the resurrection sets him forth as the conqueror over death and as the Son of God in power, yet the exercise of his kindly reign began with his entrance into his messianic calling as Mediator.

The True Man

Jesus not only reveals God to us but he simultaneously makes manifest what true humanity is. He did not strive to be some sort of ideal man. He chose the name "the son of man" which combines his high calling as Head of a new humanity with the status of one who was satisfied to live on the plane of common manhood. He would be the Servant of Jahweh who lives by God alone, "who can do nothing of his own accord, but only what he sees the Father doing." [14] In Jesus we have the portrait of a true man, man as God intended him, a man whose life in every part was the workmanship of the Holy Spirit. From him, whom Philippe Vernier calls "the earthly face of God," we learn indeed the grandeur of the gift of God in the creation of man, the profound meaning of *humanitas*. We come to appreciate the true greatness of man, his nobility as a child of God.

[13]Heb. 10:5, 7 and 10.
[14] Heb. 12:2.

In Jesus we see man in the full realization of the divine image, the full stature of mature manhood. Humanity as it appears in the man of Nazareth claims the obeisance of all humankind. By all who know what true humanity is, he is acknowledged to be the unquestioned King of humanity. Poignantly it comes home to us in his presence how far our lives fall short of the glory of God, of what they might have been. As we look upon him, we become filled inwardly with the deep yearning to be like him, to live a life which honors God as God and serves humanity in love. His life, lived in unbroken loyalty to God in a completely selfless service to his brothers in the world, teaches us what the Holy Spirit does to a human life. He embodies what true religion means, "to do justly, and to love kindness, and to walk humbly with thy God." [15] Just therein that Jesus as man depended on God in all that he was and in everything that he did, that he was ready to be simply man—man as God wanted him to be—the New Testament witnesses of Jesus came to see the manifestation of his God-sonship in his earthly existence.

Before the profound mystery of the incarnation—God manifested in the flesh, in a human life, in divine humility and grace—we shall forever stand wonderingly, in adoring amazement. This great miracle of divine love for us is beyond the grasp of human comprehension. All of our Christologies are but feeble approximations of the great truth embodied in Jesus, the Christ. He who existed in the form of God accepted the form of man. He our Lord became our servant. Jesus of Nazareth, who received from above divine wisdom and power to fulfill all of our human needs, humbly acknowledged all of his miracles to be the work of his Father.[16] Though being the Son he did not grasp at being on an equaliy with God but, emptying himself

[15] Mic. 6:6–9.
[16] Cf. John 5:19–24.

of self, he walked after his Father. In his obedience he humbled himself to die on the cross.

How Jesus came to be what he was, the man after God's heart, no one has told better than St. Paul in the classic passage Philippians 2:5-11. It is the profound self-humiliation involved in the incarnation, manifest through his whole earthly existence, which St. Paul points out to us in portraying the mind of Christ Jesus. His disciples came to know him and to call him the Christ and yet he lived among them as one of them, yea, as their servant. They came to accept his humility as something self-evident. St. Paul sees in Jesus' humility, in his complete self-denial, and in his obedience to his Father's will unto death the stamp of godliness. His divine sonship shines through his humanity revealing to us simultaneously the secret of true humanity. What St. Paul points out as the reflection of the glory of God in the mind of Christ is what Jesus enjoined upon his disciples and followers, "If any man would come after me, let him deny himself, and take up his cross, and follow me." [17]

The secret of true humanity, which is to walk the way of the narrow gate and the hard road that leads up to the holy hill of God, the disciples learned by what they saw their Master do day by day on that way which led him to Calvary and Easter Morning. "He that loveth his life loseth it; and he that hateth his life in this world shall keep it unto life eternal." [18] Jesus the Christ, the man in whom the kingly reign of God became a reality in a human life on earth, has become the true measure of manhood, the norm by which the lives of all will be judged and are being judged inescapably day by day.

Here was a man who chose poverty on purpose. He chose poverty, not on the moralistic basis of an ascetic (for he was no

[17] Mark 8:34.
[18] John 12:25.

ascetic) but because he would live his life in utter dependence on God who feeds the care-free sparrows and clothes the lilies of the field in their entrancing glory. A man's life does not consist in possessing things but in that his life comes to be something for God, for some child of God in the world.

He who is humanity's King, the bringer of the Kingdom of God on earth, eschewed worldly greatness on principle. To his ambitious disciples he said: "The kings of the Gentiles have lordship over them; and they that have authority over them are called Benefactors. But ye shall not be so: but he that is the greater among you let him become as the younger; and he that is chief, as he that doth serve. For which is greater, he that sitteth at meat; or he that serveth? is not he that sitteth at meat? but I am in the midst of you as he that serveth." [19]

The kingdom Jesus wanted was not the kind which destroys equality between man and his brothers. He reverenced in every man "an original thought of God." He scorned the desire for human honors and the ambition to raise oneself above others. He deplored the action of those who cared more for the approval of men than for the approval of God. "How can ye believe, who receive glory one of another, and the glory that cometh from the only God ye seek not." [20] The kingdoms of this world in all the areas of life and their glamorous glories Jesus flatly refused from the start. He fled from those who offered him the kingly crown of popularity, who sought to make him the national hero, and to enslave him to their secular ambitions.

Yet a king he is indeed. Truth is his royal scepter. "To this end have I been born, and to this end have I come into the world, that I should bear witness unto the truth." [21] None has

[19] Luke 22:25–27.
[20] John 5:44.
[21] John 18:37. Cf. A. Schlatter, *Das Evangelium Johannes* (Stuttgart, 1930).

this office as he, who is the light of the world, has it. He has a Kingdom, though he never had an army behind him. "Everyone that is of the truth heareth my voice." There are men who are of the truth, seekers after God and righteousness. They are men who are of God whose deeds have been wrought in God. All of these that live by the truth belong to him. They constitute his kingdom. No kingdom of this earth has ever wielded a comparable influence and become such a power over the minds and hearts of men as Jesus and his followers with their witness to truth. From the man Jesus who never aspired to reign or rule there has emanated, and continues to emanate, an authority which extends his sway over a realm without boundaries. Before the might of his spirit all the bulwarks against truth and righteousness erected by man in revolt against God, such as the false pride of nationalism and the cruel injustices of racialism, are doomed to crumble.

He has become to us what he is by divine prerogative: our Lord; not, however, as one who compels us or lords it over us, but as one who loves and serves us, who helps us in our utter helplessness, who never demands what he does not give, and who builds eternal life into the structure of our souls. The secret of his authority and influence over us lies in his unique relation with the Father as the eternal Son and in the quality of his humanity. Jesus was so completely grounded in God and so entirely God-directed that his every thought, word, and deed strike us as breathing the holy will, the divine nature of the Father in heaven; they come to bear for us the character of finality. However, the thoughts and actions of Jesus were no automatic reflection of a fixed character. They appear to us to be the constant current of his innermost being and living; yet they involved the unparalleled struggle of one who resisted sin unto blood and who was made perfect through suffering. He conquered every temptation by refusing admission to sin. Therefore he knew no sin. Everything that determined his life was derived from above. God was the source, the content, and the goal of Jesus' existence. His obedience, his service, and the humility of his character are not the outcome of some kind of human ethics or religious mechanics, they arise out of his worship of God and constitute a living sacrifice of self-offering.

The man Jesus, portrayed in the New Testament as the one to whom the dominion of the world is given, is the diametric opposite of the great man idolized by the world: the self-made man (more apparent today than ever) to whom power and eminence are accorded as a reward for his own merits. The goal of the self-made man is self-aggrandizement. What St. Paul says of Jesus in Philippians 2:6 is the extreme opposite. It constitutes one of the profoundest insights into the nature of him whom we call our Lord. Speaking of the mind of Jesus, in the totality of his person as revealed to the outreach of faith, St. Paul uses the following language: "Who, existing in the form of God, counted not the being on equality with God a thing to be grasped, but emptied himself . . ." What do these words mean? Are they not a clear reminder of another man who did grasp at equality with God, a reminder of that man from whom we, who are from below, all stem? Is not the story of the fall of man a true picture of man as we know him, empirical man whose life day by day is a confirmation of the most tragic event in the history of our race? In the seductive words of the tempter, "Ye shall be as God," [22] the fateful suggestion is contained which St. Paul calls "grasping at equality with God." Since the fall of man, his life no longer has its fountain-head in God his Creator but is dominated by self. His selfish personal interests taint all his striving. What Christian Dogmatics calls original sin is the

[22] Gen. 3:4, 5.

evil inclination in our will which manifests itself not only in
the outbreak of badness but also in the broken efforts for goodness. It is always with us, just as the call to perfection continues
to be heard within our heart. The sin from which all our sins
and all our woes result is precisely that man attempts to live his
life without God. It is evident not only in man's pursuit of his
sinful ambitions but also in his self-made pieties. The practical
atheism of our lives manifests itself therein that we live as if
there were no God. But the very anxieties which daily burden
and enslave us are witness of the abnormality of leaving God
out of our life. Original sin is man's refusal to honor God as
God, to acknowledge him as his Creator, as the Judge of his conduct, and as the Lord over life and death. Man tries to get along
without God because God works at cross-purpose to his own
sinful selfish plans. Even the religious man discovers in himself
this proneness to shape things according to his own notions. He
refuses to let God be God and tries to bring God down to the
plane of his thinking and acting.

Our lives are so full of misdirection because original sin is in
us; its taint is upon all our works. We must confess: there is no
true goodness in us, for our goodness is not the goodness of
God. Therefore, the eternal Son of God came into our humanity
to bring us the goodness of God, to deliver us from the curse of
our disobedience, from the impotence of our enslaved will, and
to lead us by the grace of his empowering Spirit on to the way
of freedom, the power to do the good through the obedience of
faith. How Jesus accomplished his tremendous mission St. Paul
tells us in Philippians 2:6–8, "He humbled himself, becoming
obedient even unto death, yea, the death on the cross." He conquered sin in the flesh. "For it became him, for whom are all
things, and through whom are all things in bringing many
sons unto glory," says the author of the epistle to the Hebrews,

"to make the author of their salvation perfect through sufferings. For both he that sanctifieth and they that are sanctified are all of one." [23]

In profound language St. Paul describes in the epistle to the Romans the conquest of sin by Christ Jesus: "The law of the Spirit of life in Christ Jesus made me free from the law of sin and of death. For what the law could not do in that it was weak through the flesh, God, sending his own Son in the likeness of sinful flesh and for sin, condemned sin in the flesh: that the ordinance of the law might be fulfilled in us, who walk not after the flesh, but after the Spirit." [24] In his utter humility, in his willingness to live his life as the obedient Servant of God, Jesus is the absolute antithesis to the self-seeking man of disobedience. In Jesus' life we see the radical repudiation of the ages-old striving of Adamitic man to become a superman. What St. Paul seeks to point out in the Philippian passage is precisely that the uniqueness of Jesus as true man consisted just therein that he, in contradistinction to everyone of our fallen race, did not seek to be a sort of God in his own right. He did not seek a kingdom for himself; he flung away the suggestion of satanic pride to bend the wills of men to his own. Instead he bowed to the will of God, even though it meant the cross. He knew what the prodigal learned from bitter experience: the humblest servant—speaking pictorially—in his Father's house could desire nothing better, no greater joy, than to serve such a Father in whatever lowly station of life it may be and at whatever cost to self. Jesus saw man's glory in his likeness to God, in his knowing God. As the one to whom the dominion of the world was intrusted, it was man's high mission to glorify God, to fill the earth with the song of gratitude and joy in profound adoration and worship

[23] Heb. 2:10–11.
[24] Rom. 8:2–4.

of the glorious Creator of the world and the loving Father of mankind. Jesus saw the meaning of life in looking up to God, and in making the glorious God the pattern of our life, in gaining dominion over self by walking the way of holy obedience in humility and loving service. He exemplified it in his own life by refusing to direct the course of his life by self-chosen ways or to seek the accomplishment of his task by self-initiated action. He declined to exercise the divine powers intrusted to him in his messianic ministry for personal use and self-glorification. His miracles of healing, of raising the dead, and exorcising of demons are the gift of his Father, signs of the kingly rule of God intended to make known to men the power of God for the salvation of humanity.

So completely did Jesus depend on his Father that he relied altogether on prayer. That explains the marvelous knowledge and wisdom which mark his life as free from any groping in the dark, or straining for solutions. He never needed to recede from steps once taken. Never do we see him given to vacillation or uncertainty as to the course before him or its final outcome.

This Jesus of Nazareth, who in all things, excepting sin, made himself alike unto man, was indeed the man from heaven, as St. Paul designates him. He is the man of the life-giving spirit who has become the inaugurator of a new race on earth. The irrefutable sign of Jesus' divine sonship lies in the perfection of his humanity as a perfect reflection of the image of God. What humanity can become in attaining the goal of sons of God, is revealed to us in the humble man from Nazareth, in the unspotted manhood of Jesus, in the self-denying obedience of the Son to his Father, in this fairest son of man.

In this self-humiliating Servant of God obedient unto death we see revealed the self-sacrificing love of God for a world of arrogant sinners. He who left all behind and came to us to be the bearer of the burden of our infirmities; who suffered by entering into conflict with us through resisting sin unto blood, who finally surrendered his pure, innocent life for us and in our stead that the judgment of our sins should fall on him and not destroy us—this man God has highly exalted and given him "the name which is above every name; that in the name of Jesus every knee should bow, of things in heaven and things on earth and things under the earth, and that every tongue should confess that Jesus Christ is Lord, to the glory of God the Father." [25]

Thus, Jesus, whom we have come to know as our Savior, became the author and perfecter of our faith by coming to be in the sight of God what man, made in the image of God, really is, but what man, the sinner, refuses to be. As Son of Man—the representative of the true *humanitas,* identified with humanity at large, and destined to be the creator of a new humanity— Jesus took over for us before his Father in a ministry of vicarious service which culminated in the act of supreme obedience when he who knew no sin was made sin in our stead. In that man on the cross God is present reaching out to every sinner in the misery of his lostness. In Christ the Crucified, God reduces himself to the state and fate of the sinner in order to reconcile sinners to himself. He deals with us in judgment aimed at our salvation in that he does not spare the Son of his love but lets him complete his life in the offering of himself for the sin of the world.[26] In pure self-giving love for his Father and for his brothers the Son accepts the cup that can not be removed if mankind is not to perish but live. Upon him lay the sin of us all; he died that we might live. In the profoundest act of grace God offers forgiveness of sin to all who accept his Son, who,

[25] Phil. 2:1–11.
[26] Rom. 4:25, 8:32.

for the joy that was set before him, endured the cross, not heeding the shame, and is seated at the right of God's throne.[27]

This divine love revealed in Jesus the Christ, which expresses as nothing else can the freedom of God's absolute sovereignty, has proved to be the greatest power in the world in that through it God has conquered the enmity of man the sinner from within and has created for himself a new humanity, a fellowship of true sons. The life of Jesus Christ, lived for us and consummated on the cross, leaves man in revolt against the holy God absolutely no ground on which to stand. The divine demand of righteousness engraved in the living flesh of Jesus before the eyes of the world lays completely bare the deceit of man's sin and its damnableness in the eyes of God. Moreover, Jesus exercises his sovereign power as Savior and Lord on earth in the lives of men in that he transforms their sin-bent will so completely as to effect in them reconciliation with God, to remove their guilt and to separate them inwardly from their sin.

When we accept him, we find in him salvation; if we reject him, we condemn ourselves. "And in none other is there salvation: for neither is there any other name under heaven, that is given among men, wherein we must be saved." [28] "God has allowed us to know the secret of His plan, and it is this: He purposes in His sovereign will that all human history shall be consummated in Christ, that everything that exists in heaven or earth shall find its perfection and fulfilment in Him." [29]

[27] Heb. 12:2.

[28] Acts 4:12.

[29] Eph. 1:10 as paraphrased by J. B. Phillips, *Letters to Young Churches* (New York, 1948).

SACRAMENTAL FELLOWSHIP

Elmer J. F. Arndt

ONE of the significant characteristics of contemporary Protestant church life is a renewed interest in and appreciation of the sacraments. There are a number of indications of this renewal and a variety of factors which have occasioned and stimulated concern with the Christian sacraments. The ecumenical movement has contributed to the renewed interest. It has provided the context for a deeper realization that our unity is to be found in the Lord who meets us in the Supper. It has also brought home to us the shame and scandal of our separation. Again, the moralism which was so characteristic of the recent past prepared the way, by its own inadequacy, for a revival of interest in liturgical and sacramental worship. Moreover, participation in the Communion was and is a Christian witness, a declaration of loyalty and an act of commitment when many other forms of witness were not possible. However occasioned, the unmistakable fact is that the sacraments are no longer on the outer periphery of Christian interest and appreciation. If two or three decades ago the sacraments were widely regarded as little more than traditional rites, such is no longer the case.

The renewed appreciation of the place of the sacramental in religion has provided the conditions for a sympathetic and a critical appropriation of the complex heritage of the sacramental doctrines of the Reformation. It also provides justification for a restatement of the doctrinal teaching. It is certainly no dishonor to the Reformers to suggest that our appropriation of their contributions should be critical as well as sympathetic. They themselves taught us that the New Testament is to be the norm of doctrine and practice; they sought to develop a body of doctrine which would be truly evangelical, and, because evangelical, genuinely catholic. Fidelity to the Reformers certainly does not consist in erecting their teaching—for all the insights and truth their teaching embodied—into a tradition on the same level with, much less superior to, the New Testament itself.

One aspect of the complexity of the legacy left by the Reformers' teaching on the sacraments was their inevitable involvement in controversy. While we might wish with Hooker "that men would more give themselves to meditate with silence what we have in this sacrament, and less to dispute the manner how" and deplore with Melanchthon the *rabies theologorum,* it would be obtuse not to recognize that the controversies were themselves testimonies to the importance attached to the sacraments. But also, recognition of the controversial character of much of the Reformers' writings on the sacraments is important if their fundamental motifs are to be appreciated and a comprehensive appropriation of their diverse insights made possible.[1]

Readiness to recognize the controversial character of a large part of the writings of the Reformers is important in three respects. In the first place, the Reformers were involved in the historical conditions of their generation. Historians point out that social and political considerations were associated with the

[1] With the exception of his earliest writings on the Lord's Supper, e.g., *De digna praeparatione cordis pro suscipiendo sacramenti eucharistiae* and *Ein Sermon von dem hochwuerdigen Sakrament des heiligen wahren Leichmanns Christi und von den Bruderschaften,* Luther's writings are largely controversial, being directed against either Roman teaching and practice or Zwinglian teaching. Zwingli's writings also were highly controversial, directed especially against the Roman conception of the mass.

controversy between Luther and Zwingli on the Lord's Supper.[2] It would be prideful pretension on our part to claim a perspective free from all the relativities of history. It is also a form of pride to attribute to the one or the other Reformer complete freedom from historical involvements. Secondly, the necessities of controversy usually involve an emphasis on the point of difference between the parties and a relegation to the background of those matters held in common (although they may be of great importance to one or both parties) which are not under attack. For instance, Luther's early emphasis on the element of fellowship in the Supper was pushed into the background in his later controversial writings. Finally, to recognize the controversial character of much of the Reformers' writings prepares the way for a better understanding of the agreements and differences between them. Certainly, such recognition will not dissolve the differences between Luther and Zwingli on the Lord's Supper; it does suggest, however, that it is worth inquiring whether their teaching is, perhaps, complementary rather than irreconcilable.

In 1540 Calvin published his *Short Treatise on the Supper of Our Lord*. It closes with a brief history of the controversy on the subject between Luther and Zwingli and Œcolompadius. On the controversy Calvin comments:

Both parties failed in not having the patience to listen to each other in order to follow the truth without passion, when it would have been found. Nevertheless, let us not lose sight of our duty, which

[2] T. M. Lindsay wrote, "It was something more than the meaning of the Holy Supper or the exegesis of a difficult text which rent Protestantism in two, and made Luther and Zwingli appear as the leaders of opposing parties in a movement where union was a supreme necessity after the decision at Speyer in 1529. The theological question was complicated by social and political ideas, which, if not acknowledged openly, were at least in the minds of the leaders who took sides in the dispute." *A History of the Reformation* (New York, 1911), II, 53–54.

is not to forget the gifts which the Lord bestowed upon them, and the blessings which he has distributed to us by their hands and means. For if we are not ungrateful and forgetful of what we owe them, we shall be well able to pardon that and much more, without blaming and defaming them. In short, since we see that they were, and still are, distinguished for holiness of life, excellent knowledge, and ardent zeal to edify the Church, we ought always to judge and speak of them with modesty, and even with reverence, since at last God, after having thus humbled them, has in mercy been pleased to put an end to this unhappy disputation, or at least calm it preparatory to its final settlement.[3]

If the generosity and modesty urged by Calvin had prevailed in the sixteenth century, and in the ones to follow, instead of an acrimonious and bitter polemical spirit, the concord Calvin hoped for might have been realized. Surely, the record of controversy on the Supper as it stands reinforces Calvin's plea for a grateful reverence joined with a discerning willingness "to follow the truth without passion."

Such an approach certainly does not suggest compromising of differences any more than it recommends contemptuous repudiation of the centuries of Christian experience and teaching. Ideally, what is required is the appropriation of the whole heritage of the church and its evaluation as legitimate development or aberration, as the case may be, of New Testament sacramental doctrine and practice. What the church, or some branch of the church, has taught on the sacraments has been part and parcel of the understanding of the nature of Christianity. The sacramental doctrine of any period has not been isolated from the total complex of doctrine. There has been a mutual interaction. Sacramental teaching has reflected the total interpretation of Christianity and sacramental teaching and practice have

[3] In Calvin's *Tracts,* trans. by Henry Beveridge (Edinburgh, 1849), II, 197.

influenced the total interpretation. Such was also true of the Reformers. It would appear, then, that a brief sketching of the bearing of two basic Reformation positions on the understanding of the sacraments might better serve to exhibit fundamental convictions than a recapitulation of sacramental doctrine in isolation from the total interpretation.

BASIC REFORMATION POSITIONS

Whatever their differences, the Reformers were united in their apprehension of Christianity as a religion of grace, in their thought of God as the Holy Love who receives sinners into fellowship with himself, and of Christ as the sole and sufficient Mediator between God and man. These fundamental themes conditioned their teaching on the sacraments. They were the impelling motive of their criticisms of medieval sacramental doctrine and practice. They were the inspiration for their positive affirmations.

The radical apprehension that salvation is *sola gratia* affirms the utter dependence of man on God for the fulfilment of his destiny. On the one hand, it involved the surrender of every pretension that man is able to "justify" his own existence. Man's virtue is ever ethically ambiguous; he is unable to break through the circle of egocentricity; he cannot transcend the ambiguities of his situation as a child of nature and of history. He is a sinner and his sinfulness means not merely that he commits sins but more fundamentally that his nature is perverted and corrupted. For man the sinner, there is no escape from despair. On the other hand, the grace of God is the promise of the fulfilment of life so that despair of self is not the ultimate word. What man is unable to do, God freely offers to him in Christ. God removes the barrier of sin; he accepts into his fellowship the sinner in all his unworthiness; he meets the sinner as the suffering and victorious love who offers forgiveness, sonship and eternal life. Repudiation of any claim upon God based upon one's goodness (since to assert such a claim would be an assertion of man's independence of God) and humble acceptance of the reconciliation and life which God freely bestows (which is to confess our dependence on him) are the central notes in justification by faith.

In such a context, the sacraments are gifts of God for the nourishing and strengthening of our trust and confidence in the divine mercy and victory over all opposition. Any thought that observance of the sacraments is a good work by which merit is acquired is set aside. For to think of the observance of the sacraments as a meritorious work is, under the cover of a means of grace, to affirm a ground for security outside of grace. Sacraments themselves do not justify; they do not confer grace. They are not rites which effect a good or by themselves confer a benefit if only no obstacle is put in the way of their operation. Such a view of the sacraments, to put it mildly, obscures the fact that man's salvation is solely a gift of God, initiated and completed by him. God, and not the sacraments, is the "cause" of man's redemption.

The grace of God, revealed in Christ, is his love and the gift of his love is his self-bestowal. God's gift is nothing less than himself. It is through and through personal as well as altogether a gift. Luther's attack on the medieval conception of the Eucharist which required the mediation of a sacerdotal church and Zwingli's attack on the mass as a repetition of the sacrifice on Calvary both had their motivation in their affirmation of the grace of God in Christ as the sole ground of man's confidence and as the central element of the gospel.

Grace means the personal character of the relation between man and God. Hence, any mechanical view of the sacraments, any false objectivization of them, and the necessity for the mediation of a sacerdotal institution were all inevitably rejected. The Reformers' common insistence on faith as necessary for the appropriation of the offered blessings emphasizes the personal and ethical character of grace.

The constant and consistent emphasis on the importance of faith in the teaching of the Reformers does not by any means imply that the sacraments are subjective in character. Faith is certainly not subjective, if subjective is taken to mean a physical state or activity which has no objective reference or basis. Faith, moreover, is neither creative of its object nor the condition of its presence. It is the divinely created response in the person by which what is offered by God is apprehended and appropriated. "That such bestowed righteousness should be in us . . . this comes to pass alone through faith for it must always be received and accepted by us." [4] Faith is a receiving, a taking, a having, a practical confidence by which "Christ is apprehended." It is a response generated by the Holy Spirit in the heart, a confidence grounded on the revelation of God in history, and an expectation and hope of the consummation of the kingdom. The presupposition of faith is the promise, the activity, the proffered blessings of God.

The denial that the sacraments possess a virtue efficacious of itself (*ex opere operato*) is not tantamount to a "subjective" view of the sacraments. The insistence that without faith the participant receives no blessing does not make the sacraments depend on faith. But that insistence does mean that without faith the benefits of the sacraments are not *appropriated or received* by the participant. The point of the insistence on faith as necessary to receive the blessings proffered in the sacraments

[4] Luther's *Werke*, Erlangen ed., XII, 118. Quoted in Seeberg, *Textbook of the History of Doctrines* (Philadelphia, 1905), II, 254.

is to affirm the ethical character of the process and to repudiate any mechanical or magical conceptions.

A second basic position, significantly common ground for the Reformers, concerned the relation of the Word and the sacraments. Both the Word and the sacraments are means of grace; only through them does the Spirit come to us. The recognition of the Word as a means of grace does not empty the sacraments of significance or render them peripheral in the life of the church; but the way in which the Reformers described the connection between the Word and the sacraments does deny that anything is given in the sacraments which is not also given through the Word.

The Word of God is, for Luther, in its primary meaning, the proclamation of the gospel whose content is the revelation of God in Jesus Christ. Where the gospel is proclaimed, there Christ and the Spirit are active. It is God's power. Through the internal working of the Spirit, the Word brings all the blessings of God's redemptive work in Christ. Consequently, there is no deficiency or imperfection attaching to the Word which must be made good by the addition of the sacraments. Calvin's statement, "Wherefore, let us abide by this conclusion, that the office of the sacraments is precisely the same as that of the word of God; which is to offer and present Christ to us, and in him the treasures of his heavenly grace . . .",[5] is the common standpoint of the Reformers.

For this reason, Luther and Calvin emphasized the Augustinian formula: "a sacrament is a visible sign of a sacred thing," "a visible form of invisible grace," and "the word joined to the element makes the sacrament." A sacrament is thus a "visible word." Thus, Luther declares in *The Large Catechism* that

[5] *Institutes of the Christian Religion,* trans. by John Allen (6th Am. ed., Philadelphia, 1928), IV, XVII.

baptism is "not mere ordinary water, but water comprehended in God's Word and command, and sanctified thereby, so that it is nothing else than a divine water; not that the water in itself is nobler than any other water, but that God's Word and command are added." [6] Likewise, he declares concerning the Sacrament of the Altar: ". . . The chief point is the Word and ordinance or command of God." "The Word must make a Sacrament of the element, else it remains a mere element." And the chief thing, the Word, "is spoken for the soul to apprehend," and without the apprehension of the Word the benefits of the sacraments are not appropriated.[7]

If the sacraments confer no blessing which the Word does not confer, why should the sacraments be observed? The "spirituals," who did not regard the sacraments as of central importance, had raised the question for the Reformers. Their answer is three-fold. In the first place, the rites of baptism and the eucharist—unlike the other sacraments of the seven, which the western church observed—had been instituted by Christ himself and commanded in the Scriptures. In the second place, since we are not pure intellects but sense-bound, God has given us the external signs of water and bread and wine so that these sensible elements may be apprehended by the senses and understood and so the heart be moved. Finally, the sacraments confirm and increase faith through the accompanying work of the Holy Spirit. The sacraments, at least for Luther, bring home to the individual, the promise generally declared in the preaching of the Word. As Dr. Jacobs wrote concerning baptism in his essay in *The Ministry and the Sacraments*: "All that is included in the word 'salvation,' all that the Gospel offers to the world, or

---

[6] The translation used is that of F. Bente and W. Dau, *Concordia Triglotta* (St. Louis, 1921), p. 735.

[7] Cf. *ibid.*, pp. 753 ff.

to any man in the world, is offered here to a single individual, in a solemn act that Christ has commanded to be performed. That is the simple meaning of the somewhat ambiguous terms that theology has traditionally applied to this sacrament when it has called it a 'sign' or 'seal.'" [8]

The emphasis on the Word as a means of grace and on the central position of the Word in the sacraments themselves reflected not only the Reformers' rediscovery of the proclamation of the gospel as constitutive of the church but also their rediscovery of the nature of evangelical Christianity. Everything is concentrated in the gospel: the divine love revealed in Christ in whom we have forgiveness of sins, peace with God, and eternal life. This promise is given in and through the Word which is God's Word. It is this same promise which is declared in the sacraments. Thus, though there are several means of grace, there is but one grace. The same grace is mediated through the Word and through the sacraments. The grace of God is not to be thought of as divided into a number of gifts. That would seriously weaken the conception of grace. God's grace is his love in all its fulness. Appropriate as it may be to point out how God has provided for our several necessities and occasions, it is a diminution, not an enhancement, of his goodness so to present his grace as though one grace supplemented another.

Further, the connection of Word and sacrament provides a safeguard against the materialization of God's grace. It affirms the wholly personal character of grace, the confrontation of spirit with Spirit. For where "the Word is spoken for the soul to apprehend," there man in his spiritual being is addressed. He is called to decision and commitment. He is in the presence of the Holy, which is both sacred and ethical, and of the Love, whose

[8] Edited by R. Dunkerley and A. C. Headlam (London, 1937), p. 140.

free and unconditioned quality compels response. By putting the Word into the very center of the sacraments, the Reformers asserted the sovereignty of grace. And is not the sovereignty of grace the bulwark against and judgment upon the incursion of magical and materialized notions into sacramental thought and practice?

It would not be easy to find a better summary statement of the Reformation position on the relation of the Word and the sacraments than that given by Calvin in the *Institutes*:

> . . . the office of the sacraments is precisely the same as that of the word of God; which is to offer and present Christ to us, and in him the treasures of his heavenly grace; but they confer no advantage or profit without being received by faith . . . It is also necessary to guard against being drawn into an error allied to this, from reading the extravagant language used by the fathers with a view to exalt the dignity of the sacraments; lest we should suppose there is some secret power annexed and attached to the sacraments, so that they communicate the grace of the Holy Spirit . . . ; whereas the only office assigned to them by God, is to testify and confirm his benevolence towards us; nor do they impart any benefit, unless they are accompanied by the Holy Spirit to open our minds and hearts and render us capable of receiving this testimony: and here, also, several distinct favors of God are eminently displayed. For the sacraments . . . fulfil to us, on the part of God, the same office as messengers of joyful intelligence, or earnests for the confirmation of covenants on the part of men; they communicate no grace from themselves, but announce and show, and, as earnests and pledges, ratify things which are given to us by the goodness of God.[9]

THE PERSONAL-SOCIAL CHARACTER OF THE SACRAMENTS

The evangelical emphases on the personal and ethical character of the prevenient grace of God reconciling man to himself,

[9] IV, XVII. Trans. by John Allen.

on the connection between Word and sacraments, and on faith as the condition for the appropriation of the gift of God suggest the basis and character of communion with God in Christ. The same gift of God—his loving-kindness reconciling us to himself, bestowing on us the status of sonship—and membership in the new humanity, which is proclaimed in the Word is proffered in another mode in the sacraments. The evangelical emphases necessarily (as well as actually) give a central place to fellowship in sacramental teaching and practice; and that fellowship is both personal and social. Indeed, it is a fellowship better described as personal-social in order to indicate the inseparable character of the two aspects.

The traditional view of the sacraments emphasized their visual character. The stress was put on the visible elements (the water and the bread and the wine). The Augustinian designation of a sacrament as a visible Word to a large extent determined the development of sacramental theology both in the medieval church and in Reformation and post-Reformation protestantism. It may not be too far-fetched to suggest that the concentration of the visual element had a connection with the various theological preoccupations centering around the question of the relation of the divine presence to the elements. So far as the theology stemming from the Reformation is concerned, attention was centered on the important affirmation that the Word and the sacraments offer the same grace; the same gift is given through the sacraments as is given through the Word. The difference between Word and sacraments was then presented as a difference in mode of setting forth the gospel, the sacrament having a visible character.

The emphasis on the visible character of the sacraments has tended to obscure their character as acts. This is its chief defect. Action rather than visibility is a more comprehensive description of the character of the sacraments.[10] The sacraments are divine actions, acts of God, of Christ, of the Holy Spirit; they are acts of the church of Jesus Christ; they call for action from those who receive them—not only the act of faith but also the "external" and "public" actions of being baptized, of taking and eating and drinking. They are actions which are intelligible actions (for they also include the Word—the words of institution and the words of promise). Yet they are also concrete actions which are not only spiritual but physical as well.

The sacraments are acts of fellowship, in the first instance, as signifying God's purpose in bringing us into fellowship with himself. They declare his grace revealed in Christ. They present the gospel of reconciliation, exhibit his initiative in seeking out the sinner and his suffering and victorious love, and are the instruments by which the Holy Spirit seals, to those who have faith, their inclusion in the covenant of grace.

The Christian sacraments have their basis in the reconciling work of God in Christ. They point to his action in redeeming his people, and, significantly, to an act of God in human history. They proclaim that "while we were yet sinners Christ died for us." [11] The Christian sacraments are not rooted in the mysterious powers of nature but in God's self-disclosure in history in a historical person. The historical character of the Christian revelation has given the question of the institution of the sacraments by Christ its significance. Often, indeed, the connection between Jesus Christ and the sacraments was conceived in an external manner. The Protestant restriction of the sacraments to baptism and the Lord's Supper was frequently justified on the

[10] Cf. Gustav Aulen, *The Faith of the Christian Church,* trans. by E. H. Wahlstrom and G. E. Arden (Philadelphia, 1948), p. 376: "It may be argued, however, that the formula, 'a visible word,' too strongly emphasizes the visual element, and that it does not call to attention the most essential character of the sacrament, viz., the action."

[11] Rom. 5:8.

ground that these two, and only these two, were instituted by Jesus himself. The decisive question, however, is not the purely historical one (which will in all likelihood remain problematical) but the question of the meaning and the content of the sacraments for faith. Their connection with the work of Christ is an organic one; they express the content of the gospel. On such considerations, which point to the historical facts and their interpretation as the saving act of God, rests the validity of the sacraments.

The connection of the sacraments with the historical facts of revelation has been emphasized especially, if one-sidedly, in the conception of the Lord's Supper as a memorial. The Lord's Supper points back to the Last Supper of the Lord with his disciples. He who enters into fellowship with us in the Supper is the same Lord who broke bread with the disciples, gave himself for those he loved, and sealed his love with his blood. The "words of institution," belonging to the very center of the observance of the sacrament, are the living memory in the church of the historical facts through and in which God declared and accomplished his saving purpose.

This emphasis on the historical element of the sacraments defines in a significant way the character of the Christian's fellowship with God. It is a fellowship with God mediated through Jesus Christ. It is not a fellowship achieved through a descent into the depths of the soul; it is not found in isolation. Not in the inmost center of existence, not in flight from history, but in Jesus Christ, the crucified and living Lord, the soul is confronted by God. It may be suggested that this indicates one of the fundamental reasons why the churches of the Reformation so strongly emphasized the sacraments against those who, in the interest of immediacy, would deprecate or even abolish the observance of the sacraments.

The divine activity in connection with the sacraments is underscored not only by their historical content but also by the genuine divine presence in the sacraments. God the Holy Spirit uses the instrument (as Calvin says) of baptism for vivification, regeneration, and sealing to the believer the promises of the gospel. In the Lord's Supper, Christ the Host, whose guests we are, gives himself. It is not a particular blessing which the Lord of the Supper bestows, but all his benefits; and where all his benefits are bestowed, there is Christ himself.[12] If Luther, as is well known, emphasized the forgiveness of sins as the blessing of the Supper, forgiveness of sins is to be understood as inclusive of all the benefits of Christ and not as a particular benefit. The sacraments declare Christ's intention to unite us to himself, to have fellowship with his own, to be at one with us. And that this fellowship is experienced has been and is the testimony of the church. Indeed, in the Communion devout men and women have found again and again a direct, if mediated, experience of God in Christ. This is the living substance of the affirmation of the presence of Christ in the Supper.

That Christ is present in the Supper for communion with us is widely affirmed by the Christian churches. It is worth pointing out that Luther, Zwingli, and Calvin were all agreed on his presence. Their disagreements revolved about the connection between the presence and the elements, not about the fact of his presence. Just this sense of the personal presence of Christ is the source of the sense of mystery which so often, and rightly, finds expression in theology and liturgy. He is present as the holy

[12] Cf. R. M. Adamson, who writes discerningly in his *The Christian Doctrine of the Lord's Supper* (Edinburgh, 1905), pp. 152-3: ". . . No catalogue of special blessings received can suffice to express the fulness of the gift offered in the Holy Supper. The nature and the greatness of that gift can be expressed only by saying that it consists of Christ Himself. The real gift to be obtained through the Sacrament is the Lord Jesus Christ Himself."

One before whom we are constrained to acknowledge our own unworthiness. He is present as the gracious One who endured the cross for our redemption. He is present as the Victor over sin and death, the living Lord of an eternal kingdom. In his presence, we are in the presence of the Eternal. Awe, reverence, wonder, adoring love possess us. Is it really surprising that the presence of the Lord and the fellowship he enters into with those who respond to him with faith cannot be contained in conceptual statement or be exhausted in verbal expression?

If it is kept in mind that Christ is present and has fellowship with his faithful people in the Supper as an integral whole, we shall have taken what may prove a step that will remove one of the barriers to fellowship between various bodies of Christians. Christians have been divided by their conflicting views concerning the relation of Christ's presence to the elements. Our view is that he is present in the sacrament of which the elements are a part. The elements, indeed, are the things in the Supper which symbolize the body and blood of Christ. Yet it is in the whole sacrament—itself a complex—that Christ makes his presence known to faith. The assembly of people, the worship of God in prayer and praise, confession of sins and confessions of faith, the reading of the Scriptures, the preaching of the Word, the words of institution, the invocation of the Holy Spirit, the breaking of the bread and the distribution of the elements: all these contribute to our apprehension of the cardinal fact. Christ himself, our Judge and our Redeemer, our Lord and our Elder Brother is with us.

The personal character of the fellowship afforded in the sacraments is indicated by the fact that it is a fellowship on condition of faith in the participants. The blessings of baptism require for their appropriation faith in the person baptized.

The Lord's presence in the Supper is a presence for faith. The emphasis on faith—not merely apprehension by the mind but also trust and confidence of the heart—involves both the personal character of the relation and the setting aside of any magical, mechanical, or materialistic conceptions of the sacrament. Faith itself as trust and confidence as well as intellectual apprehension is intensely personal. It is a response of the whole person and it is a response that is thoroughly personal in character. Faith is love responding to love. It is the reorientation of the whole self turning from its self-love to commitment to him who broke into our egocentricity by the power of his invincible love. The self, owning the constraint of holy love and recognizing in that holy love *the* good as well as *its* good, finds its true freedom in responding to that love.

To recognize that the sacraments are for fellowship and that fellowship requires from us the attitude of faith is, again, not to deny the objectivity of the divine presence in the sacraments. It does deny a false objectivity which would result in a sub-personal relation. In the sacraments Holy Love in all its initiative, redeeming, and revivifying power claims us for its own. Its claim on us is not for a part of the self but for the whole self, the self itself. It is a call to self-renunciation, to consecration, to adoration and to obedience. It is a claim on us to unite ourselves with him who unites himself with us. As in the Word, so also in the sacraments we are confronted by the living Lord; the whole pressure of his holy and gracious person is brought to bear on us through the total action by the work of the Holy Spirit. Yet as he freely offers himself for fellowship so he asks of us a freely given response. Faith is grateful and humble acceptance of the gift of grace, the owning of his claim, the acceptance of his fellowship. To participate in the sacraments unbelievingly is not to annihilate the divine presence; it is, by rejecting his claim on us, to remain in our isolation and false independence. It is to face the Lord as our Judge whose mercy we have spurned.

Understood as a means for personal fellowship between the living Lord and believers, the basis is laid for a deeper view than the symbolical or realistic views of the presence afford and also for a better, more evangelical conception than one which would interpose the church as an institution between God and the soul. The sacraments are *for* faith, for the nurturing and strengthening of faith, which is itself the gift of God. The sacraments, indeed, are not private acts; but they are personal. The condition of faith, as necessary for the appropriation of the gift offered, and the character of faith, as directed upon "the Son of God, who loved me and gave himself up for me," [13] point away from an "institutional" sort of fellowship, though not at all away from a social conception of fellowship.

The fellowship of Christ with the believer and the believer with Christ is distinguishable but inseparable for the fellowship of believers. The individual and corporate aspects of the sacraments are neither separate in practice nor separable in faith. The sacraments exemplify characteristic aspects of the nature of God's self-disclosure and of Christian faith in the conjunction of God's redemptive activity, personal response and togetherness with other men. As God of old spoke his Word through the prophets and as the Word was incarnate in the man Jesus, so in the sacraments he speaks and gives himself through the ministry of men. The sacraments, which declare and offer his grace to faith, make it evident that faith in the Lord Jesus Christ also includes a relation of love and unity with our fellowmen in the Holy Spirit. As the sacraments are grounded in the activity of God in Christ reconciling us to himself; as the

[13] Gal. 2:20.

activity of God the Holy Spirit uses the sacraments to bring
home to us our salvation; as the receptivity and activity of faith
is the condition for appropriating the gift offered; so also the
sacraments are the activity of the fellowship of believers expressing, initiating into, nurturing, and requiring that fellowship. The sacraments by their very observance as well as by
what they demand, by what through the Spirit they give as
well as what they require, witness to the truth that union with
the Lord includes union with our fellowmen. To be in fellowship with him includes fellowship with the brethren. Incorporation into Christ is incorporation into his Church.[14]

The social or communion character of sacramental fellowship
is a complex, a cord woven of several strands. We note three of
those strands: the sacraments as activities of the church, the
fellowship of believers; the sacraments as incorporating and
nurturing the fellowship of believers; the sacraments as provid-
ing not only the witness to fellowship actualized but also as
including the demand and promise of a perfected fellowship.

From the very beginning of the Christian church, the administration of the sacraments has been an act of the Christian
community. They have always had the character of a corporate
act, an act of the community which had its unity in Christ.
From the day of Pentecost, baptism has been administered as
an act of the community of believers. Through this ministry of
men, others have been united with them "in the name of Jesus
Christ." The Lord's Supper has likewise had from the beginning
the character of a corporate act, whether the emphasis was on

[14] Cf. Emil Brunner, *Our Faith* (New York, 1936), p. 130: "One cannot have
faith alone. Indeed the aim of the Word of God is to conquer their solitude by
leading us out of our isolation into fellowship with one another. God's Word and
fellowship are inseparable. Therefore our Lord instituted the Sacraments that we
might not make a private concern of His Word, but come together *actually,* not
simply in spirit."

its character as the memorial or fellowship or mystery or eucharist. Individuals as individuals neither baptize nor celebrate communion; such a conception or practice of the sacraments is foreign to their nature. The presence of the church—the fellowship—belongs to their observance. The error of the view which regards the sacraments as official acts of the church is not in their recognition of the corporate activity characteristic of the sacraments but in the conception of the church implied. In the sacraments, we are met by Christ and his church, both coming to us in union.

Likewise, we, as individual persons unite with both Christ and his church in receiving the sacraments. We are baptized into Christ and initiated into the church. We commune with Christ in the Supper and commune with the members of the congregation gathered together in adoration, praise, and thanksgiving. The "one baptism," like the "one faith" and "one Lord," unites all not only with the Lord but with each other and the participation in the Supper is a common bond both with Christ and all who belong to him. Those who participate in the Supper are "one bread, one body: for we all partake of the one bread." [15]

Sacramental fellowship is an actual fellowship with a concrete, actual congregation of Christian people. It is a fellowship of mutual service as well as common worship. No more than fellowship with Christ is separable from fellowship with his Church is fellowship with others separable from actual fellowship, being together with them and in actual union with them. Such actuality or concreteness belongs to the essence of sacramental fellowship just as the sacraments are inseparable from the ministry of the Church. Yet it is also profoundly true that this or that particular, local fellowship does not exhaust the

[15] I Cor. 10, 17.

fellowship offered in the sacraments and witnessed to by them. Baptism in the name of Christ is baptism also into his holy Church, the whole community of redeemed people of all ages and places. "We, who are many"—many individuals, many congregations, many historical churches—are "one body." The one fellowship—so broken, incomplete and even perverse in our concrete historical situation—extends beyond the limits of history to the eternal and perfect fellowship of Christ and his saints. Nonetheless, the fellowship in our concrete situation is real; and its reality—imperfect, indeed—is the earnest of its perfect consummation in eternity.

The sacraments are acts of fellowship by way of manifestation and nurture; they are also incentives to fellowship, to a perfect communion which ultimately has its fulfilment beyond history. It belongs to the sacraments to express both what is actual and the hope for the completion of the actual; and this is true of the communion with the Lord and with those who also belong to the Lord. An element of tension belongs to sacramental fellowship. It is a tension which is exemplified in the sacraments because it belongs to the fundamental character of Christianity as at once a religion of grace and an ethical religion. Baptism is incorporation into Christ, into "newness of life," into the holy Church, of all the saints redeemed by Christ. It is incorporation not merely into this branch or part of the church but into the body of Christ, whose unity is not apparent to observation and is even a "broken" unity in historic fact. Nevertheless, just as Paul declares that in baptism we were buried with Christ into death and so are no longer in bondage to sin and then urges upon his readers the obligation to walk in the newness of life in which they have participated sacramentally, so there is the tension in the fellowship between its real, though partial, realization in actuality and the demand for and promise of its fulfilment.[16] The Lord's Supper likewise contains this tension between the actual fellowship and unity of the company of guests at the table of their Host and the consummation of that fellowship which will "be fulfilled in the kingdom of God." [17]

As Paul's first letter to the Corinthians makes evident, the actual fellowship of Christians with each other was then as now far from ideal. Yet the Apostle neither revised downward his affirmations concerning the reality of the fellowship nor relaxed his exhortations to Christians to actualize more fully their fellowship with each other. In the present time, in spite of the divided, separated churches which actually administer them, the sacraments also bear their witness, to the one fellowship in the Lord and Savior. As a matter of fact, a number of the churches, even in their separation, have been constrained to recognize the validity of baptism in the name of the Triune God even though administered by another church. Thus they recognize both that our fellowship is in Christ and that the Church into which we are baptized is wider and more inclusive than the church which baptizes. The Lord's Supper, despite the evidence of the separation of the churches its observance provides, yet is the renewer of Christian conscience and the ever-flowing source of the impetus to a more inclusive unity of Christian people. He, the Lord of the church, is the Host; all who come are his guests. And who are guests to bar other guests? At his table the earnestness of his prayer "that they may all be one" is borne in upon us so that we are shamed in our separation and constrained to find a fuller embodiment of the unity he has given us. There our pretensions are humbled and in his grace we find both the solace and dynamic of our lives.

[16] Cf. Rom. 6:3–11.

[17] Luke 22:16. The same eschatological note is in I Cor. 10:26: "For as often as ye eat this bread, and drink the cup, ye proclaim the Lord's death till he come."

Whether our separation be on the basis of nationality, or class, or race, or cultural level, or tradition, or institutional loyalty or whatsoever, the sacraments unmask the disorder in the world and in the church. We are shamed because of our acceptance of disorder in both world and church. The sacraments do more than shame us. As we meet Christ in the power of his love there is given also the power to wrestle with the principalities of evil in obedience to his will. And in the presence of the living Lord we are assured that ultimate victory belongs to him whom God has made Lord over all.[18]

The sacraments, used by the Spirit of God and received by us in faith, are concentrates of the gospel of God. They are means to fellowship, witnesses to the fellowship, and nurturers of the fellowship; in them, fellowship is given and its fulfilment in eternity promised. They include the range and nature of Christian fellowship: communion with us of the Lord Jesus Christ who gave himself as sacrifice that we might be reconciled with God; our communion with him in the responsive service of adoring love and self-sacrifice of obedience; our communion with each other who confess loyalty and faith to a common Lord and who are bound to each other because he has bound us to himself; a communion in time whose fulfilment lies beyond

[18] In a noble and tender passage in the *Institutes,* IV, XVII, XXXVIII, Calvin writes: "We have derived considerable benefit from the sacrament if this thought be impressed and engraven upon our minds, that it is impossible for us to wound, despise, reject, injure, or in any way to offend one of our brethren, but we, at the same time, wound, despise, reject, injure and offend Christ in him; that we have no discord with our brethren without being, at the same time, at variance with Christ; that we cannot love Christ without loving him in our brethren; that such care as we take of our own body, we ought to exercise the same care of our brethren, who are members of our body; that as no part of our body can be in pain without every other part feeling correspondent sensations, so we ought not to suffer our brother to be afflicted with any calamity without our sympathizing in the same. Wherefore, it is not without reason that Augustine so frequently calls this sacrament 'the bond of charity.' For what more powerful stimulus could be employed to excite mutual charity among us, than when Christ, giving himself to us, not only invites us by his example mutually to devote ourselves to the promotion of one another's welfare but also by making himself common to all makes us all to be one with himself."

time; a communion here which contains within it the assurance of the triumph of the kingdom of Christ and the promise of an indefeasible fellowship with the Lord of all together with all his saints in the Church triumphant.

In observing the sacraments, the Christian Church witnesses to its faith in Jesus Christ, its Lord and Savior; to its hope in Christ; to the holy love of God, Creator and Redeemer. In observing the sacraments, the Christian Church responds to God's love in Christ ever assured anew by the Holy Spirit in adoration, in penitence, in joyful thanksgiving and self-consecration. The fellowship to which the sacraments testify and which they serve is nowhere better expressed than in words of one who knew so well the mind of the Father: "And the glory which thou hast given me I have given unto them; that they may be one, even as we are one; I in them, and thou in me, that they may be perfected into one; that the world may know that thou didst send me, and lovedst them, even as thou lovedst me." [19]

[19] John 17:22-23.

PROCLAIMING THE WORD

Frederick W. Schroeder

SINCE its very beginning the church has regarded the proclamation of the Word to be its foremost function. When the apostles discovered that too much of their time was consumed by an expanding program of administering relief within the fellowship, they let it be known that they did not regard it proper to "forsake the word of God, and serve tables." [1] Though there are many activities which properly come within the realm of the church's total ministry, the proclamation of the Word is its very *raison d'être*. If it fails at this point it will be unfaithful to its great commission to make the gospel known throughout the world.

It is important to recognize that the proclamation of the Word includes more than preaching. The life of the church, its corporate acts of worship, specifically its observance of the sacraments, its ministries and institutions of mercy, its efforts in behalf of justice and righteousness in human affairs are all, directly or indirectly, forms of proclamation; nevertheless, in Protestantism the sermon is the foremost vehicle of proclamation. In practice, though not in principle, the Reformers placed the spoken Word in preaching above the acted Word in the sacraments. As Dean Sperry points out, Protestantism "for better or worse has cast its lot with the prophetic type of religion";[2] which is to say that it has stressed preaching. The sermon has been and still remains the high point of public worship. Even

[1] Acts 6:2.
[2] Willard Sperry, *We Prophesy in Part* (New York, 1938), p. 3.

the altar-centered sanctuary and the revival of interest in liturgy have changed this very little.

Unfortunately the practice of preaching does not always match its prominence. This is evidenced by the fact that both within the church and without there is a widespread feeling that preaching, as a means of propagating the faith, has lost its effectiveness and outlived its usefulness. One hears caustic remarks about the futility of preaching; and several decades ago the proposal was made that there be a moratorium on preaching. About the same time some churchmen, despairing of changing the life and habits of adults through preaching, were on the verge of giving up the pulpit to concentrate on the more promising task of teaching the young to walk in the ways of the Lord. More recently it has become somewhat of a vogue to rate personal counselling above preaching.

Such criticisms and misgivings regarding preaching are due, in no small measure, to the mediocre quality of many sermons. There is reason to say that there are many within Protestantism who have retained the preeminence which the Reformers gave to preaching without either understanding its nature and function or giving it the attention which is its due. For instance, many sermons can hardly be regarded as proclamation; they are either essays on morality and religion, learned discussions of current issues with the major emphasis on diagnosis, or pious exercises which traditionally have belonged to a service of worship and are therefore continued to make the service complete. To this one might add that some sermons are so predominantly moralistic in content, language and delivery that the "ought" completely overshadows the "is" with the result that the message, from beginning to end, has the flavor of a religious harangue or an unwelcome exhortation. The fact that well-meant criticisms in man-to-man relationships are sometimes turned back with the remark, "Don't preach to me," is sufficient evidence to indicate that preaching is regarded to be synonymous with moralizing.

Strangely enough, however, though preaching falls short of its purpose and possibilities, and in many quarters has become something quite different from what the Reformers conceived it to be, the fact remains that the people in the pew are not ready to dispense with the spoken word. Within the Protestant tradition there is a deep and abiding conviction that the sermon is, in intention at least, a proclamation of the Word. And in this their desire to hear the Word, however ineptly and ineffectively it may be proclaimed, the faithful are not mistaken. This abiding demand for preaching fully corroborates the Protestant Confessions when they declare that the Church is "where the Word of God is rightly preached and the sacraments are rightly administered." The proclamation of the Word belongs to the very *esse* of the church, not just its *bene esse*. A church that does not proclaim the Word—and in Protestantism preaching is a vehicle of the Word—by that very omission ceases to be a church.

The Word of the Lord

The Word that is ours to proclaim is God's Word to man, whether spoken in the past or the present. But this Word is not to be equated with a book or a set of propositions and statements about God; neither with a series of divine oracles handed down from God and carefully reported and recorded by man, nor with a body of well-formulated beliefs and doctrines however true and useful. To think of the Word in these terms is to imprison it in a dead letter, but the Word "is living, and active, and sharper than any two-edged sword." [3] Perhaps some of our

[3] Heb. 4:12.

difficulties regarding a right conception of the Word would be avoided if we did not think of it so exclusively in terms of an audible sound. The Word, which the church is to proclaim, is that which becomes known to man in what Martin Buber has called the "I-Thou" relationship, or what Emil Brunner speaks of as "the divine-human encounter." Such an encounter can and does take place without benefit of audible words, though ultimately words will be employed to describe or convey the experience. He who makes "winds his messengers and flames of fire his ministers" [4] can speak in many tongues and also without any.

Israel's prophets and poets understood this perfectly; as the author of Hebrews reminds us, the divine Word came to them "in divers portions and divers manners." [5] But this diversity in portion and manner did not disturb them. Neither did it move them to question the authenticity or the meaning of the revelation received. For example, an ancient poet heard the voice of the Lord in the raging storm that destroyed the cedars of Lebanon; Elijah, on the other hand, heard nothing of the divine in the wind, the earthquake and the fire, but responded in faith and obedience to the still small voice that came after the violence of the storm had subsided. Isaiah, surrounded by the beauty of holiness in the temple, saw the Lord high and lifted up; but he saw the hand of the Lord just as distinctly in the defeat of his nation. The historian, looking back upon the deliverance of his people from the bondage of Egypt, recognized this event to be fully as much a Word of the Lord as the Law received by Moses on Mt. Sinai. In none of these instances are we dealing with words spoken and heard in the sense of verbal communication, but rather with events and deeds. That

[4] Ps. 104:4.
[5] Heb. 1:1.

each event or experience was in its own unique way a Word of the Lord was accepted to be a fact beyond doubt.

To our matter-of-fact minds, nurtured on scientific data and formulae, mathematical equations and demonstrable evidence, such a word might seem to be rather nebulous and too subjective to be reliable. There are those who seemingly want a word spoken audibly at a given time and place; they would believe, they claim, if the church could say: "These are the *ipsissima verba dei*." But that is not the way the Word of the Lord comes to man; it comes as an encounter, confronting man with his sinfulness and God's holiness, with his inability to atone for his sins and the all-sufficiency of divine grace, with his responsibility to both God and man according to his talents and opportunity. The Word is always in the first instance the encounter rather than the record of the encounter, though the latter, as we shall see, may communicate the Word.

Were our definition of the Word to stop here the most important thing would remain unsaid; for the Word that confronts us and that is given to the church to proclaim is the Word-made-flesh. That God was in Christ, judging the world, redeeming the world, reconciling men unto himself, revealing his wisdom and power, puts the stamp of validity upon the Word spoken at the beginning of time when God said, "Let there be," and there was; it gives meaning to God's covenant with Abraham and his descendants; it validates the Law delivered unto Moses and the Word spoken through the prophets. In the incarnation the Word is so direct and dynamic that it leaves no room for doubt. What need, one might ask, has any man of further evidence? Jesus Christ is the Word *par excellence*.

In the incarnation the Word takes on in unmistakable fashion the kind of objectivity that can be communicated. "That which was from the beginning, that which we have heard, that which we have seen with our eyes, that which we beheld, and our hands handled, concerning the Word of life . . . declare we unto you." [6] What St. John writes about the Word-made-flesh is true of every other revelatory Word given to man. True as it is that the highest cannot be spoken it is equally true that it compels men to speak. The prophets of the old covenant and the apostles of the new, though unable to share everything they saw and heard and knew, could not remain silent concerning the mighty deeds of God. The Spirit moved them to speak and write. And what they spoke and wrote has been preserved for us in Scripture.

It is not necessary, therefore, for any one to wait for some special rending of the skies to hear the Word of the Lord. God has already spoken. And though he continues to speak in diverse portions and manner as in days of old, he speaks most distinctly and dynamically through the record of his mighty deeds in history as we have it in the Bible. Word and Scripture are unmistakably and intimately related; not in the sense that the Word is confined to Scripture, or that Word and Scripture are one and the same but rather in the sense that Scripture is a record of the Word, a witness to the Word, and a vehicle of of the Word.

To say that Scripture is a record of the Word is putting the matter in minimal terms, but even that is important. The mere knowledge that something occurred at a given time and place, and that it had sufficient meaning to be remembered and to be preserved for posterity has value. It is important to know, for instance, that certain men of old conceived themselves to be under the compulsion of a Word not of their own choice or imagination. They spoke as men who were divinely confronted; Scripture leaves no room for doubt on that score. And when it

[6] I John 1:13.

is remembered that something has happened to man's outlook and conduct wherever the Bible has become known this takes on added significance.

What this says at once is that Scripture is more than a mere record of the Word; it is a witness to the Word. John, summarizing his account of the many signs that Jesus did but of which he recorded only a few, declares: "These are written, that ye may believe that Jesus is the Christ, the Son of God; and that believing ye may have life in his name." [7] Some such statement might be made of the Bible as a whole. It is a generally accepted fact that the authors of our canonical Scriptures did not write to preserve a record for posterity, but to bear witness to what God had wrought or spoken in a given moment of time. In short, the Scriptures were written, as it has often been said, from faith to beget faith.

Because Scripture begets faith it is not only a witness to the Word but at the same time a vehicle of the Word. When Scripture is read or interpreted the setting is created in which a divine-human encounter, not unlike that of which it speaks, may be re-enacted. Is there a minister of the gospel who has never had the exhilarating experience of having some well-known passage of Scripture suddenly come to life, illuminating his mind with flashes of insight and warming his heart with the compulsion to proclaim its message with zeal and joy? Such experiences, though all too rare, are sufficient evidence that the Word speaks through Scripture with remarkable effectiveness. They also put the stamp of validity upon the apostle's claim that "every Scripture inspired of God is also profitable for teaching, for reproof, for correction, for instruction which is in righteousness." And it is profitable in this respect for no other reason than that the Word speaks through Scripture, making men "wise

[7] John 20:31.

unto salvation," or, to use the other phrase, making "the man of God complete, furnished completely unto every good work." [8]

THE SUBSTANCE OF PREACHING

It is apparent, therefore, that the use of Scripture in proclaiming the Word rests upon something more than tradition. If the Word is found in Scripture and if the Word in turn finds man through Scripture it follows that those who would proclaim the Word cannot by-pass Scripture without sustaining a vital loss. This is not to say that the Word is imprisoned in Scripture. God can and does speak to man without benefit of Scripture. Those who humbly and honestly seek to know his will, who live as hopefully in expectation of his revealing Word as the devout of old looked for the consolation of Israel, are rewarded with glimpses of truth and visions of glory that leave no doubt or uncertainty as to the reality of a divine-human encounter. At the same time it is true to say that such experiences are as meaningful as they are because of Scripture's prior witness to the Word. In his final message to the pilgrims about to sail for America John Robinson voiced the confidence that God had "yet more light and truth" to give to his people, but it is worth noting that he said it would "break forth out of his holy Word"; and it is safe to assume that the reference was to Scripture.

We could begin, therefore, by saying, that Scripture provides the substance of preaching. No servant of the Word need rely on his personal discovery of the divine will, much less on his ingenuity to say something new or wait for some fresh revelation of truth. There is much to be said for achieving contemporaneity in content and language, but it is not necessary to sacrifice or neglect Scripture to achieve this end. The cult of

[8] II Tim. 3:16, 17.

trying to be original has carried the pulpit far afield. Although there was something distinctly original and direct about the Word of the Lord that came to the later prophets, there is no evidence at hand to suggest that they disdained the revelation that had been given to Abraham, Moses, Samuel and others before their time. Neither is there any evidence at hand to suggest that God spoke to them at regular seven-day intervals. In this respect no modern prophet may presume to be more favored than those in whose tradition he considers himself to stand.

The fact of the matter is, that it is difficult to understand how the Word can be proclaimed without the use of Scripture. This need not be taken so literally that the use of a passage of Scripture as a text is either the indispensable medium or the absolute guarantee of the Word. Beyond doubt, the Word can be and is proclaimed without benefit of a biblical text, but scarcely without benefit of the insight and impact of Scripture's witness to the Word. As a general rule, therefore, the use of a text is an essential prerequisite. "If within the ample range of biblical literature a preacher cannot find a text for what he wishes to say," writes Henry Sloane Coffin, "the chances are that he is deviating from the historic faith of which he is a teacher." [9] A sermon is more apt to be a faithful proclamation of the divine will if it is well-grounded in Scripture.

To be quite specific, this means that Scripture must be taken seriously—the text, the context, and its testimony as a whole. With a little ingenuity or by some *tour de force* it is rather easy to find a text to support a preconceived idea whether it be true or false, in harmony with or contrary to the Word. Such use of Scripture is nothing short of the abuse of Scripture whereby the Word is obscured and men are deceived. Evidences that this

[9] Henry Sloane Coffin, *What to Preach* (New York, 1926), p. 21.

practice is rather common are not difficult to find. The rise of numerous religious and semi-religious cults, many of which are rooted in a misinterpretation or a very fragmentary use of Scripture, might be cited as an example. But it is not necessary to go to the cults to discover evidences of the abuse of Scripture; even those who stand squarely within the main stream of Christian thought have been known to do violence to some biblical incident or saying for the sake of making a point or fortifying a position. Brunner makes the observation that the sacraments are almost "the only biblical element that has been able to withstand the caprices of the gifted minister who lives by his own wisdom rather than from Scriptures." [10]

Lest the herald of the Word fall under this condemnation it is worth remembering that "no prophecy of Scripture is of private interpretation." [11] The faithful observance of this principle is a kind of minimal guarantee against that excessive subjectivism that leads to vagaries of one sort or another. If it is true that no passage of Scripture really comes to life without "the inner witness of the Spirit," it is also true that this inner witness of the Spirit, on which some have placed so much emphasis, is constantly in need of the correction or verification of what God spoke through the prophets of old and in particular through the Word-made-flesh. Any unique experience, though it have all the earmarks of a genuine revelation, is in need of some touchstone of objectivity lest under the impact of an exalted moment one facet of the Word be emphasized to the exclusion of everything else in what St. Paul called "the whole counsel of God." [12]

This phrase, which came from the lips of St. Paul in defense

[10] Emil Brunner, *Our Faith* (New York, 1936), p. 128.
[11] II Pet. 1:20.
[12] Acts 20:27.

of his ministry and message, merits special emphasis. It calls our attention to the fact that the Word has many facets. The whole counsel includes law and gospel; and the gospel is both personal and social, rich with the promises of God and exacting in what it demands of man; it speaks of man's sin and God's salvation, of judgment and grace, of punishment and reward. People who come to hear the gospel have a right to expect that those who preach shall include "all things commanded . . . of the Lord," [13] to use the word of the Roman centurion, Cornelius. There must be no intentional or inadvertent omissions. No theological hobby-horses are to be saddled and ridden to the neglect of affirmations of the faith that are less congenial.

Now it is obviously impossible to proclaim the whole counsel of God in any one sermon, but each proclamation can be a true and correct segment of the whole so that it is in harmony with the total testimony of Scripture. Preaching is often found wanting at this point. Violence is done to Scripture by what might be called key-hole interpretation. That which can be seen through a key-hole may be accurate in regard to the area that is visible, but the very fact that only a very small area is visible may produce a totally false picture of the proceedings as a whole. To condemn or convict a man on key-hole information is a travesty on justice. And to take one little segment of Scripture, perhaps tearing it out of its context or interpreting it without regard to the testimony of the Bible as a whole, is to run the risk of distorting the Word by neglecting some aspect of the whole counsel of God.

This leads to a second consideration regarding the place of Scripture in the proclamation of the word. It is this: Scripture will not let us forget that the heart of the Christian message is what God wrought in Jesus Christ. This was the heart of preach-

[13] Acts 10:33.

ing in apostolic times. The thorough study which C. H. Dodd [14] and other scholars have made of the sermonic fragments found in Acts leaves no doubt on that score. A common pattern is clearly distinguishable in the apostolic *kerygma*. The story of the suffering, death and resurrection of Jesus, set in the framework of Old Testament history and prophecy and concluded with a call to repentance, was its core. To this were gradually added such facts concerning the teaching and healing ministry of Jesus as the apostles remembered and considered essential to insure an understanding of their message. By frequent repetition this spoken *kerygma* became enshrined in an oral tradition, which in turn was preserved in written documents, known to us as the gospels. What we have in the gospels is the sum and substance of preaching in apostolic times. And apostolic preaching, as Hugh Thomson Kerr points out, "defines and determines for us and for all time what the content of Christian preaching really is." [15] In some way or other preaching must always point to this one great affirmation of faith, that God was in Christ reconciling the world unto himself.

This means that God's action rather than man's ideas about religion and morality is the sum and substance of preaching. Only that which God has wrought and revealed comes properly within its orbit. And foremost among these deeds and words is the good news of the gospel. To this everything else is subordinate. Moreover, the one word which men need to hear and know above every other word is precisely this that God so loved the world that he was willing to give himself for its redemption. This is not something that men will come to know by the process of reasoning; this can only become known by telling the story of what actually happened when the Word was made flesh

[14] C. H. Dodd, *The Apostolic Preaching and Its Development* (London, 1936).
[15] H. T. Kerr, *Preaching in the Early Church* (London, 1942), p. 40.

and dwelt among men. John Baillie reminds us that "the Christian knowledge of God is not given to any man save in conjunction with the telling of an old, old story." [16] And the old, old story, it may be observed in passing, is not as well known as is generally assumed. It bears telling; in fact it bears repetition, for even "those who know it best seem hungering and thirsting to hear it, like the rest."

Now telling the old story is not to be thought of as though it were simply a matter of reciting what happened a little more than nineteen hundred years ago. History *per se,* even if it is sacred history, is not the concern of the Christian herald, for he is not a historian intent primarily on preserving a knowledge of the past for its own sake; as a herald he is interested in the meaning that sacred history has for us and our time. That which happened in Bethlehem, Nazareth and Jerusalem concerns him because it illuminates and transforms life as it is lived in London, Berlin, Chicago, and every other place in the world today. The story of the life, death, and resurrection of Jesus is of such tremendous importance because all this was accomplished for us and our salvation. Such a story has the merit that it never grows old.

Moreover, the telling of this story is not to be thought of as a wearisome repetition of the same message Sunday after Sunday. True as it is that preaching has but one great theme, it is a theme with many variations. The New Testament itself bears witness on that score. The different Christological formulae found in the gospels and the variety of interpretations in the New Testament as a whole provide ample evidence that the mystery of godliness with which men found themselves confronted in Christ was so profound in its depth and so comprehensive in its breadth that no single approach was adequate to

[16] John Baillie, *Our Knowledge of God* (New York, 1939), p. 180.

express what the believers had seen and experienced. Similarly, no herald of the Word will ever exhaust all there is to be said about the height and depth, the length and breadth of the love of God that was in Christ; neither will he ever be able to do justice to the wisdom and power of God that meets us on Calvary.

In spite of this reassuring word that the central message of the Christian faith is inexhaustible the objection is apt to be raised that such a restriction fails to allow for sufficient variety in preaching. It will be pointed out that the church is losing the interest of countless numbers because its message lacks sufficient diversity. In so far as this criticism has validity it is more apt to apply where men rely on their own wisdom and neglect Scripture. Scripture is the best guarantee of variety for the very reason that it brings us the whole counsel of God. Where it is taken seriously in the sense that all of its treasures are explored sameness is inconceivable, for the diverse facets of insight and interpretation inherent in the Christian message make for variety of content and emphasis. However, this does not relieve the Christian messenger of the responsibility of finding the media of idiom and illustration that will introduce variety, and especially contemporaneity, in form and language. To be quite specific, the use of archaic language, of numerous biblical quotations and time-worn religious cliches—regarded in some quarters to be the *sine qua non* of good preaching—is apt to be a liability rather than an asset in making the good news of the gospel known. As a matter of fact, it will not really become known unless it is presented in a way that its relevance to life is clearly seen and fully understood.

A reading of the Old Testament prophets is instructive at this point. They spoke to a specific need or situation, never in vague generalities. Apostasy, idolatry, ceremonialism, injustice, hopelessness and despair are some of the situations to which they spoke. To discern and proclaim the timely within the timeless, to bring the resources of the age-old gospel to bear upon the needs of men in a particular time and place is the prophet's task, whether he be ancient or modern. And this gives him the responsibility as well as the opportunity to be original and creative without either adding to or substracting anything from the God-given Word, which, though always relevant, is not always relevant in the same way for the reason that the human situation is never quite the same from age to age. Even within one generation the changes are so profound that many sermons which were relevant a decade or two ago strike us as being very irrelevant today. Reduced to its simplest terms this means that while we are telling the same old story we are not telling it in precisely the same way. The old story can be given a setting that will make it as contemporaneous as the day's most recent event.

Wherever this is done the Word is not only understood but it is also dynamic in its effect. Men are compelled to decide either for or against its demands. Neutrality is impossible, for the Word of the Lord is powerful. Jeremiah compared it to a hammer that breaks the rock in pieces.[17] What happened on the day of Pentecost fully substantiates the prophet's claim. It was the story of the crucified and risen Christ that stirred the multitude to repentance and faith. St. Paul also adds his testimony on that score. As a result of his failure at Athens, where he appears to have relied on excellency of speech and wisdom, he went to Corinth with the determination to know nothing save Jesus Christ and him crucified,[18] and on this foundation he established a church. Where else but in Scripture will you find

[17] Jer. 23:29.
[18] I Cor. 2:12.

a word of such power? This is another reason that Scripture is is so important to preaching.

Considering the ineffectiveness of the church in our time the question might be raised whether it may not be due, at least in part, to a lack of fidelity and fervor in proclaiming the Word, specifically the Word of the cross. Evidences are not wanting to warrant the statement that up to the time of the revival of interest in theology in general and in Christology in particular, preaching in the twentieth century had become largely a matter of exhorting the faithful to be more faithful, discussing the evils of men and society, and proposing panaceas—many quite unrealistic—for ushering in the millennium of universal peace and prosperity. The sermonic literature of this period is not marked in any conspicuous way by a witness to what God did and does for man; its emphasis is upon what man is expected to do for God or what he has neglected to do. The fundamental mistake of such preaching is that it summons men to action without first bringing them to the point where they come under the compulsion of the constraining love of Christ. Is the church today perchance reaping a rather meagre harvest of devotion and consecreation to the Kingdom because of yesterday's shallow, moralistic preaching?

While no one may presume to answer that question with finality, this much is certain, that in so far as the pulpit neglects the great biblical affirmations it fails to be true to Protestantism's cardinal principle that the church is "where the Word of God is rightly preached"; for the Reformers— whether Luther, Zwingli, Calvin or Knox—the Word of God had its focal point in the Word-made-flesh. In this Word there is power. Where this Word is proclaimed the church grows. To this Reformation principle Protestantism must return with a greater measure of fidelity, not merely for the sake of being true to its heritage, but for the purpose of bringing to bear upon a sin-sick, suffering world the dynamic impact of the one and only Word that is able to bring health and healing.

It goes without saying that every truly consecrated servant of God is sincere in his desire to proclaim this Word. There may be those who deliberately use the pulpit to exalt themselves or display their wisdom, but they constitute a very small minority. Most of us are troubled by the knowledge of our limitations, both intellectual and spiritual. Like Isaiah we are aware of having unclean lips and dwelling among a people of unclean lips. How is it possible under such circumstances for listeners to sense something of that divine presence and imperative which confronted men through the prophet's "thus saith the Lord"? Paradoxical as it may seem that God should use the words of sinful men to make his purposes known, the fact is that he does. He did it in days of old, he does it today. Just how or when this occurs is not for men to say.

Much less is it for any one to say, "Now I will proclaim the Word of the Eternal." That would be presumptuous. No mortal may arrogate unto himself a role that God alone has the right and the power to bestow. The times and seasons of the Word are not for us to determine. The Word of the Lord is not an object or substance which we control; on the contrary, it controls us. And when it takes possession of us it leaves us no option whether we will speak or not; at least not without becoming disobedient to the heavenly vision. There were times when the Old Testament prophets would have preferred to remain silent, but the Word overpowered them. Jeremiah speaks for every man to whom the Word has come: "If I say, I will not make mention of him, nor speak any more in his name, then there is in my heart as it were a burning fire shut up in my bones, and

I am weary with forbearing, and I cannot contain." [19] It may
not happen very often that the Word controls us as completely
as that; one might wish that it did, for if it did the quality of
preaching would be improved materially. But be that as it may,
the point of emphasis here is that the Word is as independent
of man's contriving as the wind that blows "where it listeth."

This need not leave us with a sense of helplessness or futility.
We may not be able to determine when the divine Word is
heard through the medium of human words, but if we speak
with fidelity and fearlessness concerning the wonderful things
which God has wrought and revealed we may have the confidence that our effort will not be in vain; for there is a power
resident within the Word that is independent of human effort
and achievement. Eloquence of speech is undoubtedly an asset;
but also those who are slow of tongue, if warm in heart, can
send it on its way on the wings of words. Wherever the Word is
preached in purity it will go forth with power and prosper in
the thing whereto it is sent.[20] The history of the church fully
confirms this scriptural claim.

[19] Jer. 20:9.
[20] Isa. 55:11.

LITURGICAL FREEDOM AND LITURGICAL REFORM

Purd E. Deitz

DIVINE worship is among the loftiest and noblest of man's activities, especially when it is freed from the compulsions of self-interest and motivated by thanksgiving and a longing for communion with the unseen Giver of life's blessings. It is not to be confused with form and ritual, which are merely vehicles to carry forward the activity of the spirit. Their value is always proportionate to the earnestness and receptivity of the worshipper; and the reality and worth of the worship are to be measured not by the vehicles used but by the ends sought and attained. In private worship the acts of devotion must be brought under a certain measure of rule and discipline, if for no other reason than to prevent neglect, on the one hand, or over-emphasis, on the other. But the form is not greater than the experience. Likewise, in public worship, there is always the need for common and disciplined expression, but the reality of the devotion is found in something other than in its form or ordering. Worship is the service of God, yet for the Christian it is not so much in obedience to his law as in response to his gospel—"a sacrifice of praise to God, that is, the fruit of lips that acknowledge his name." [1]

The problem of worship has always been to keep it free and vital without having it run into excesses of many sorts, sentimental or emotional, spectacular or magical, even didactic or verbose. Christianity has given expression to its genius for

[1] Heb. 13:15.

ordering worship in forms as diverse as the magnificent choral music of the Eastern Orthodox Church and the simple silence of the Society of Friends. But it has always sought a measure of attestation of these various practices in the New Testament, and has refused again and again to maintain forms or rituals in rigid molds when they seemed to differ from the standards of authentic and spiritual Christian faith. Rebellion against unchanging and outmoded practices of worship has always had some part in the reforming and purifying movements which characterize the church in its human aspect.

OUT OF UNIFORMITY

The Protestant Reformation was not initially directed against the prescribed forms of worship which characterized the Roman Church in the sixteenth century. It struck first at the most obvious points of theological error and ethical confusion. It aimed particularly at the recovery of obedience to the Scriptures and at the experience of saving faith in the New Testament sense of a free gift of God's grace. But such an attempt could not long overlook the visibly unscriptural and corrupt practices so prevalent in the services and organization of the church. In connection with the hierarchical system, the attack upon venality and simony in the church led to courageous resistance to Rome and an earnest effort to lift the level of the priesthood—an effort so successful that after the Protestants had withdrawn or were forced out, a great wave of purification ran through the Roman Church in the Counter-Reformation. In connection with worship, the attack upon the Mass was first from the side of doctrinal connection with the cardinal New Testament teaching of salvation by faith and the inefficacy of work, but soon came the necessity of introducing changes in the form and manner of corporate worship. How successful the

Reformers were in this effort may be a matter of difference of opinion, especially since the Mass itself, with most of its doctrinal and ritualistic trappings, persists virtually unchanged in the Church of Rome. The Counter-Reformation did little to conserve for Rome what Wittenberg, Zurich or Geneva offered by way of reconstruction of the Mass.

Yet the success or failure of the Reformation in the matter of public worship need not be judged by the response of the Council of Trent. Everything depends upon the standpoint from which public worship is viewed. If the main concern is for historic continuity, it would seem important to preserve the essential features of the Mass in western Christianity. But if the canon of judgment is derived from the spirit of freedom in the New Testament, an entirely different result is to be desired. On the whole, the Reformers took the latter viewpoint, and probably would wish their work to be estimated in accordance with such standards as flow from the teachings of the Scriptures. But the matter is not so simple as such statements would seem to suggest; for the Reformers were not gods, but men, and the whole movement was greatly affected by the widespread stirrings of the times as well as by the personal situations and proclivities of its leading spirits. It is necessary to look at the matter more closely.

The oustanding developments of medieval worship in Europe were the Gothic cathedrals and the Roman Mass. They were, in a sense, parts of the same great structure of life and thought which dominated the Middle Ages. The life of the community was centered in the worship of God, and a tremendous symphony of arts was called into the service of this worship. Ceremony and symbolism, light and color, music and movement, vestment and ornament, were employed with creative skill and effectiveness. Yet the cathedral did not represent a true community of aspiration, since the worship which should have expressed the common longings and thankful offerings of the people had become a spectacle controlled entirely by the priesthood. Mighty as the cathedral was, dominating the landscape and towering over the homes of the people, yet it was a false symbol, since the church, by Roman definition, was not the fellowship of the redeemed, but the hierarchy—the priesthood. The people were held by the power of a miracle, the "unbloody sacrifice" of the Mass. They did not often partake of the Lord's Supper, and the cup was invariably withheld from them. The sense of corporate worship had been lost, except perhaps in the monastic establishments or among the clergy, where the "Divine Office," or daily services of prayer and Scripture, bound them together in a common rule.

The Mass itself presented little which would remind the people of "those mighty acts by which God had brought salvation to his people," except in a narrowly conceived sense. What the priest was offering at the altar was the important transaction. This in itself was a propitiatory sacrifice, and was of value as a work of devotion. Its efficacy was not limited to those who shared in the service, but could apply to the absent and even to the dead. The service was in an unknown tongue and invested with all manner of superstitious ideas common among the people. Add to this the general illiteracy and lack of knowledge of the Bible, and it becomes evident that the Reformers could not long avoid dealing with the issues raised by the corrupted worship of the Church of Rome.

Of the various approaches to this corrupt worship, Zwingli's attack was most frontal and direct. His first reforming act, in 1516, it is said to have been preaching salvation through Christ alone instead of through the Virgin Mary; for he was located at Einsiedeln, where a famous shrine had been erected to the

Black Virgin, with an image supposedly fallen from heaven. In this he was pointing out one of the greatest weaknesses in the Roman worship, namely, the unscriptural worship of Mary and the saints. It is extremely probable also that the reforming tendencies of Zwingli came not only from his study of the New Testament in the Greek text but also from such incidents as his observation, while serving in Italy as a chaplain with Swiss troops, that the Mass at Milan was said according to a different rule from the one he was using at Glarus (1506–1516). Luther had also made the same discovery that the Ambrosian Mass at Milan differed from his Mass at Wittenberg. Zwingli reasoned: "Either Ambrose, from whom this book came, made changes in the Roman Mass without being visited with censure, or the Roman ritual had taken its shape since the time of Ambrose. In either case the liturgy was the work of men and subject to change." [2]

Another incident of interest is reported by Zwingli: "It was while pastor at Glarus that I came across at Mollis, north of Glarus, an Obsequial which, although old, was complete. And there stood a Latin rubric which said that immediately after the infant had been baptized, then shall the sacrament of the Lord's Supper be administered to the child, including the chalice containing the blood. How long this practice was observed in the canton of Glarus I have not been able to find out, but surely it was not two hundred years since, in Mollis, the Lord's Supper was administered in both kinds." [3] It is scarcely to be wondered at, if Zwingli, animated by his clear understanding of the scholarly approach to the New Testament and convinced of the tremendous discrepancies between what he saw in the church life of his time and that of the apostolic period, should have

[2] Good, J. I., *The Reformed Reformation* (Philadelphia, 1916), p. 45.
[3] Quoted by Good, *op. cit.*, p. 45.

become rather drastic and thorough in his suggestions for doing away with the Mass and substituting for it a service of reading, preaching, and prayer. Such a service, in which God's Word was magnified and exalted, was the goal towards which all the Reformer consistently were moving. Zwingli happened to be less conservative than some others, and the Swiss Reformation resulted in such drastic changes as reducing the observances of the Lord's Supper to four times a year, eliminating music and art from services and places of worship, and basing the liturgy principally upon the preaching of the Word.

In Germany, similar tendencies were at work, especially among the Anabaptists, and Luther (because of the radical activities of Carlstadt and others) had to overcome his initial reluctance to try his hand at reforming worship. According to Moffatt, it was not only "a natural conservatism and an instinct for continuity in worship" which made him slow to break away from medieval customs and admit the need of drawing up any new forms, but also it was "partly due to his own experience— had he not found his way to God through the Word, and not through breviaries and missals—and partly due to a superb confidence in the Word." [4] Preaching the gospel was to Luther, as it was to Zwingli, the supreme need of the hour, and he was driven to make some positive contributions to the reform of worship only by the needs of those who were turning their backs upon the superstition of the Mass and had no substitute for it. With many varieties of changes being made by those who realized that faith always expresses itself in the forms of worship, Luther felt compelled to offer his suggestions also. They are of tremendous importance, and have been avidly studied by Lutherans of a later day as a guide to modern reforms in wor-

---

[4] Moffatt, James, "Luther" in *Christian Worship*, N. Micklem Ed. (Oxford, 1936), p. 121.

ship. Yet it is quite permissible to call attention to the fact that they did not gain anything like the response which his translation of the Bible, his catechisms, or his hymns and music had among his followers. Church orders were issued in such numbers that it is stated that between 1523 and 1555 as many as 135 appeared in the various states and cities of Germany.[5] These varied all the way from ultra-conservative, which sought to retain "as many as possible of the pre-Reformation forms and ceremonies," [6] to mediating or radical, which reflected the influence of the Swiss Reformers. However deplorable this great diversity may seem to the students of liturgy as they look back upon it, the fact remains that the Reformation was a liberating force which could not be contained in any given vessel of worship-expression.

Many Lutherans wish that Luther had been more positive at the point of worship, and had imposed his moderate ideas upon the church which followed his movement. In like manner there are Presbyterians who regret the outcome of the Zwinglian and Calvinian Reformation, especially as it found radical expression under Knox and the English Puritans. The extreme simplicity of the Reformed services on the Continent became, in the British Isles, an attempt to do away with any suggestion of art or beauty in vestments, music or musical instruments, altars, stained glass, or any ornamentation of worship, as being either Romish or pagan. Incalculable and irreparable damage was done through this perversion of the Reformation principle of New Testament truth and freedom. Yet should the principle itself be repressed because it may be subject to perversion? There was great risk in the whole movement of the Reformation, but it could not be evaded.

[5] Luther D. Reed, *The Lutheran Liturgy* (Philadelphia, 1947), p. 88.
[6] *Ibid.*, p. 89.

The researches of Maxwell, the eminent Scottish liturgical scholar, have made it clear that Calvin was not nearly so radical in his reform of worship as had hitherto been believed. It was not by his wish that the Lord's Supper service was separated from the regular Sunday worship, but by the will of the magistrates; and his Genevan ritual for Holy Communion was derived from the German rites of Strasbourg, which kept fairly close to the eucharistic structure of the medieval Mass. Thus the principles (but not the practice) of Calvin have become a rallying point for those who desire to bring about reforms in worship based upon historical development. Calvin is being invoked as favoring weekly communion and a much richer content in the liturgical service after the ancient patterns.

Yet the question may still be raised: To what extent does the knowledge of preference or taste of one person—even of so able and learned a leader as Calvin—outweigh the clear testimony of history that the reforms in worship wrought by Calvin and the Calvinists were noted for the reduction of the number of Communion services to four times a year and the utmost simplicity in everything connected with public devotions? Except for their involved doctrine and verbose statements, the reformed orders of worship are extremely bare and simple. The descendants of the Reformed reformation have to live with this fact of history just as the children of Lutheranism must accept the partial character of Luther's work and the multiplicity of Lutheran forms. It may be quite desirable to do something about it in either case, but for different reasons than those which look back merely to the possible wishes of a leader who has had his day and who, under God, has made his contribution as best he could in the midst of his own situation. All honor to the Reformers for what they did! To appeal to what Luther or

Calvin might have wished to do seems only faintly relevant to our present situation.

The central fact of the Protestant contribution to worship is diversity. Over against the imposed uniformity of Rome was set the freedom of the Christian spirit, that inevitable product of the rediscovery of the New Testament standard of salvation by the grace of a sovereign God. For all the Reformers the standard was the Holy Scriptures, and it was precisely because of this agreement that the differences arose between them. The teaching of the New Testament is by no means so specific and well-defined upon the subject of worship as is often claimed by those who may have their own ends to serve. The Spirit-filled, Spirit-led disciples of the early chapters of the Acts give the impression of a different pattern of worship from the council at Jerusalem or Paul undergoing rites of purification in the temple. The kind of church life described in the Corinthian correspondence seems quite unlike that implied by the Epistle to the Ephesians. There are many elements common to all, of course, and it is certainly not impossible to gain a coherent view of early Christian worship as set forth in the New Testament; but the main impression is of freedom within a wider order and diversity within a wider unity.

For the Reformers themselves it is doubtful if such an idea of diversity within unity would have been very impressive. They all felt the exhilaration which had come to them with the opening of the Bible and the discovery of the Word of truth; the temptation of each was to feel that he had found the authentic teaching, and therefore to refuse to another the same freedom of interpretation. *Ad fontes* was the watchword of the leaders of the movement, but they did not seem to realize that there might be several sources of the mighty and free stream of the spirit of worship in the New Testament. With the gospel had come a loosing of the spirit so that it is impossible to find in the first century the one complete and authentic formula for worship. There are many glimpses given and many suggestions offered; from among them one may select the type of service which seems to be most consistently presented and overlook the others. But the diversity is still there, and instead of refusing to admit it, one might better inquire what general principles underlie the outward expressions.

Reformation Principles

Wherein can be found the unity upon which, for all its diversification and disagreements among the various parties, the worship reforms of Protestantism finally rested? It lay in principles which flowed from the Reformation's respect for the Scriptures as containing the true guide to doctrine and action. Three of these principles deserve mention in this connection, beginning with the simple, but amazingly fertile concept of the *sola fide*. If salvation is by faith alone, any thought of worship as earning merit must be abandoned. The Roman Mass was peculiarly vulnerable at this point as well as the daily offices and many customs associated with the Christian year. How could the Mass be purified? How could the whole sorry business of works-righteousness be stripped from worship? Different answers were given by different Reformers, for the same principle operated in more than one way.

For an impulsively generous and brave man like Luther, who loved the services of the Church, it was enough to cut out most of the Canon of the Mass, because of the ideas of "obligation, sacrifice and good works" which it contained, but to retain practically all the rest of it, so long as the Gospel should be preached "purely, clearly, and without admixture." When the Elector Joachim II of Brandenburg sought to retain the priestly

eucharistic vestments, with processions and the like, Luther
wrote to Bucholzer, the elector's chaplain, to advise him that if
he kept certain principles and practices such as preaching and
the two sacraments, and gave up worship of the saints and
masses for the dead,

then, in God's Name, go along in the procession, and carry a silver
or golden cross, and a chasuble or an alb of velvet, silk, or linen. And
if one chasuble is not enough for your lord the elector, put on three
of them, as Aaron the high priest, put on three, one over the other
. . . and if his Electoral Grace is not satisfied with one circuit or
procession, in which you go about and ring and sing, go around
seven times, as Joshua and the children of Israel went around Jericho
shouting and blowing with trumpets . . . For such matters, if free
from abuses, take from and give to the Gospel nothing: only they
must not be thought necessary to salvation, and the conscience dare
not be bound to them . . . And if the pope would let these matters
be free, and the Gospel be preached, and commanded me to hang
my breeches about my neck, I'd do his pleasure.[6]

It is difficult to imagine Zwingli or Calvin making a similar
suggestion (or a similar offer!), yet they all agreed in condemning any thought of merit as being gained by works of worship.
Pure devotion springs out of the heart's response by faith to the
gracious acts of God. Worship as the service of God must never
be confused with worship as winning something from God.
Indeed, worship is a duty only insofar as it is freely offered as a
witness to God's salvation and power. Despite differences in
application, the Protestant principle of justification by faith
alone provides a deep channel for all true worship.

A corollary of this truth is the common Protestant idea of

---

[6] Enders, *Dr. Martin Luther's Brief Wechsel*, XVI, 316 ff. Quoted by Reid, *op.
cit.*, p. 98.

obedience to the Word of God, arising out of thankfulness to him for his grace. In this doctrine, good works are given their proper place in life, and the believer is delivered from the burden of legalism. As a redeemed man, he cannot do as he pleases; but he pleases to look to God in faith and to trust and obey. This faith is wrought in him by the Holy Spirit through the preaching of the gospel, and confirmed by the use of the sacraments. It makes of life a constant procession of gratitude and praise. Worship is the outpouring of the soul filled to overflowing by the grace of the Eternal.

Although the services proposed by many of the Reformers were quite bare of anything like a festival spirit and Luther himself eliminated the entire Roman canon from the Eucharist (as he often called it, significantly), yet this spirit persists in the teachings and practice of various Reformation groups and finds expression in hymn-singing and private devotions. Moreover, Protestants worship *because* of the promises of God and not merely to receive them. Thus the spirit of compulsion or uniformity is foreign to the Reformation genius.

Again, there can be no doubt that all phases of the Reformation held, in some degree, to the idea of the priesthood of all believers. By its very wording, this doctrine is essentially liturgical, having to do with the mediation of grace, not only in salvation but also in worship and the acts of worship. The Reformers thought to restore the service to the congregation. They were agreed in their opposition to the rigid Roman sacerdotalism which controlled all the expressions of worship. Thus they invited congregational participation and encouraged it by the introduction of singing by the people and responsive readings and chants. In regard to music Zwingli was a strange exception to this rule, for although he was a skilled musician he undertook to forbid all music, vocal or instrumental, in the churches.

Yet Zwingli, like Calvin, was keenly aware of the corporate nature of worship, and both of them placed the great act of proclaiming the Gospel at the center of the fellowship of Christian people. As with Luther, the gospel was proclaimed both by preaching and by the administration of the sacraments, but the former dominated the regular Lord's Day service, and the latter (contrary to Luther's custom) was limited to very infrequent observance. Yet, curiously, the reduction of the number of administrations of Communion was for the express purpose of increasing the number of communicants and emphasizing its corporate character. This later became the general Lutheran pattern also, and for the same reason. Worship is a function of the community of believers; it is one of the expressions of their fellowship in Christ. Here are contributions of tremendous importance—the re-emphasis of the New Testament conception of *koinonia,* along with full and free access to the throne of God by every earnest believer.

In this connection, attention should be drawn to the place of music in the service. As part of the break with a priestly system of worship, congregational singing was encouraged, especially by Luther and his followers, with spiritual and cultural results that are astonishingly great. Calvin's limitation of suitable hymn texts to the Psalter was a retarding factor along this line, as was also Zwingli's radical omission of music (later restored) from the services. There is no doubt that Luther's work established hymn-singing as an important part of Protestant worship everywhere, as well as leading to the development of the musical spirit which finally culminated in the mighty works of Bach. Its basis was in the simple idea that worship is the function of all the congregation and one of the signs of its fellowship.

The third great characteristic of Protestant doctrine which found common expression in the way worship was dealt with by the Reformation is that of freedom within order. It is a principle which seems to have opened the door to confusion, but liberty is of the very essence of the New Testament faith which the Reformation hoped to restore and, even more importantly, of the living faith which is ever being created by the Holy Spirit. The confusion need not blind our eyes to the great gains made by the application of this principle, as individuals and groups sought to find the way of worship which would have most meaning for them as servants of a living God. To the whole sum of Christian devotion, Lutherans, Reformed, Anglicans, Anabaptists, Separatists—of many kinds and degrees of emotion and understanding—each brought his own contribution of form and materials. Even those who desired no form at all made a kind of form out of their very formlessness, but they were powerless to impose this "form" upon all others.

To emphasize the differences is to erect barriers to a larger fellowship of worshipping Christians; but to recognize the common unity beneath the differences is to lay a firm foundation for ecumenical relationships. It must be remembered that the New Testament freedom which the Reformers sought for themselves is not freedom for man's sake; it is freedom under God, for God's purposes. It is freedom under order; or, as is sometimes said, in secular affairs, "freedom with responsibility." The responsibility, however, for the Christian, lies in the realm of obedience to the Word of God; the freedom comes from the impelling power of the Spirit of God. It is only fair to note, on the one hand, that sometimes there are Protestant groups in which the spirit of freedom seems to burst the bonds of order, thus becoming something other than true freedom. Given a little time for maturity in religious experience, however, and the growth of a certain measure of institutional life, the original liberty begins to find normal channels for its activity in worship as well as in other group functions. But, on the other hand, let it become too rigidly ordered, and it will periodically spill over into enthusiastically new, free, and formless ways.

It is interesting to note that outside of Anglicanism, only a few large bodies of historic Protestantism have adopted a fixed ritual of worship. In passing, it may be pointed out that the *Book of Common Prayer* allows a larger measure of liberty in usage than is generally supposed to be the case. Liturgies have had to win their way by popular acceptance. Now popular acclaim is not always the equivalent of the voice of the Holy Spirit; nevertheless, there is a sense in which, by the loosing of the spirit of man, the Spirit of God is given more leverage in moving him. When the advocates of formal expressions of worship seek to win their case by an appeal to the Word of God and the spiritual victories they have won, and at the same time those who plead for less form in worship use the same arguments, the way would seem to be wide open for some kind of unity in approach. Certainly they are both free to try a more excellent way.

TOWARDS UNITY

At present this search for unity is taking the form of seeking to assess the contributions which each communion brings to the service of God through worship. In the World Council of Churches the Protestant bodies have been joined by representatives of the Eastern Orthodox Churches in such an endeavor, although in the initial stages of this process the emphasis is largely upon the broader questions of the nature of the church and its witness to the gospel of God in the world of our day. Nevertheless, there is a growing sense of the kind of Christian unity which can bear the strain of differences and disagreements; the kind of unity, indeed, which can rejoice in diversities

and utilize them for the greater glory of God. When the
churches come together, they recognize that they have a common vocation to worship God in his holiness and that this
worship is not to be separated from the witness of the Christian
community. The "Findings and Decisions" of the First Assembly of the World Council of Churches contain this clear statement about the necessity of vital and genuine worship:

> Worship and witness . . . belong inseparably together . . . When
> the ordinary man speaks of the Church he thinks of a group of
> people worshipping in a building. By what that group is, the Church
> is judged. Effective witness becomes possible only as each worship-
> ping group is so filled with the joy of the risen and living Lord that
> even the outsider becomes aware that, when the Church speaks, it is
> of real things.[7]

From this it would follow that through vitality in worship, the
church can approach unity in witness.

It is true that in the ecumenical gatherings which have been
held in recent years it has been impossible for the representatives
of all faiths to unite in one form of the Holy Communion. This
fact has shamed and perplexed many who look for the token of
our inner unity in an outward act of worship. The presence of
adherents to the ancient catholic churches as well as of those
who accept widely differing evangelical or Protestant confessions makes it extremely difficult to find common ground for
complete fellowship at the Lord's Table. But at least in certain
services of confession of sin and preparation for the Holy Communion, Christians of all kinds have found it possible to combine, and perhaps this is the most important point of agreement!
To recognize ourselves as sinners who must all come to a

[7] World Council of Churches, *Findings and Decisions of the First Assembly*
(New York, 1948), p. 29.

common Lord for forgiveness is the first requisite of ecumenical fellowship. The true unity which we may find beyond our diversity is in Christ Jesus our forgiving Lord.

In considering the measure of unity which the major Protestant groups may bring into such a situation of ecumenical fellowship, attention must be called to some evidences among the "Reformation Churches" of a more dynamic approach to the matter of public worship through which the "joy of the risen and living Lord" may speak to our needs. There occurred among the Lutheran and Reformed Church in America during the nineteenth century a liturgical revival which both kindled a great interest in worship forms and their theological undergirding, and, at the same time, awakened strong opposition. Out of these movements have come certain tendencies which may be of great value in the present situation, if they can be kept under the essential principles which make unity possible.

True to the pattern of the mother churches in Europe, the Lutheran Churches in the New World found themselves using a variety of forms of service and many with little or no form. However, in 1748, Henry Melchior Muhlenberg introduced a liturgy which was adopted by his newly organized Ministerium of Pennsylvania; and which, although greatly modified in later forms and English versions, became the basis for the preparation of books of worship in the latter part of the nineteenth century which are proving now to be the generally accepted standards of Lutheran worship. Certain groups in Eastern Pennsylvania issued a *Church Book* (of the General Council) in 1868, which represented a definite return to the more complete liturgical services first suggested by Muhlenberg. By 1888 other Synods had joined in a movement which produced a *Common Service* issued in varying editions by various Synods. In this movement there were drawn together the forces working for a return to the worship principles of the Reformation and the forms of the early centuries. The *Common Service* had many affinities with the English Prayer Book of 1549. Also, the choral parts of the service were greatly elaborated, and the pattern for Lord's Day worship was fixed as a Eucharistic service, stopping short, however, of actual communion except upon the Sundays when this was indicated. Additional Lutheran bodies, including the Missouri Synod, the Norwegian bodies and others, adopted it, and it became a unifying factor in American Lutheranism.

The joint work of the bodies which originally provided the *Common Service* was continued until in 1917 the *Common Service Book* was issued, containing the Liturgy, the Hymnal, a series of Occasional Services, and musical settings for the liturgy and hymns. It is a monumental work, and has been hailed as the most complete and authentic Lutheran liturgy in vernacular ever issued. It represents a victory for the liturgical party within Lutheranism—in many respects a mildly conservative party, eager to bring the scattered elements of Lutheran confessionalism together. They refer to the spirit of their liturgical endeavors as that of "progressive conservatism." The tendency is to make this work the authoritative worship of the churches, despite certain liberties in minor matters. Its strength is largely the strength of liturgical scholarship; of accepted Protestant formularies it is closest to the historic Western Mass although it suffers a defect, admitted even by some of its admirers, in the lack of any eucharistic prayer—that is, prayer of consecration. Its weakness is that it represents only one stream of historic Christian worship, the priestly, official, and artistic type, and thus may have difficulty establishing itself as a popular and dynamic expression of religious faith.

The Reformed Churches (Swiss and German) in America had only the simplest of liturgical forms. The Palatinate Liturgy of 1563 which they brought with them was little more than a directory which conceived of worship under the didactic forms so customary to the more thoroughgoing Reformers. But through the middle period of the nineteenth century a movement gained headway among the German Reformed congregations known as the "Mercersburg Theology," so named from the theological school at Mercersburg, Pennsylvania, where influences from England and the Continent became focussed in a Christocentric, churchly view of theology, and flowered in a liturgy which claimed to be of the essence of the Reformation without following any special Protestant pattern except that of preserving the heritage of the early church.

Issued first as a "Provisional Liturgy" in 1857, this formulary was revised and published in 1866 as the *Order of Worship,* a book which still persists in some places as a living rite, although never officially adopted and often revised or officially superseded. This is due, probably, not only to its intrinsic liturgical strength, but also to the intense opposition which it aroused among the non-liturgical groups, which led in turn to the development of an intense loyalty on the part of its proponents. It differed from the Lutheran service in seeking to introduce elements not only from the Western Church but also from the Eastern Churches and in partaking of a more festival character than the services patterned on the Roman model. Because it made some attempt to go back to a fourth century kind of pattern, it has been referred to as "ecumenical" in spirit, meaning that it tries to recapture the spirit of the time when the Body of Christ was not divided between East and West, Orthodox and Roman. With more congregational independence to contend with in the Reformed churches than is the case within Lutheranism, this liturgy did not fare so well as the Common Service. Its strength was in the liturgical taste of its authors and in their sound historical sense; but it seemed far too priestly and altar-centered for those whose views were more evangelical and pulpit-centered.

After the Prussian Union of 1817 which brought together Lutheran and Reformed congregations in Germany, many of the emigrants to the United States preferred to be "Evangelical" rather than exclusively Lutheran or Reformed. The success of the union movement, however, had been marred in 1830 by the Prussian King's insistence upon a union "Agende" or church order. Consequently the Evangelicals did not insist upon any old-country worship forms when they organized the Church Society which later became the Evangelical Synod but laid plans for a book of their own. Their first *Agende* was published in 1857, and revised in 1887. Although the Lutheran influence is evident in the order for the Lord's Supper, this is partly counter-balanced by the introduction into the English version of a brief but heartfelt eucharistic prayer following the words of institution. Many of the prayers betray, delightfully, the pietistic spirit of their writers in the address to the Lord Jesus Christ rather than to the Father. In 1916 a revised *Book of Worship* in English was adopted. The custom of formal prayers was continued, and the official liturgy was widely used, although few of the churches were actually liturgical in spirit and there was little of the high church movement as compared with Lutheranism.

The moderate and irenic spirit of the Evangelical Synod was matched by the willingness of the Reformed Church to try to reach agreement upon forms of worship as well as upon confessional standards and ecclesiastical polity in the Evangelical and Reformed Church, brought into being by their union in 1934. A *Book of Worship* was drawn up which drew heavily upon the 1866 "Order" of the Mercersburg group, yet represented the clearly evangelical piety and faith of the *Agende,* and borrowed some features from the Lutheran service. In accordance with the essential character of true Protestantism, congregations are permitted full freedom of worship, and the *Book* is offered as containing the "accepted norms" of the Church. In the Preface, this is stated to be "in harmony with the evangelical ideal of worship, which affirms authority without bondage and freedom without license and requires truth, beauty, and propriety in the services of the House of the Lord." [8]

This *Book of Worship* endeavors to meet also the requirements of the Reformation principle of the corporate nature of the church's worship by encouraging congregational participation and minimizing the priestly or ritualistic character of the minister in the services. This aspect of the minister's function (especially as pastor-priest) is not left out entirely, and in the eyes of some may seem to approach more nearly a fourth century pattern than one derived directly from the New Testament. This is always the dilemma of liturgics, whether to take its starting point with the patristic age, thereby gaining the benefits of the first glorious centuries of development in the church, or to go back to the apostolic period and start with almost nothing that can be established as normative. Perhaps the true dynamic of worship can best be realized through the "ecumenical" patterns of the fourth century and the free and vital spirit of the first century, with both of them measured and informed by the situation in which we find ourselves today.

The principle of salvation by faith alone must likewise always be revealed in the explicit expressions of glory and praise to the sovereign God and in the implicit spirt of complete trust and confidence which are breathed in the devotions of the congregation. So long as worship is purely duty, it is in danger of legalism; insofar as it is propitiatory, it is Roman; wherein it

[8] Evangelical and Reformed Church, *Book of Worship* (Cleveland, 1947), p. 3.

depends too much upon man's activity, it is less than Christian. In this is seen the danger of all ritualistic worship, that it may lose the sense of grateful spontaneity in the presence of the living, risen Christ.

LIVING LITURGY

What makes a liturgy a living thing is not the form of words which it uses but the spirit which is breathed into it. This spirit comes from the ability of the liturgy to express actual religious feelings and attitudes and to form a vehicle for the interaction of God's Word and man's response. It is meant, therefore, both to awaken familiar memories and to stimulate new interest.

Hymnals contribute to this same end. Therefore it is gratifying to find the new hymn collections of Methodists, Presbyterians, Baptists and Disciples combined, Evangelical and Reformed, and Episcopal alike striving for a truly ecumenical and universal character. The hymns and tunes represent the long centuries of Christian devotion, although in modern dress, as well as the contributions of contemporary poets and composers. Hymns like Ferdinand Q. Blanchard's "Before the Cross of Jesus" take their place beside "Christian, dost thou see them?" by eighth century St. Andrew of Crete. The chorale tunes are being revived, and even arrangements of plain song appear in these hymnals. The principle of freedom may admit much substandard music and poetry of the sentimental and jingle-rhythm type into many congregations; but it also leads to a recognition of the finest and best that can be offered in the service of the Eternal. There is an increasing body of hymns which seek to express the concerns of the church for a world-wide ministry and for the application of the gospel to all the social relationships of men.

Likewise in prayers and liturgical materials generally, the

Reformation spirit fosters the highest type of contemporary expression. The essence of liturgy is not necessarily in the stately English prose style of Cranmer and the *Book of Common Prayer* or in the use of formal pronoun and verb endings. More and more the manuals of worship include prayers like those of Walter Rauschenbusch. His stirring prayer for the church, beginning, "O God, we pray for thy Church, which is set today amid the perplexities of a changing order, and face to face with a great new task," is becoming as well known as some of the older intercessions "for the whole state of Christ's Church." Prayers by Joseph Fort Newton and W. E. Orchard, as well as by John Hunter, Henry Van Dyke and others, are frequently found in books of public worship now being issued. An interesting example of such prayer expression is the following, attributed to Reinhold Niebuhr,

O God, who hast bound us together in this bundle of life, give us the grace to understand how our lives depend upon the courage, the industry, the honesty and the integrity of our fellow-man, that we may be mindful of their needs, grateful for their faithfulness and faithful in our responsibilities to them; through Jesus Christ our Lord. Amen.[9]

It is probable that the denominational bodies which might be characterized as "semi-liturgical" hold in their hands the future of sound public worship according to the Reformation genius. There is a real liturgical movement abroad among the churches. Unfortunately to some it is merely a liturgical "revival," looking backwards almost exclusively; but to others it is an effort to recover in our own time the dynamic which thrust forward the great movement of the Reformation, the power of the living

---

[9] Evangelical and Reformed Church, *Book of Worship* (Cleveland, 1947), p. 360.

Christ which has invested the church in every age with the urge to express praise and devotion in forms worthy of the great acts of a saving God. As such, it also looks forward and upward, placing itself under the judgment of the Word of God and the leadership of his Spirit. What the liturgical movement of our time will bring forth depends upon the extent to which the forms and practices proposed are kept under the vital guidance of the principles to which we owe so great a debt to the Reformers and by which we may be led afresh into the way of truth and unity. We need not hope to see the churches fall into step like ranks of soldiers trained only in uniformity; but we can labor for a symphony of worship in the whole Christian world, with many diverse instruments of praise blending their skilled and directed efforts to one glorious and harmonious end.

THE NEW REFORMATION AND PRAYER

JOHN BIEGELEISEN

ALMOST every present-day writer and speaker seems to know that the present generation is characterized by crises and confusion. What does not seem to be common knowledge is that underneath our crises and confusion there flows a great prophecy and promise of re-birth and re-union of the most vital forces in the Christian heritage. There is a sense in which all creation is under oath of loyalty. The past refuses to be buried. Every new age carries within it the essentials of the preceding age. The superstructure may require centuries for its completion; countless generations may have to contribute their own quality and mode of labor, but the foundation, in design and structure, contains the essence of the *Form,*[1] which is the structure's strength, symmetry and beauty. Our world may have always existed, as Bertrand Russell and Julian Huxley and others would have it. But we are told: "The earth was waste (without form) and void; and darkness was upon the face of the deep. And the Spirit of God moved upon the face of the waters."[2]

It was *form* which gave our world meaning. That *form* is God-given. Man, inspired by the *form,* creates formations. The formations, when true to the original *form,* always reflect the Creator. When the formations become obstructional and eclipse the original they become obsolete; it is then that we get re-

[1] "Form" is here used in the sense in which Plato and Aristotle and Kirkegaard use it.
[2] Gen. 1:2.

167

formations. Every Reformation seems to be an attempt to recapture the original *form*. The success of the attempt is contingent upon depth, not distance; not how far back a certain reformation goes is important, but how deeply it penetrates to reach the purity of *form*.

The Christian Church between the evening of Pentecost and the morning in October, 1517, on which Luther nailed the Ninety-Five Theses to the door of the Castle Church at Wittenberg, had accumulated a vast amount of beliefs which would have astonished the apostles if they could have heard about them. The Protestant Reformation, as part of the Renaissance, was an attempt to melt the frozen streams of large parts of Christendom and to unstop the wells of true *form* which the Spirit of Life had dug, but which an ecclesiastical philistinism had stopped up. The Reformation of the sixteenth century released religious people from a load of ornate and lifeless superstitions and ritualistic accretions and caused them to re-examine the foundations of their faith. That the Reformation, after 400 years, is still an unfinished task needs no further argument. Any reformation worthy of the name has within itself a dynamic element which refuses to let it become static. The Protestant Reformation is an on-going process.

THE NEW REFORMATION

But all is not well with Protestantism. Voices are being heard, both in religious and secular camps, which give expression to a widespread feeling that Protestantism has lost its vitality; that it has become an institution and, like all institutions, is growing old and is dying. The symptoms of the sickness of Protestantism are, so it is maintained, first, a sentimental secularism, or as St. Paul would say: "We have minded the things of the flesh instead of the things of the Spirit." [3] The remedy prescribed is "genuine repentance with sorrow and change of mind." The second symptom of the sickness is paralyzing doubt, which undermines the high convictions of the revealed truth. The remedy recommended by Andrew H. Osborn is the re-thinking of Protestantism and all that it involves.[4] The same author tells us that a new Reformation is on the horizon; that Protestantism is taking a new lease on life. The last statement is corroborated by the papers and reports of the First Assembly of the World Council of Churches,[5] particularly by the paper entitled, "Evidences of New Life in the Church Universal," by Miss Olive Wyon.

As one reads the various sections of the report of this Assembly at Amsterdam, one notices that the idea of a new way is present in every section, either explicitly or implicitly. In every section of the report the assumption is obvious that the old order has come to an end; that a new era is at hand, and that the new order is present in embryonic form in the Christian inheritance of the West; that the new order is revealing itself for the churches of the world in the ecumenical movement itself, in the striving of the churches towards unity. One is aware that the "new way" is proclaiming itself as the legitimate heir, not of the West primarily but of the Christianity of old, and is seeking to saturate mankind, in its bewilderment and despair, with a new and resolute hope. Even more one notices in every section a determination to action, i.e., to earn in order to possess what we inherited from the early Christians.

The primitive Christian church was conscious of occupying a peculiar place in history. The Christians knew themselves as a

[3] Rom. 8:5, free rendition.
[4] Andrew H. Osborn, *Christianity in Peril* (New York, 1942), pp. 58–68.
[5] *Man's Disorder and God's Design* (Omnibus volume, New York, 1948).

new people, a new creation pursuing a new way; they were neither pagans nor Jews; they were a new race.[6] The early Christians had an eschatological understanding of history. The church, eschatology, and history were inseparable. The proclamation of the gospel of Jesus always began: "The time is fulfilled, the Kingdom of God is at hand." [7]

The conception of the Church as a new race, which is peculiar to primitive Christianity, is only to be understood on the basis of the eschatological interpretation of history. The pagan era and the era of the Jews is over; the time of Christ and his community has come. It is a conception which is revealed and fulfilled in the very foundations of the meaning of history. It needed but one last step to the coming of the Dominion of God, and history would be at an end. The Church as the new race already preaches to the old era the coming of the new. The Church is the forerunner, the prelude, to the Kingdom of God, or as Paul, James and the author of Revelation have it: "These have been redeemed from mankind, as first-fruits for God"; [8] "They who have the first-fruits of the Spirit"; [9] "a kind of first-fruits of His creatures." [10]

For primitive Christianity, the Church is the new race, its way the new way, which leads to the goal and reveals the meaning of God's plan of salvation for his people. It is as if we of today were rediscovering this eschatological interpretation of the history of the Church and of the nations. At this point we see the new Reformation linked up not only with the Reformation of the sixteenth century, but going through it, also with the beginning of the Christian movement. When taken seri-

[6] See I Pet. 2:9, 10.
[7] Mark 1:15.
[8] Rev. 14:4.
[9] Rom. 8:23.
[10] Jas. 1:18.

ously such movements reveal the eternal elements in religion, elements which are not inheritable; they are never ours; they are part of the *form,* which is God-given. The basic elements of faith become ours when we are sufficiently desirous to possess them so as to be willing to be possessed by them.[11]

There is always a harking back to the century of power, unbounded consecration, authentic vision, and adventurous action. The inner connection between faith and prayer and the present-day need of both cause us to seek the renewal of the former by deepening the life of the latter.

The devout student of history and life ultimately comes to the conviction that mysterious forces play upon the lives of individuals, nations, and movements whose coming and going take place unannounced and cannot be determined. Life, in retrospect, appears to be the result of a number of forces, some partly understood, others leaving even the most diligent student baffled. The events and forces, it appears, are held and guided by an invisible but mighty arm.

We may not know whence the guidance comes, or what is the nature of that invisible power by which men and events are kept in their orbit. But it is not altogether out of harmony with spiritual experience to liken this invisible arm of God to the power of prayer. We need to disabuse our minds from the misconceptions generally held concerning prayer.

To begin with, prayer does not mean the making of words. The most dispensable element in prayer are words. The indispensable elements are: a sincere belief that God is; that he is a God who speaks and is waiting for someone who really listens, and that unless his spirit prays within us we do not know how to pray. Many are the definitions of prayer; few are satisfac-

[11] For a more historical exposition of this point see the essay by Prof. C. E. Schneider.

tory. Something so dynamic and penetrating as prayer in which God is always the benefactor and we the beneficiaries, he the actor and we the ones acted upon, will always defy analysis and evade definition. For prayer is power. It is the means by which a man enters into intimate conversation with God and learns to know and to use the spiritual resources and the secret of invisible forces, which are his gifts.

It is unfortunate, to say the least, that prayer and the life of devotion are widely regarded as a sort of reserved occupation for the few exceptional folk who "happen to be made that way." This is the view which has made the treatment of biblical characters unnatural and unhistorical. Some of the most alive and most vital personalities in the story of mankind have been mangled beyond recognition, starched up, and ironed out to a common pattern of conventional piety. The Bible characters are intensely interesting human beings. What makes them specially worth studying is that they were men of prayer. That does not mean that they spent most of their time in devotional exercises; rather it means that they lived their lives "as seeing him who is invisible"—conscious all the time that they were citizens of a spiritual as well as of the material world.

The invisible arm, the prayer which is power, has been undergirding the inner structure of Christianity through the centuries. Like an immovable rock stands the prayer of the Lord: "Keep them . . . that they may be one even as we are." [12] The ecumenical movement, in which many see the beginning of the New Reformation, is most desirous to be "a strategy of worldwide evangelism" and not merely "an interesting academic exercise." [13] The movement seeks to see the Church's mission in its universal dimensions and to confront the whole church with the challenge of the Gospel.

[12] John 17:11.   [13] Man's Disorder and God's Design, II, 116.

The Amsterdam report, in speaking of the offices of the Church, mentions "the diaconal office" which demands of the Church, and above all of each individual layman "to speak boldly in Christ's name both to those in power and to the people," and to learn afresh "what is the duty of the Christian man or woman in industry, in agriculture, in politics, in the professions and in the home."

This is part of the New Reformation. But even as there is no spontaneous generation so there can be no spontaneous reformation unless it is preceded by a regeneration which takes place in the secret intercourse where the Lord of life is creatively active and we, the raw material, respond to his *form* or pattern.

The New Reformation sends out a clarion call to all thoughtful believers to unite in Christ and acknowledge him Lord *in all things*. Since the unity which Western civilization claims is based upon technological achievements, the Assembly at Amsterdam let it be known that "man cannot live by technology alone." It will be one of the greatest tragedies if the present-day church fails to sense the true relevance of the New Reformation and falls short of teaching its preachers and laymen to think ecumenically. Ecumenical thinking is defined as "taking seriously the Gospel as that act of God which cannot be understood except as His proclamation of salvation for the whole world, and as that Word of God which awaits for its final interpretation, the contributions to be made by all the nations of the world as they are gathered into one fellowship of the world-wide Church of Christ." [14]

BIBLICAL PRAYER

In order to succeed in the task of conditioning church people for ecumenicity the church will have to teach them the art and

[14] *Ibid.,* p. 116.

the significance of prayer. Prayer is one of the highest and deepest modes in which religion seeks to express itself. It is only natural, therefore, that the man of religious temper turns to the great religious classic to discover what it has to teach him concerning prayer. If prayer to him is wrapped up in question marks, he is likely to be disappointed with the biblical records; for the Bible does not answer all the questions concerning prayer which are being asked by present-day religionists. The Bible confronts us with reality instead of with controversy. It is always good to face reality and to have the facts thrust upon us which are dwarfed or lost in the labyrinth of argument. Instead of discussions about the nature and value of prayer, we have, in the Bible, perplexed and persecuted men pouring out their hearts to a God, who is as real to them as their sorrow, and finding in that communion the strength that cometh in the night.

The Bible assumes the existence of God. Perhaps that is the reason why prayer in the Bible is spontaneous. The questions, which weigh so heavily upon the educated man of today when he discusses prayer, are barely raised, never answered in the Bible. The difficulties which are felt by the modern mind in relation to prayer—such as the universality and relentlessness of natural law countered by the omniscience, the love, and the wisdom of God—seem to combine to make prayer little better than idle words or at most a pious exercise, whose influence is limited to the character of the man who offers it. But these considerations do not seem to disturb the biblical men of prayer. The progress of exact science has produced a scientific temper which is shared by hundreds of thousands of people who have no technical knowledge of any particular science. The increasing complexity of our world is making more difficult the readjustment of ideas of a simpler world to new situations.

However, it would be a serious loss to our religious knowledge to regard the religious thought and practice of such men as Jeremiah and Paul as irrelevant or sterile just because we fail to find in their prayers an adequate answer to modern problems.

The problems to which we have alluded are never formally discussed in the Bible. Its world is not our world, and the ancient Hebrews had little genius for philosophical discussion of any kind. Even the book of Job, which gives the impression of a continuous discussion, is really only a series of eloquently reiterated assertions rather than a connected argument.

Here and there one finds in the Scriptures traces of sceptical moods in which problems of a sort are born. When one considers the moods in which Ecclesiastes writes: "That which has been is that which shall be; and there is no new thing under the sun," [15] one finds it expressive of a world view which regards history as an endless inexorable cycle. What place would there be for prayer in such a world?

Again, no Hebrew would have dreamed of denying that there is a God; but there were many, among the rich and poor alike, who had their doubts as to whether God played any real and active part in human affairs. The easy-going and comfortable plutocrats in Israel were quite certain that God leaves the world to run as it pleases, or rather as they please; that he can be trusted not to interfere.[16]

Two centuries later, men of a different make are forced to the same conclusion by the cruel silence of heaven.[17] Honest though this doubting is, it seems to be the result of a too utilitarian view of religion, which finds expression in Job. "What is the Almighty, that we should serve him? And what profit should we have if we pray unto him?" [18] But this doubt is

[15] Eccles. 1:9.
[16] Zeph. 1:22.
[17] Mal. 3:14.
[18] Job 21:15.

refuted by Malachi: "They that feared Jehovah spake one with another; and Jehovah hearkened and heard." [19] Once more, it might be true that God gave good things to those who asked him; [20] but no one could deny that many good things were given to men whether they asked him or not. He caused his sun to shine and his rain to fall no less upon the unjust than upon the just. Thus while the impartial beneficence of nature might draw a prayer of gratitude from a devout heart, it would probably confirm the indifferent in their indifference.

The unbroken sequence of cause and effect in the physical world, by which we modern people are overwhelmed, would have left the ancient Hebrew unmoved. Apparently the phenomena in nature did not spell a stern law to him, but gave him a sense of rhythm and regularity. That is why the Hebrew of old could never have understood the problem of prayer as it presents itself to the modern mind. To him God was directly responsible for every phenomenon; and if a modern problem had been presented to him, his reply would have been: "With God all things are possible." [21]

His God was a living God, whose ear was not heavy, whose arm was not short; and why should he be less able than man to command and control his resources? The ancient Hebrew was in no danger of involving God in nature. Nature was not God, it was God's. The earth was the Lord's, and the fulness thereof; might he not do with his forces what he pleased? There was no limit to the divine possibility, for God was "able to do exceeding abundantly above all that we ask and think." [22]

What has been said thus far ought to convince us that the Bible had no theoretical solutions for modern problems. But, by the utter simplicity and naturalness with which the pious heart

[19] Mal. 3:16a, b.   [21] Matt. 19: 26c.
[20] Matt. 7:11.   [22] Eph. 3:20a.

turns to God in every conceivable situation, a conviction is borne in upon us that prayer is not only reasonable but has an indisputable place in the life of vital religion.

Prayer, therefore, is regarded throughout the Bible to be as natural as the existence of need and the sense of God; and as the need is universal, prayer is the privilege of all. Out of the depths any man may cry for himself to God. Sometimes, overwhelmed by their own unworthiness, men felt that they needed a prophet to intercede for them.[23] But as a rule, a man confesses his own sins and craves help for his own need. Public men, e.g., David and Solomon, appear as leaders in prayer. However, the greatest masters of prayer appear to have been the prophets. With the exception of Jeremiah, their prayers are seldom recorded, but there are many incidental allusions which suggest that prophecy had its roots in prayer.[24]

Again, as need is universal, prayer must be equally possible to the foreigner and the Israelite: the Roman Cornelius may pray to God as well as the Hebrew Peter. And though the foreigner may be disposed to pray to his own God, the religious thinkers of the Bible cherished the hope of a time when Jehovah would be worshipped by the whole world. "Many peoples and strong nations shall come to seek Jehovah of hosts in Jerusalem, and to entreat the favor of Jehovah." [25] It is to be noted that when foreigners pray to Jehovah, their prayer does not take the form of petition but of acknowledgment—a recognition of something that Jehovah has done for Israel.

Jethro said, Blessed be Jehovah, who hath delivered you out of the hand of the Egyptians, and out of the hand of Pharaoh; who hath delivered the people from under the hand of the Egyptians. Now I

[23] Jer. 42:2.
[24] See Jer. 32:16-25.
[25] Zech. 8:22. See also Jonah 1:11-14.

know that Jehovah is greater than all gods; yea in the thing wherein they dealt proudly against them.[26]

The triumph of the Gospel of the Lord Jesus dealt the death-blow to every particularistic view of religion. He taught men to pray not to the God of Israel, but to "our Father in heaven." That was the true prayer which was offered "neither in this mountain nor yet in Jerusalem," but everywhere in the wide world where men worship God in spirit and in truth.

The quality of biblical prayer does not improve with time but with insight. That is particularly true of the Old Testament prayers. The later prayers in the Old Testament are not generally nobler or profounder than the earlier ones. Prayers for vengeance, for instance, are among the latest as well as the earliest in the history of the Old Testament. But generally speaking there is an advance from the material to the spiritual. In the earlier times, God was seen mostly in his gifts. Men longed for them partly because in them they found him. The descendants of the men who had prayed for abundance of corn, wine, and oil learned to pray for the nearer presence of God and for the spread of the gospel of Christ.

A perusal of Deuteronomy 28 and Leviticus 26, where the blessings and curses are seen to be entirely of a temporal nature, will convince us that what the Lord Jesus said of the Gentiles in Matthew 6:32, "After these things do the Gentiles seek," he might have said it also of the average Hebrew. The words of ancient blessing stated in Genesis 27:28, "God give thee of the dew of heaven, and of the fatness of the earth, and plenty of grain and new wine," find an echo in Nehemiah 9:25. Solomon in the great prayer of dedication recorded in I Kings 8 utters many petitions but not for spiritual things as we understand

[26] Exod. 18:10 f. See also I Kings 10:9; Dan. 4:17; Ezra 6:12.

them. The petition most characteristic of the Bible prayer is "Save us." But in the Old Testament the prayer for deliverance is not usually for deliverance from sin, but from enemies of a more tangible sort. Within the Old Testament, however, there are also prayers for other things than bread and victory. The seers of Israel knew that men did not live by bread alone, and prayers rise for wisdom and forgiveness, for guidance and a closer walk with God. The deliberate rejection of riches and honor by Solomon and the request for wisdom instead, is regarded in the narrative as touching unusual heights.[27]

The highest note in petitionary prayer is expressed in the 73rd Psalm: "Whom have I in heaven but thee? and there is none upon earth that I desire beside thee." The defects found in the prayers of the Old Testament are derived from the weakness of Old Testament religion, which is earth-bound; but this is also its strength.

There is an occasional mysticism about Hebrew poetry nobly expressed in the 39th Psalm. But that is not the dominant note of the older religion. It did not lose itself in the distant heavens. The earth was the Lord's and he had given it to men. The treasures of the field and the vineyard, the delights of home and country were regarded as blessings from his good hand. History was but the march of the divine purpose; and when virtue seemed to be defeated and vice triumphant, faith was put to a terrible strain. It seemed as if God had left his world. But within its limitations Old Testament religion was intensely and passionately real. Its healthy this-worldliness was one manifestation of its faith. It expected and found God in the world, because it claimed the world for God.

In the New Testament, as we might expect, prayer is predominantly for things spiritual. Doubtless material things could

[27] Deut. 8:3; I Kings 3:11, Cf. Jas. 1:5.

not be altogether ignored or forgotten; had not the Master himself taught his disciples to pray for bread, and had he not made upon them the impression that any request they made in his name would be answered? But requests by such men and in such a name would be overwhelmingly for things spiritual. Those whose ambition was to "abide in him" would not be sorely troubled by ambitions of a worldly kind.

All requests were to be made in accordance with the divine will, and since that will is the salvation of all men through the gospel of Jesus,[28] many of the New Testament prayers are but for the success of that gospel among those to whom it is preached, for boldness in proclaiming it, and for the further strengthening and undergirding of those who have already accepted it.

One of the earliest prayers in the book of Acts is that the servants of the Lord may be enabled to speak with all boldness, and that signs and wonders be done through the name of Jesus.[29] Paul, like his Master, prayed that his converts should be prevented from all that was evil and perfected in all that was good, that they should be filled with knowledge of the divine will and with the desire to do the same.[30] In the early church this spiritual note is the dominant one. Epephras prayed earnestly that the Colossians "may stand mature and fully assured in all the will of God," and in almost the same words the author of the epistle to the Hebrews prays that those whom he addresses may be made perfect in every good thing to do his good will.[31]

THEOLOGY IN PRAYER

But however noble the quality of prayer, it is but one aspect of the way in which religion expresses itself. Prayer may be the

---

[28] I Tim. 2:4.
[29] Acts 4:29 f.

[30] Col. 1:9, Cf. John 17:15.
[31] Col. 4:12, Heb. 13:21.

heart of religion even as social action expresses the ethic of religion. But when you converse with religion in its thoughtful moods you find a theology. Intelligent Christian prayer might, therefore, be defined as the heart and mind thinking upon God and conditioning the will to action.

There may be no theology of prayer, but there is theology in prayers. It has often been said that the theology of any people is influenced more by the hymns they sing than by the direct instruction they receive. The stirring hymns of Luther did more to spread the principles of the Reformation throughout the Germany of his day than all his polemical writings. The hymns which Charles Wesley wrote are said to have been more effective in spreading and preserving the doctrines which were the inspiration of the Methodist revival than the sermons of his brother John. Competent observers of the successes of the so called "sects" in our own country point out that their hymn-singing attracts many more people to their meetings than their particularistic doctrines. The influence of hymns upon popular theology is not always for good. As one listens to some of the so called revival preaching and the testimonies for Christ, one surmises that their idea of Jesus Christ is derived not from the Gospels but from the gospel hymns. There can be little doubt that the crude sentimentalism of many of the popular evangelistic hymns of the past generation has had an effect on current ideas of religion.

But there is theology in hymns, not in formal definition and precise statements, but as it has been vitalized by personal experience and clothed in the forms created by a devout or poetic imagination. It is in the personal experience that we may look for theology in prayers as well as in hymns. Some one, whom Dr. James Denny quotes,[32] expressed his difficulties with the Bible in this fashion:

[32] "The Way Everlasting" (London, 1911), p. 1.

The Gospels are story, and a story may conceivably be untrue; the Epistles are arguments, and arguments may conceivably be unsound; but the Psalms are the immediate reflection of personal experiences, and we can take them as they stand without asking any questions.

There is much truth in this when the prayers and psalms of the Bible are under consideration. It is true that the experience of different men, living under different circumstances and at various times will use a variety of modes of expression; but there is a deep underlying unity which can be recognized by every serious-minded student of biblical prayers; and such a unity seems to have been recognized by the collectors of the devotional literature of the Bible. It is therefore neither correct nor helpful to lift out an individual prayer or a single psalm, or the psalms belonging to a single author or to a certain period in order to demonstrate a certain religious view; one must ask for the conceptions which characterize the prayers as a whole.

All religious experience centers in God, and the Psalms are dominated by the consciousness of his presence, his glory, his grace. There is no argument to prove his existence, because poetry is not the expression of argument but of spiritual experience; moreover, to the Hebrew mind, as to the mind of all the ancient world, no such argument was needed. The existence of God was taken for granted. It is true that there are references in the Psalms to those who say in their hearts: "There is no God." [33] But that is only said by the fool, the morally worthless man, and his attitude is that of a practical, rather than a theoretical, atheism; for what he really seeks to deny is the possibility of retribution. Against any such attitude the biblical writers do not attempt to reason, though there is one passage that looks so much like it that it has been said to contain the germ of a philosophy of religion:

[33] Pss. 14:1 and 53:1.

Consider ye, brutish among the people; and ye fools, when will ye be wise? He that planted the ear, shall he not hear? He that formed the eye, shall he not see? He that chastiseth the nations, shall not he correct? Even he that teacheth man knowledge? [34]

But this is not the reasoning of a philosopher: it is the indignant expostulation of a poet, who has a vivid consciousness of the presence of an all-seeing and all-knowing God, with those who think they can escape his judgment. One might also refer to Psalm 19:1, "The heavens declare the glory of God; and the firmament showeth his handiwork," which sounds like a formal argument for the existence of God. But here again the Psalmist is not pointing out a proof of God's existence; he is disclosing a sacrament of it. The truth he already holds in his own heart, and as he looks up to the heavens he sees the sacred sign or symbol by means of which he can hold it firmly and give it fresh expression.

For a theology which is grounded in spiritual experience there can be only one God, and, though the Psalms contain passages in which the God of Israel is contrasted with other gods, they do not show any acceptance of the primitive belief in the existence of such gods. When the Psalmist says: "There is none like unto thee among the gods, O Lord," [35] he is simply using the poet's license to borrow images from beliefs he does not share, to set forth his conception of the uniqueness of the divine majesty and power. The gods of the nations are mere idols of silver and gold, the work of men's hands.[36]

But while scorning the gods that are the work of men's hands, the Psalmists are not afraid to speak of God in terms that suggest a human form and the powers possessed by a human personality. They are not philosophers trying to express spiritual

[34] Ps. 94:8–10.
[35] Ps. 86:8.
[36] Ps. 115:5–7; also Ps. 135:15–17.

realities in colorless abstract words, but poets using concrete and familiar imagery. So they can speak of God's eyes beholding and his eyelids trying the children of men; of his strong hand and stretched-out arm leading out his people; of his ears attentive to their cry. They can describe him as seated in the heavens with the earth as his footstool; as bowing the heavens to come down, and as riding upon a cherub. They can picture him as a warrior, as thinking and speaking, knowing and willing, loving and hating. With a boldness that shocks our sense of reverence they can even speak of God as sleeping, awaking from his sleep, shouting like a drunken man as he smites his enemies, and laughing in derision of them. By such means they express the reality and fulness of personal life in God in the only way in which the popular mind can grasp the truth; they bring us nearer the presence of the *living* God than we get anywhere else in the Bible except in the life and teaching of the Lord Jesus Christ. People, who pretend to be superior, may talk about survivals of mythological conceptions or raise objections to what they call anthropomorphic or anthropopathic language, but it is only through such figures of speech that any personal experience of God can be expressed. The metaphysical abstractions of the philosopher do not express it; at best they are negative and give no hint of the warmth and intimacy of such an experience. Professor Hocking has said: "Philosophy, when it speaks of God at all, speaks of Him as 'he.' Religion always speaks of God as 'thou.' " [37]

What the theologians sometimes call "the metaphysical attributes of God" are not, however, dimmed in any way. With the aid of the poetic imagination of the Psalmist they find expression that is immeasurably more adequate and satisfying than any abstract definition could possibly be. Where has the

[37] Quoted by W. L. Sperry, *What We Mean by Religion* (New York, 1940), p. 76.

eternity of God been described in human language equal in power and majesty to that of the opening verses of the 90th Psalm? And who has ever stated the conception of the omnipresence of God, or what we today call divine immanence, so majestically as the writer of the 139th Psalm? These are outstanding illustrations of the way in which poetry accomplishes what is utterly beyond either philosophy or theology.

It might be added that such expressions of what we label "metaphysical" truths always have a practical reference for the Psalmists. That can be seen by anyone who reads the two Psalms just referred to. Or it may be illustrated by verses 3 and 4 of the 147th Psalm, where the thought of God's omnipresence is linked to the thought of his grace. The truths expressed in the Psalms are no mere speculative conceptions unrelated to the conditions and necessities of life; the value of the truths has been tested in experience.

The Psalmists saw something of the glory of such a God of whom the Christian declares: "God is love," and to whom the believer has the relationship of child to father. For the clear and steady shining of the light of that revelation men had to wait until they saw it in the face of Jesus Christ.

The ecumenical Church of Christ has accepted the prayers of the Bible to the extent of molding its prayers after the biblical pattern. It has thereby borne witness that the biblical prayers were made for all ages, for all places and for all souls. But the New Reformation is not bound by words but submits to the spirit which permeates the ancient prayers; it aims at a fellowship which remembers always that "the multitude of them that believed were of one heart and soul." [38]

While the nations of the world are *trying* to come together, allowing fears, suspicions and reservations to keep them hesi-

[38] Acts 4:22.

tating, the Christian churches *are* coming together. Having joined with heart, mind, and will in the prayer of their Lord, "that they may all be one," they clasped hands at Amsterdam and resolved never to let go. The granite walls which divided Protestant Christianity are cracking because the New Reformation is a positive power; it is not a movement *against* somebody or something, it is a movement *for* Christ and *for* unity of believers in him. By praying together, working together and thinking together a fullness of faith will be given to the churches which none may ever have alone; and in united witness there will be given a spiritual dynamic greater than the sum of the power given to the churches in their separation.

EDUCATION, CHRISTIAN EDUCATION, AND THE REFORMATION

HAROLD A. PFLUG

PROTESTANT parents are in a critical situation with regard to the education of their children. This crisis has been of some duration; a series of recent happenings has made Protestant Christians aware of it. Moreover, it is not superficial or fragmentary; it is rooted in the very nature of the culture in which the Christian life is to be nurtured and lived.

A public school educator recently writing on the evolution of the school curriculum points to four dominant motives for education in the United States: first, the religious motive; second, the political; third, the utilitarian; and currently, the mass education motive. He then points out that the religious motive ceased to be *primary* by 1850, and makes the assertion, as fact, that the religious motive is the only one of the four that is *"entirely inoperative"* today. If only partially true, this development is serious for Protestants who have established, supported and furthered the public school for the nurture of their children in a democracy. It is the substitution of one basis of education for another; and more, the substitution of a basis which is, in at least some respects, hostile to the other.

Early American settlers, coming from the Old World, were rooted and grounded in Reformation thought and ideas, which in turn influenced the development of education. We propose to look back to that rootage; to note its transplanting process to a New World environment; to trace something of its develop-

ment as it sought to take account of the factors of religious freedom and religious diversity; to sense the chaotic relationships of
religion and education in our own time; and to contemplate
possible roads for further traveling. The awareness that we have
reached the time in American life and culture when separation
of church and state has come dangerously near to meaning separation of religion and education prompted forty-two Protestant
denominations in the International Council of Religious Education to establish a Department of Religion and Public
Education. When our great grandchildren study the history of
education, and more specifically the history of Christian education in the United States—and it is not without significance
that we must write two parallel historical accounts in our time—
the document undergirding this action taken by representatives
of the great majority of Protestant Christians may well be an
important one. It will be important because of its discernment
of the road which we have traveled, and because it points out
clearly the forks in the road ahead.

This document declares that Protestants affirm, after studied
deliberation, their commitment to the public school for the
education of their children; that this commitment is rooted in
loyalty to basic principle and not a matter of expediency or of
institutional inertia; that they take sharp issue with those who
maintain that public schools must become completely secular
and who by deliberate attempt, or unconscious tendency, elimi-
nate from the educational process any acknowledgment of the
theistic faith of the great majority of American citizens. There
is no tendency to deal lightly with an attitude of "lofty neutrality" between a religious and a non-religious philosophy of
life, as if it did not matter which one was chosen by pupil,
teacher, and parent.

If it has seemed to some here and abroad that Protestants have been drifting with the current cultural and educational philosophies, in their policy-shaping document Protestants take a definite stand. In replying to the question, "Has the trend toward separation between religious education and general education tended to weaken both religion and education?" an affirmative answer is given and supported. To separate religion from education does violence to both of them. Education is weakened and made inadequate; it cannot possibly treat life as a whole when religious faith and presuppositions are avoided. Indeed, the sectarian varieties of organized religion must be avoided in public education; but basic religion must be included if education is not to become a flabby, weak, and anemic interpretation of life and history. Religion, too, is seriously weakened when it is not intimately related to general education, for real religion must be taught and caught and nurtured in the daily, hourly processes of living and learning; it cannot exist in a vacuum, separate from day by day experience.

Since Christian public school laymen helped to write this basic statement of policy, the following assertion is all the more significant: "There is nothing in our laws, nothing in our Court decisions up to and including the McCollum opinion, nothing in our traditions, which prevents the school, within its own program, from making adequate provision for the religious interpretation of life."

In connection with this basic statement of policy for Protestants with regard to the relation of religion and education, our great-grandchildren will also read of Supreme Court decisions and state court judgments affecting religious instruction in the schools on released or dismissed time; free text-books and free transportation provided Roman Catholic children attending parochial schools from state educational funds; bills for Federal

Aid to education involving decisions on aid to private and parochial schools; and varying attempts made to answer the question of what constitutes *sectarian* religion in the school classroom. Such issues and movements make up the social context in which the validity or non-validity of Protestant Reformation principles and policies are tested and developed.

A well-grounded and careful historian, taking these incidents and affirmations and tracing them back, step by step, could unravel the strands of history back into the Reformation and pre-Reformation era. It would be an enlightening study to follow the process stage by stage. We will need to short-cut this process considerably. We shall, however, take several of the great ideas of the Reformation to show how they have brought about the present status in the relationship of education and religion.

THE REFORMATION ROOTS OF MODERN EDUCATION

Readers and writers of the human pilgrimage through the centuries are more and more prone to underline the truth of the statement that nothing is so powerful as an idea whose time has arrived. We must look at several such ideas associated with men and movements in the first days of the Protestant Reformation without holding them responsible for the ways in which we today interpret these ideas. A great idea, through the understanding and vision of one man, or a little group of men, starts rolling down through the centuries. We, living in another generation, need to note how that idea has been qualified, compromised, over-stressed or lightly treated in the social context of each era of history. Thus it becomes valuable, when original ideas in their travels become cluttered with social baggage, to look back and attempt to see them as they first appeared. The Reformation embodied principles of such importance for education that no secular history of education can disregard the influence of the Reformers on subsequent educational theory and practice.

Luther and the other Reformers lived in an age that was seeking an escape from the binding restrictions of authority, for the individual had been taught that he had no existence apart from institutions. The church taught that apart from it the individual possessed little worth or significance, no hope of salvation; and the feudal society certainly gave individuals little status or hope apart from the feudal system. In response to this mood, which we can sense because of counterparts to it in our present world situation, Renaissance leaders began to emphasize the individual's place in life and to free expression of individuality in various areas. The humanists pointed to human reason as the individual guide to life. They were very critical of whatever rested on authority and had little respect for tradition. They attacked beliefs, customs and institutions that had outlived their day. Because the Church had so largely controlled the lives of men for a thousand years, it, too, was bound to come under the questioning temper of the time. Then, too, the humanist emphasis of studying the Old and New Testaments and the Church Fathers in the original sources inevitably raised questions about the doctrine and practices of the church. They, before Luther, demanded reform in the church, asking that the clergy lead better lives, that they perform the duties attached to their high incomes, and that more evidence of social usefulness come from the monasteries. The Reformation carried further these ideas of the Renaissance, and Protestants have carried still further the Reformation ideas for the past four hundred years.

Overlapping ideas stated in phrases which have come to be associated with the Reformation period and the developing

Reformation spirit, have had, and still have, far-reaching educational implications. Such slogans as "the dignity and worth of the common man;" "freedom and independence of the individual;" "the sacredness of personality;" "the right of conscience;" and many others, are influential ideas in all modern education, even in modern secular education where their sources are little known or acknowledged by the educators who use them.

When Luther repeated in his own experience the spiritual history of Paul and Augustine, experiencing the free grace of God in his own life, affirming that the just shall live by faith, and finding union with God through prayer, meditation and faith, then it was that he asserted to the church, and to his age and culture, the teachings of Christian liberty, the necessity of individual judgment, and the validity of personal inner religious experience. From the authority of the church, Luther moved to the authority of inner experience, for the Spirit of God had enlightened and enlivened his own spirit and conscience. Since he had come to freedom in and through his study of the Scriptures, it is understandable that the necessity for all to be able to read the Scriptures loomed large as his concern. The import of this was a demand for education of *all* the people. Luther's work was primarily religious and only incidentally educational. Therein lies its real power and significance for education.

Before the Reformation, ecclesiastical schools were designed chiefly for candidates for the priesthood; in addition, there was knightly education which gave training for chivalry and physical culture and burgher or town schools which were intended for the commercial and artisan classes of the cities. The few parochial schools taught doctrine, worship and church practices, but not reading and writing. The Middle Ages neglected the common people and the laboring classes were left to toil on in ignorance and want. Then came the revolutionary dictum that all people must learn to read the Bible because it was involved in their very salvation.

So that the Bible could reach the people Martin Luther made his famous translation into the vernacular. There were other German translations before Luther, but in dialects which were used by only a limited group of people. Now the Bible was put in the hands of the laity. No longer was it regarded as an unsafe volume.

The educational implications of these dominant early Protestant ideas or convictions are many. A few of them may lend significance to our discussion at this point. People were increasingly able to *read* the Bible, and the invention of the printing press sped this process considerably. Emphasis was placed on the vernacular languages. There was a growing demand to make elementary schools available to all, in order that all might attain at least the ability to read the Scriptures. Girls as well as boys—a revolutionary change—were given educational opportunities, for "they too had souls to save." The base of secondary education was broadened to train leaders to teach the people to read. A desire for education and a realization of its importance was fostered because of the responsibility placed on each individual to study the Scriptures and the belief that contact with them would produce a conviction of truth. Educational work was implicit in Protestant thought and increasingly became explicit as Protestantism developed and grew.

Melanchthon, Zwingli, and Calvin, as well as Martin Luther, were active in educational work. Here we note particularly some contributions of Martin Luther. To his translation of the Bible already mentioned, as a distinctive educational contribution, must be added his two catechisms, one for adults and one for children; devotional materials for use in both church and home; his hymns, Luther often writing both words and music, and his published hymnals which made it possible for the people to sing the great Christian convictions.

The schools furthered by Luther were not only conducted in the language and dialects of the people, but also the schedules were arranged to enable the children of the common people to come at such times as would fit into the carrying on of their practical duties at home. The repressive harsh discipline of the school room in the Middle Ages was replaced by school rooms that were made attractive and by study made more enjoyable. No longer was language study the sole or main diet in the class room, for Luther believed it was part of the natural activity of every child in work and play to handle concrete things. The study of various phases of nature was introduced in the belief that the knowledge acquired in the study should be used in the service of men. That all be helped, and that all "come to the knowledge of the truth" was a very different motivation for the educational process from one which made the well-being of the institution (church), rather than the person, the aim of all activity.

Far-reaching also were the educational contributions made by Luther in sermons which he preached to parents on the duty of sending their children to school and the duties and privileges they had in teaching religion both directly and in-directly in the home. Many of his writings in this area have a peculiarly modern sound with our present-day re-emphasis on the basic nature of the home in the religious nurture of children and adults.

But Luther went beyond the specifically religious purpose of the schools and wrote letters to mayors and aldermen of all the major cities in Germany to make them aware of the necessity for Christian schools in their communities. He said in one of these documents:

Even if there were no soul, and men did not need schools and the languages for the sake of Christianity and the Scriptures, still, for the establishment of the best schools everywhere, both for boys and girls, this consideration is of itself sufficient, namely, that society, for the maintenance of civil order and the proper regulation of the household, needs accomplished and well trained men and women. Now such men are to come from boys, and such women from girls; hence it is necessary that boys and girls be properly taught and brought up.[1]

Here, in embryo, are the ideas of public education for all the children; of education by the State for the welfare of society; and of compulsory education.

Philip Melanchthon, sometimes called the "Instructor of Germany," was called upon to make a survey of the schools in Saxony. In his Report, or *Book of Visitation,* he outlined a detailed plan for state education. Reading, writing, counting, sacred music, and religion were included in the curriculum of the elementary schools which he projected. In his secondary schools, which gradually evolved into the famous Gymnasiums and influenced early American secondary education, Latin and Greek grammar, dialectics, rhetoric, and ethics were taught.

The educational influence of John Calvin was probably more international than that of Luther. Geneva, his home, became a kind of Protestant Home for Christian exiles from France, England, Holland, Scotland, and other countries. Exiles, returning to their homelands, took with them the pattern of the German schools and greatly influenced the type of schools

[1] "An die Burgermeyster und Radherrn allerley-stedte inn Deutschen landen," 1524, W.A., XV, 45.

developed among the French Huguenots, the Dutch Reformed, and the people of Scotland.

To feel the pulse-beat of the English Reformation we must go back to Wyclif and note some of the ideas which he propounded and which grew out of his thought. Thomas Hall says of him:

Wyclif seems to have been no preacher like Luther, no organizer like Calvin, no skillful rewriter of creedal faith like Melanchthon, but he set to work to translate the Bible and to train "Poor Preachers" for the work that is still being carried on over the prairies of a land Wyclif did not know existed, by men and women speaking his tongue and holding fast to his faith. Yet these simple folk often do not know where they got their inspiration.[2]

Because Wyclif believed that the state could never bring in the kingdom of God, he concluded that a lasting separation of church and state was necessary and made demands for a "free Church in a free State." Wyclif, more than Luther and Calvin, swept away for the common man the whole historical church and in its place put the individual interpretation of the English Bible by each reader; everyone was entitled to find in the Scriptures "what commanded his heart and conscience." Each person was a priest of God, without the mediating church, and the sacraments were not necessary for salvation. Wyclif is known as the "Father of Lay Preachers," for he encouraged the more advanced laymen to preach—quite in contrast to the ordained preacher and teacher movement of Continental Protestantism. Wyclif thus laid the foundation for many types of Protestantism still in existence.

The Reformation within the Anglican church was more concerned with matters of government, church organization,

---

[2] *The Religious Background of American Culture* (Boston, 1938), p. 19.

and worship. England, therefore, tended to keep and develop a church education system with a narrowly humanistic curriculum in which the Anglican faith was substituted for the Catholic faith.

EDUCATION IN THE NEW WORLD

The American colonies, quite early, became the scene of conflicting religious groups with differing implications for educational theory and practice. Our forefathers brought with them their traditions of religion and education. In New England schools were established by and for the community. Adequate place was given to the Christian faith in the schools; the minister was often the teacher in the school; the curriculum was predominantly religious with such texts as the *New England Primer* and the *Hornbook* being widely used. But New England communities refused to give dissenting individuals and groups the religious freedom they desired for themselves. Roger Williams and others, banished because of their non-conformity, founded colonies where free expression for all religious groups was possible.

In the Middle Atlantic states, because of the diversity of religious loyalties, education was largely carried on by the separate religious groups in parochial schools, with some free schools for other than church children held under state auspices.

In the South, where the Church of England predominated, education was for the most part a private matter for parents. Tutors, many of them ministers or persons qualified through training in schools of the church, taught the children, and religion had its integral part in education. A few charity schools were established for Negroes and poor whites.

As the thirteen colonies came together to form the Federal Union it was a real question what particular set of patterns, embodying the relation of religion and education, should be adopted. Religious loyalties were quite diverse. Puritans, Baptists, Anglicans, Catholics, Quakers, Lutherans, Presbyterians, Methodists, Jews, and many others had worked together against tremendous odds toward establishing a common life and culture. In many respects they had become one people in this process. Two great principles became basic as the new country developed and grew. These were woven into the very fabric of American life. The first principle declared that education be provided for all the children of all the people, and that all people be taxed for education, whether or not they had children of their own, and whether or not they sent their children to the public schools. This is usually referred to as the principle of public responsibility for education.

The second principle was that of religious freedom and is best stated in the words of the First Amendment to the Constitution:

"Congress shall make no laws respecting an establishment of religon or prohibiting the free exercise thereof."

This is sometimes referred to as the principle of separation of church and state. This concept of religious freedom which withheld from Congress the power to establish a state church, to make compulsory the support of or attendance at any religious institutions, or to restrain the free exercise of expression of religious groups, was a great triumph. It went much further than the religious toleration which had been painfully wrought out for religious minorities in Europe. As states wrote their constitutions they made varying provisions for the relationship of government and religion and of religion and education.

Thus, religious diversity and an established principle of

religious freedom gave Americans a new spiritual frontier on which to push forward and venture into new solutions of problems which had their root beginnings in the Reformation. In the human pilgrimage, education related to religious faith had first been the duty and concern of the family and home almost exclusively; later it became a shared endeavor between home and church, with the church taking over more and more of the formal teaching of religion; now it had launched into the third stage where state, church, and home all shared in the education of the young and the state, through public schools, was destined to take over more and more of the formal education of children and youth.

Diverse religious groups have held their varying loyalties and beliefs with such a sectarian spirit that public education has gradually lessened its concern for the role of religion in American Life, and for the part that the Hebrew and Christian faith plays in the lives of a majority of individual students enrolled in public schools. The eighteenth century revivalistic techniques of the churches tended to underemphasize intellect and overemphasize emotion. But school rooms were not apt centers for revivals. This fact made the relationship between religion and education a more tenuous one.

Along with these circumstances there came the rise and growth of the Sunday school movement, beginning with Robert Raikes in England in response to the early effects of the Industrial Revolution in that country. The Sunday school movement in the United States began under the impetus of laymen from the churches who endeavored to meet the needs of socially, economically, and religiously underprivileged boys and girls. In its early history the movement was quite separate from the church. Gradually the churches accepted the Sunday School as their educational agency and both the home and the public school have increasingly tended to turn over all religious instruction to the Sunday Church School.

THE CONFLICT BETWEEN CURRENT TENDENCIES

These and other factors provided the environment for acceptance of the policy, the practice, and finally, the principle that public education must not provide *sectarian* teaching of religion. Public educators, many of whom were churchmen, were willing to accept this principle partly because city systems of public education, and larger units of centralization in rural areas, meant more diverse religious heritages represented in their schools and class rooms. Then, too, there had been such a rapid growth of knowledge with the expansion of the physical and social sciences, that the school had more than enough to keep it busy, and when some things had to be omitted, it was easiest to omit the controversial. No better way could be imagined to render religion innocuous to one generation after another, or to have it thought of as unimportant by the boys and girls of the schools, than to ignore it as an *essential* part of culture. As we divorced public education from ecclesiastical controls we fell into the mistaken idea that this meant that religion should be separated from education.

Only recently has the religious community come to the awareness that this principle of non-sectarian teaching has resulted in the almost complete exclusion of religion from public education. No one deliberately planned this exclusion; school boards have not voted it; school faculties have not discussed it; teachers have not consciously decided to strip their teaching of religious reference and content; but it has happened, and to an alarming extent!

Although the immediate occasion of the exclusion of religious teaching from the schools was sectarian conflict, another powerful factor has been at work in the cultural fabric for some time, namely the idea that God does not really matter in the day by day and hour by hour decisions in the lives of individuals and groups and nations. This secularization is not a denial of religion, in most quarters, but, what is worse, the denial of its relevance to the major activities of life. The development of economic and political systems not answerable to God and his purposes has produced a potently secularist climate in which education has had to function. Schools should shape the culture, and not simply be shaped by it. Realistically, however, schools of the state are usually shaped more by the prevailing culture than they manage to change it. Because this is true, public education has tended to re-enforce the secular culture about it and the results have been the more devastating because the religious bases of culture have been gradually and subtly removed.

The secular trend in American education has several sources. One of these is the tremendous development of science, which has revolutionized man's view of the natural world and of himself. Science, the accumulation of knowledge through a systematized experimental method, has become a faith for many educators. Such a faith includes extravagant claims for the applicability and adequacy of scientific method to human problems. John Dewey, the most influential philosopher of American education for many years, has furthered the development of a science of man, in which verification and expansion of moral and religious values is finally to be achieved. This faith rests on a purely naturalistic view of life and declares man to be the measure of all things, himself included. In this kind of thinking God becomes more and more irrelevant to his creatures as well as to his creation.

When "freedom from sectarian religion" becomes a demand

of persons educated in this growing secular pattern, then American education is in danger of substituting for freedom of religion the secularist freedom to indoctrinate pupils in scientism, humanism, and vocationalism—in short, freedom to perpetuate religious ignorance.

The philosophy of life developed by some educational leaders and teachers in this secular pattern and spirit rejects religion in its historical forms, for the most part, and gives little place for religious creeds, institutions, and worship in their own lives. Another much larger group no longer think of religion as *the* unifying principle of all culture or as the faith that permeates every cultural good and influences every aspect of life, but think of it rather as a phase of culture. Thus it becomes possible for educators to propose, in good faith, that the religious part of the total education of children and youth be turned over to the home and the church.

In the educational world, probably the clearest example of this "phase of culture" conception of religion is to be found in the statement of the seven cardinal principles of secondary education published in a Bureau of Education bulletin in 1918. These are: health, command of fundamental processes, worthy home membership, vocation, civic education, worthy use of leisure time, and ethical character. Worthy use of leisure time is sub-divided into recreation, fine arts and religion. Religion is a leisure time activity which one might engage in if there is time left from the main business of living. Religion becomes peripheral rather than central; it is pigeon-holed as one of many aspects of life which one can choose to do something with, or not, the implication being that it makes little difference which way one chooses. But, in a truly religious view, religion is at the heart of it all. Through this religion a man or a nation knows what worthy home membership is, what worthy vocational choice involves, which civic relationships are worthy and which are unworthy, what is involved in worthy use of one's leisure and what high ethical character involves and demands.

As a consequence of this development involving the prohibition of sectarian teaching in the public schools in order to safeguard religious liberty and diversity, the secularization of education resulting from the generally accepted secularized outlook, as well as other factors, the religious communities of the nation have had to develop their own teaching institutions and patterns for instruction. The church has found that the home—as well as the school—has become greatly secularized. The church is making new efforts to help the homes and families of the church fellowship to assume and fulfill a far greater share in the Christian education of their children. Some groups like the Roman Catholics and the Missouri Synod Lutherans have set up schools of the church for the *total* education of their children and youth. Within the past two years, this alternative has been seriously suggested by a few outstanding Protestant Christian leaders with a plan for interdenominational Protestant parochial schools. This most recent pronouncement of the majority of Protestants, referred to in the opening of this chapter, rejected this plan for Protestants because of the many problems it would create. The right of parochial education, supported by any religious group which desires it and is willing to pay for it, is defended at every level of education, but the judgment is expressed that this right should not be widely exercised at the elementary and secondary levels.

The Protestant churches have relied largely upon the Sunday church school for their teaching ministry. With all its limitations it has made immeasurable contributions to teachers, pupils, and the life of the churches in American Protestantism. The vacation church school, the camp and conference movement, the development of church youth fellowships and many other patterns, are at present the framework within which Protestantism is attempting to have persons of all ages "confronted with and controlled by the Christian gospel."

About thirty-five years ago, the Week Day Church School movement became an educational vehicle for Protestant Christians, cooperating with public schools, to reach children with Christian teaching on "dismissed" or "released time" from the school program. In three and one-half decades the movement grew to the point where it reached two and one-half million children in 2,200 different communities in the United States. This practice has now been called into question by widely differing interpretations of the Supreme Court decision of March 8, 1949, in the McCollum case. The decision was clear in denying to the churches two facilities: the use of school machinery and the use of school property.

Beyond this the decision both raises basic issues and leaves them unanswered. Several of them deserve our attention. Doubts have been expressed in some interpretations of the decision whether religious elements may be included in public education at all. Is the mention of God in the classroom sectarian teaching? What should the school do with music, art, literature, and the early history of our country? Then, too, in protecting the religious freedom of a minority that chooses to believe in no God, which is their constitutional right, must the children of the majority, who believe in God, be penalized by the practice of the religion of irreligion, or atheism in the classroom? Is not this sectarian teaching also?

Another issue raised is with regard to the validity of the Supreme Court setting itself up as a kind of Super-Board of

Education for every school district in the nation. Something precious is lost in depriving local communities of their time-honored rights in this field. Some fear that this may be an opening wedge toward more of a system of federal education. As a Super-Board of Education in this one respect, there will come a time, perhaps very shortly, when the Court will be asked where the secular ends and the sectarian begins in education, or where the religious ends and the sectarian begins. For the facing of these questions there will be guidance in no *legal* source; yet the Court will be called upon to make a decision.

The right of the parents, who desire that religious instruction be a part of the total educational experience of their children, is not adequately recognized by the Justices. Well may Attorney Charles H. Tuttle, in his "Brief Greater New York Coordinating Committee on Released Time of Jews, Protestants, and Roman Catholics" ask concerning the McCollum case: "Will the courts confine the parent to one side or the other of the 'wall of separation,' and, if so, to which side, and why? . . . Will the courts force the State to erect 'a wall of separation' between parent and child?" [3]

The rigid wall-of-separation concept of the relation of church and state is probably the most disturbing question raised. A group of eminent Protestant clergymen felt so keenly that the Supreme Court had gone far beyond what was warranted by the language of the First Amendment to the Constitution, that they issued a thoughtful statement to government and church. They said, in part, "We believe that, whatever its intention may be, this hardening of the idea of 'separation' by the court will greatly accelerate the trend toward the secularization of our culture." Also, "cooperation entered into freely by the state and church and involving no special privilege to any church

[3] June 14, 1948 "Brief to New York Supreme Court" (Bar Press Inc.).

and no threat to the religious liberty of any citizen, should be permitted. As Protestants we desire to affirm this interpretation of the American doctrine of separation of church and state, and to protest against the interpretation that has been formulated by the Supreme Court."

Through varying local interpretations of the Supreme Court decision, Week Day Religious Education continues in almost 90 per cent of the communities where it was established, awaiting further clarification in many instances. The real issues are those which appear in the chaos of opinions regarding what the relationship of religion and education should be. The continuing discussions around these issues point up the divergent philosophies of education which are struggling for primacy in the homes and the churches as well as in the schools of the state.

The types of contending philosophies of education which we here summarize have been clearly set forth in the report of the Committee on Religion and Public Education of the International Council of Religious Education to the Annual Meeting, February 1949. They are: 1) Frankly materialistic and secularist views or philosophies, where ultimate values in life are found in physical things and where it is thought and believed that life can be lived and understood without any reference to God or to any religious interpretation of life. 2) Belief in spiritual values, conceived without reference to transcendent religious faith. Acknowledgment is given to the already existing strong moral and spiritual emphases in public school curricula, teaching, and administration. Idealism, cherishing and pursuing the good, the beautiful, and the true, and seeking to further such democratic values as cooperation, tolerance, and open-mindedness, has distinct advantages as man-centered philosophy, over purely materialistic interpretations of life. But will this idealism permanently endure unless it is rooted in the life-giving soil of theistic faith? To this question the religious man, especially the Christian, will conscientiously give an emphatic "No." The idealistic, but non-theistic humanist misunderstands the "no" as he asks: "But, aren't we all working for the same values?" Ill-informed members of Christian churches also misunderstand the "no" when they naively say: "But isn't Christianity simply practicing the Golden Rule?" Both are concerned with fruits; the Christian is econcerned with roots as well as fruits. 3) "Belief in God as the Source of all spiritual values and material goods, the Determiner of the destinies of nations, and the loving Father of mankind" is a third position. In whatever language this philosophy of education is phrased, it affirms faith in the God revealed in the Old and New Testaments and faith in man as his responsible creatures. It is the faith embodied in our laws, documents and institutions which has guided and inspired our life and history from Colonial times through the early days as a nation, and is believed to be the only adequate basis of deep spiritual values for future generations.

Possible Lines of Solution

Which of these three philosophies of education is dominant in public education today? Which is dominant in the homes of the nation? Christians believe that the first two philosophies do not offer an adequate basis for education, for culture, or for life. However, realizing that the full range of religious teaching is a function of home, church and school, and that the school needs to remain nonsectarian in its teaching, the Protestant educational forces of the United States have recently gone on record as choosing to throw in their lot with the public schools and to commit their children and youth to these schools for a large share of their education, rather than to establish schools of the church. This position affirms that while the separation of church and state is an American tradition, it is also a tradition for the schools to interpret in a friendly manner the common religious heritage of their varying communities.

Protestantism is not interested in bringing pressure on public schools, nor in propagandizing them to teach Protestant views of religion. It is saying, by this action, that it will do its best to bring to the schools whatever religious resources it has for the common good and that it believes the public schools can be counted on by Catholics, Protestants, and Jews alike to be an ally, not an enemy, of religious views of life. It believes that the school will not be satisfied with a neutral position on religion, that it will not carry out a policy of silence with regard to theistic faith, nor will it negate religious faith in the process of education.

The American Council on Education, through its Committee on Religion and Public Education, has recently issued a statement which gives backing to such hopes and expectations on the part of Protestant churches. In part, it says that, if the public school accepts the responsibility of bringing children and youth "into full possession of their cultural heritage," it does not fulfill its responsibility if it leaves out the role of religion in history, the relation of religion to all phases of culture, and the way in which the religious life of American communities is expressed today. The council says further: "An educated person cannot be religiously illiterate." This represents a real advance over the conception of religion as a leisure time phase of culture.

This newly re-established Protestant position with regard to education is not without some precarious aspects. The church in every age and time has been in conflict with some values upheld by the state. This tension between church and state is a healthy relationship. But, this position is in the continuing stream of the Reformation tradition and spirit, which nurtures a free and responsible citizenry whose obligation to God involves it in continuous reformation of both church and state. Knowing that the responsibility for the development of the religious aspects of our public education lies with the people, the teachers, boards of education and administrators, Protestants, as responsible citizens, place trust in these persons and processes. Protestantism is ready to back its conviction with offers of cooperation in exploring with Roman Catholics, Jews, and other religious leaders common grounds for dealing appreciatively with religion and the public schools; offering cooperation with state teachers' colleges and departments of education in liberal arts colleges to discover possible patterns for equipping future teachers to deal adequately in the schoolroom with the place of religion in public education; offering cooperation with curriculum builders and textbook makers in preparing curricular materials which give adequate recognition to the place of religion in American life; and to work for a public opinion among Protestant people that will support vigorously the basic principle of academic freedom. These are offers far-reaching in their implications. If accepted by the educational forces in the nation, needed reformation in public education, in both philosophy and practice, may be on the way; and we may be on the way, also, to a clearer statement of the educational opportunities and obligations of home, school and church, both as separate and interrelated units in society.

Our fathers, coming to this land during the past three centuries, have lived and worked not only on physical frontiers, but also on spiritual and educational frontiers. We have noted previously that they brought with them such concepts as the dignity and worth of the common man; freedom and independence of the individual; the sacredness of personality; and the right of conscience. In the crucible of living, many of these ideas have become separated from their religious base as the nation endeavored to bring education to all the children of all the people—those related to religious fellowships and those not so related. The very idea of universal education itself came through Reformation influence. The mood of free inquiry under which scientific endeavor has made such rapid strides, the beginnings of so many lay movements by church and religious people, the measure of religious freedom that has developed and been written into the laws of the land, the authority of reason and conscience in the individual person, have all had far-reaching implications for educational development and are not unrelated to the Reformation spirit.

The question before the American people now is whether or not the Hebraic-Christian religion will continue to play any part in public education. With the American Council on Education emphasizing the necessity for the public schools to interpret the role of religion in history and in all phases of culture and its varying expressions in community life today, and with a large part of Protestantism affirming its intention to work with educators for a religiously sensitive, nonsectarian, public school, there is hope at a precarious moment in history.

The Protestant churches, motivated anew by the Reformation dynamic, are challenged to use all of their resources in witnessing to the state and nation the truth that "without religious insight and mission, educated people cannot live adequately or know sufficiently that allegiance to God is the beginning and end of all wisdom." [4]

[4] Frederick West, "Christianity and Organized Education" in *The Church and Organized Movements*, R. C. Miller, ed. (New York, 1946), p. 179.

EVANGELICAL AND PROTESTANT ETHICS

H. Richard Niebuhr

A STRANGE duality manifests itself in every human movement. Perhaps it is the inner contradiction in man which
comes to appearance in the double-minded character of political,
scientific, cultural, and religious revolutions and revivals. Mon-
archies and tyrannies arise in protests against the rule of the
strong but also as assertions of such rule. Democratic revolutions
contend for the right of the people to govern themselves but also
for the right of a special group—church-members or property-
holders or industrial workers—to direct them. Natural science
enters upon its great career under the double motto of obedience
to the laws of nature and of power over its forces. Nations and
cultures come into existence as representatives of a universal
cause and as exponents of particular interests; communism
and Russianism, democracy and Gallicanism or Americanism,
the sovereignty of law and Roman imperalism, rationalism and
Hellenism accompany each other like non-identical and competitive twins. In religious history this duality and internal contradiction are also manifest. Hebraic universalism and particularism are contradictory and inseparable. Rejecting the proposition that a particular people has been chosen by the God
of heaven and earth, the church asserts the same statement in a
new form. Catholicism and Romanism or Catholicism and
Anglicanism go hand in hand; pietism, stressing the primary
importance of heart religion, concentrates attention on external
behavior; theological idealism asserts the absolute dependence
of man on God and the primacy of the religious consciousness.

Protestantism which from the beginning has been keenly aware of this aspect of man's misery is itself subject to the law it has discerned. Some of the ways in which this internal contradiction appears in their own history have been called to the attention of modern Protestants. Historical inquiry has illuminated the antitheses and cooperations of church and sect principles, of capitalism and Calvinism, of nationalism and the Reformation, of stateism and Lutheranism, of bibliolatry and dependence on the Word of God, of individualism and the idea of the priesthood of all believers, of legalism and liberty. Yet the illusion easily arises that while the past has been subject to the sway of original sin or that, while other men and organizations are beset by internal contradiction, we, in our own theological movement or denomination, are happily delivered from the body of this death. The Calvinist can discern the ambiguity in Lutheranism; the Lutheran sees the mote in Geneva's eye; the sectarian understands what is wrong with the churchman; the Barthian analyzes inerrantly the fallacies in Brunner; the double-mindedness of *Kultur-Protestantismus* is as plain as a pike-staff to the church-theologian, etc., etc. The great fact remains that we cannot see the beams in our own eyes, and that we can only be thankful that the Lord has constituted the church a society for the mutual extraction of motes and beams.

Yet what cannot be seen in particular may be understood in general. Though each individual Christian man or group in Protestantism may be unable to discern the contradiction in himself or itself, it is possible, within limits, to understand something of the contradiction which exists in modern Protestantism as a whole. The antitheses are discernible in theology, polity and worship; but they are most evident in Protestant and Evangelical ethics.

These two terms, Protestant and Evangelical, may be used to designate the two tendencies. On the one hand we note in our answers to the question, "What shall I do?" a defensive temper which regards Protestantism as a way of life, once and for all established, which must be maintained and defended against internal and external enemies. These defensive answers in their organization we shall call the Protestant ethics. On the other hand the question may be and is answered by the simple statement, so rich in implications, "Believe in the Lord Jesus Christ and thou shalt be saved." This answer with all those implications we shall name the Evangelical ethics.

Protestant Ethics

The defensive or Protestant ethics has as many forms as Protestantism itself, yet all of them show a family resemblance. In each of them Protestant men express their pride in and their concern for the conservation of those achievements which are credited to the Reformers, however variously the nature and relative value of these achievements are defined. In each Protestants express their antagonism to destructive forces which seem to threaten those achievements and the Protestant way of life. In each there is expressed high awareness of one or the other of the negative principles of the Reformation: the doctrine of radical evil in man, the rejection of the authoritarian church, of tradition, the suspicion of reason and natural law. In each the positive content of the ethics is derived from tradition, though now from Protestant rather than medieval tradition.

One form of the defensive Protestant ethics is that which has been dubbed *Kultur-Protestantismus*. It is the socal religion of a large part of Western civilization and is intimately connected with national, political, and economic ways of thought and behavior. Sometimes it is very conservative as in the case of fundamentalist groups where Protestant ethics is often identified with the prevailing mores of a static culture and with defense against all experimental types of behavior, whether in the realm of amusements, or of property-holding and union-organization, or of ecclesiastical organization. Protestant ethics here appears as strict obedience to the traditions established in sectarian and revivalistic days on the one hand, in the days of agrarian capitalism and early democracy on the other. Dominantly an ethics of prohibitions, it seems to be founded on a deep suspicion of sinful man, especially of sinful youth and of the sinful outside "world." Its representatives live in fear of the destructive effects on the established folk-ways of communism, Catholicism and liberalism, of science and literary criticism. Avowedly biblicistic, this ethic is actually based much more on the traditions of the elders than on Scriptures, as the prominence of prohibitions against drinking, dancing, and card-playing and interest in the maintenance of rather unbiblical economic and political instiutions indicate.

The extreme antithesis of this ethics seems to appear there where Protestantism is identified with socialism and even, occasionally, with communism. Here the culture with which Protestantism is allied consists of a new set of economic institutions and practices. Yet a certain identification between Protestantism and the new culture is regarded as justified by the antagonism of both to Roman Catholicism and of defensive Romanism to both.

The most prevalent kind of culture Protestantism, however, is to be found in neither of these extremes but in the great middle where the institutions of liberal, democratic, industrial, scientific culture are closely associated with the achievements of the Reformation and where the defense of such institutions with the aid of religion is the central concern. This kind of Protes-

tantism may show more or less willingness to modify the institutions and also the religion in order that the "democratic,
liberal, and Protestant way of life" may be conserved. But one
thing stands out in its ethics: the utilitarian interest in promot-
ing a faith for the sake of saving from external attack and
internal decay the habits of life that have been sanctioned by
tradition. That it is a pleasant tradition, that the mode of life
which it enjoins is satisfying to those who follow it, that its
rules serve many human values, that it enables people of differing faiths to get along with each other in nonreligious matters,
that it provides for desirable reforms—all this may be quite
evident. But it is also clear that this great median cultural ethics
of defensive Protestantism is less interested in the transformation of life by grace than in the conservation of a kind of life
once radically changed by grace or by the proclamation of a
doctrine of grace.

It is remarkable how much of the current revival of interest
in religion expresses itself through defensive Roman Catholicism. But Protestantism is also a beneficiary of the movement.
A new interest in Puritanism is manifested by men who realize
that democracy would not have arisen without the convictions
of Puritanism and that without something like them it cannot
be maintained. A new interest in the doctrine of God may
appear in the form of concern for the foundations of modern
science. Oswald Spengler called attention to the tendency in
dying civilizations (we might better say in civilizations which
believe that they are threatened with death) to revive the religion of the culture's creative period. Cultural Protestantism
in our time seems to illustrate his thesis. Churchmen and non-
churchmen now often turn to religion—what man does not?—
with the idea that once upon a time this world was in a much
happier state than it is now, that a fall from joy and order has

taken place, that this fall was connected with the abandonment of the religion of the fathers, and that if the religion can only be reestablished all may yet be well. There may be some truth in this widespread cultural myth, though theology will point out the fallacies of equating the time of man's innocency with a cultural era, such as that of the thirteenth, or of the sixteenth, or of the eighteenth century, and of identifying the fall from grace with such an historic event as the coming of the Reformation, or the Renaissance, or the Enlightenment, or the Industrial Revolution. In any case the ethics of liberal culture Protestantism is the ethics of modern culture, restored, improved, revised. Its principles are those of anti-authoritarianism, or individual religious, intellectual, and political liberty, or of the sacredness of personality. It is a Protestantism which justifies itself by calling attention to its social works and expects to be justified in the historical judgment by its continued production of socially valued effects.

The second species of Protestant ethics is made up of many families of ecclesiastical defensive moralities. In them the moral question to which answers are sought is not, "What must we do to save our culture?" but rather, "What must we do to save our church and its way of life?" It is assumed that part of the church was reformed by the Reformers and that Christianity now consists of ordered and disordered parts. Right polity, right teaching, right belief have been established, it is believed, in Protestantism or in the particular variety of Protestantism in question. Sex life and the family, at least in principle, have been rightly ordered since the aberrations of medieval monasticism have been eliminated; a Christian doctrine of vocation has been substituted for a false one; right relations of church and state have been established. Such defensive morality may be more liberal, seeking some changes in the traditional Protestant ways of life or more conservative, resisting all changes. But in either case the emphasis is on the maintenance of tradition, though the tradition which the Reformers rejected is also rejected and the one that began with them is affirmed. So it is a characteristic of contemporary Protestant scholarship that it seeks in the writings of its Fathers—of Luther, Calvin, Wesley, Edwards—sanctions for the ethical decisions it needs to make in social life with the same avidity and inventiveness that Roman Catholic scholars employ in the exegesis of Thomas Aquinas or Jewish rabbis in the analysis of the Torah.

Defensive Protestantism, of course, appears not only in these social forms but also in highly individualized fashion. It has often been pointed out that the revolt against legalism which characterized the Reformation issued in a new kind of legalism, that is, in a new manifestation of the old spirit of rigorous obedience to laws, accompanied by the fears of punishment and the hopes of reward which mark such moralty. Where this spirit obtains, whether in Judaism or in Christianity, whether in Roman Catholicism or in Protestantism, morality has a defensive character. Man seeks to justify himself by his works; he wrestles with the problem of making God friendly toward him; he lives in fear of the divine righteousness; his activities are accompanied neither by confidence in God nor by thankfulness but by distrust of the divine good will and by the feeling that the Lord is a hard taskmaster. Men who have been nurtured in Protestantism find it hard to deny that such an attitude is widely prevalent in it or that it is not nurtured by the very manner in which Protestant doctrine is transmitted from generation to generation. The narrow and fearsome spirit which characterized the second generation of Puritans in America and was represented by a Cotton Mather manifests itself in one way or another in every group. In one case, indeed, it may appear as a meticulous concern for correct religious belief, in another case as fearsome respect for taboos in eating and drinking—especially drinking, in still a third as careful suppression of every angry or self-regarding thought. But whether it is more concerned with spiritual or with carnal sin, with perfection in conduct or perfection in belief, it is always the same spirit of negative and self-conscious morality. It is not wholly an accident or a mistake that in popular literature Protestants are more frequently chosen than Catholics to exemplify this narrow, self-defensive and uncreative morality. It is doubtless fallacious to seek for the sources of this perversion of the gospel in the Protestant formulations of the Christian creed or the Reformed doctrine of the Christain life, since moral decision and personal, religious relations are not based on conceptual propositions, whatever the service these may render the life of practical reason. Sin is not correlated with doctrines about sin; it does not abound more nor is it diminished where doctrines or sin abound. It is only remarkable that Protestantism itself illustrates the prevalence of that human moral orientation which it tends to associate in peculiar fashion with Roman Catholic doctrine and polity; and that it makes evident in its own history and actions man's unconquerable desire to defend and justify himself by his good works as well as to identify his social or personal culture with God's revelation of his will.

Evangelical Ethics

If only defensive and self-justifying morality had appeared in the Reformation that event would have little Christian significance, whatever political or cultural meaning it might have. If only defensiveness in ethics characterized its historic successors, Christian faith today would turn away from their churches and rites to find its wellsprings elsewhere as once it turned away from defensive medieval religion. Of course, the Reformation contained negative and defensive elements. Its exponents were sometimes more aware of human sin than of divine grace, more conscious of the pope's errors in granting indulgence than of the truth in Christ's forgiveness, more afraid of earthly enemies than confident of heavenly friendship. But it was also and perhaps dominantly the expression of an affirmative and joyful, a positive and creative Christian life. However much the motives of a life according to man were mixed up in it with the motives of citizenship in the City of God, the latter were gloriously present. These gave the sixteenth century movement élan and power and whenever in later days the spirit rather than the letter of the Reformation has been manifest among its "children after the flesh" these motives have again been evident, however mixed with defensiveness and fearful self-justification. We have called the positive movement and orientation of the Christian life Evangelical ethics, using a term which the Reformers themselves preferred to such words as Protestant or Reformed. The name, of course, is a matter of relative indifference so long as the thing itself is adequately located and described.

Evangelical ethics cannot be located, as a self-justifyng temper always seeks to do, by looking for it in the self and one's own community, or in any isolated person or group. We cannot fix it by looking for it in Luther rather than in Calvin or in Calvin rather than in Luther, in sectarian rather than in ecclesiastical Protestantism or vice versa. To be sure we are more aware of its presence when we read Isaiah than when we study Leviticus, when we identify ourselves with Paul than when we do so with the author of II Peter, and when we look at God and ourselves with the aid of Calvin than when we do so under the guidance of Cotton Mather. But the spirit of Evangelical ethics is not discernible in men; it exists only in the relations of men to God and of God to men. It is as erroneous to look for it in men or churches as it is fallacious to look for manifestations of magnetism in steel filings in the absence of a magnet.

The chief descriptive statement which can be made about this Evangelical ethics is that it is the mode of life which issues out of a positive relation to God, as that relation is established by, through, and with Jesus Christ. It is *theocentric* ethics. It is the ethics which accompanies a dominant orientation of the self and the community toward the action of God. This is the grand idea which pervades the utterances of a Luther and a Calvin and which is symbolized by such phrases as "The Sovereignty of God" and "Justification by Faith," which is set forth in many variations in the *Sermon on Good Works* and in the *Institutes*. As the prophets call upon Israelites to drop their preoccupation with the maneuvers of their mundane enemies and with their own religious activities to turn their eyes to the workings of the living God, so the Reformers out of their own experience of the mighty deeds of God proclaim, "We are not our own; therefore let us as far as possible forget ourselves and all things that are ours; we are God's; to him therefore let us live and die."

The distinction of this dynamically theocentric spirit in ethics from some of its specious surrogates will help make its character more evident. Because God is not known in his might and favor without the aid of a fallible authority it is easy to substitute pedagogical authority for the reality to which it directs attention. In Roman Catholicism that temptation had resulted in concentration on the church so that Roman Catholic ethics tended to become the morality of those who were always oriented toward the church, listening to its commandments in the first place, and watching its deeds as the most important in the world. The Reformers were assured that the authority of the Bible was a corrective to this tendency and that the Bible could always be counted on to point away from itself to the God-in-Christ and Christ-in-God to whom it bore witness. Yet sometimes they themselves and more frequently their successors looked away from the living God to whom the Bible pointed and oriented themselves toward the Bible itself. The consequence was then a new legalism in which the question was no longer, "What doth the Lord require of thee?" but, "What does the Bible demand?" A God-centered ethics, however, looks with the Bible and through the Bible to the Lord of the Scriptures.[1] Similar reflections about the Spirit who leads men to God-in-Christ and Christ-in-God apply to the spiritualistic and subjectivistic perversion of Evangelical ethics, to the confusions of the authority of religious experience and of conscience with the God to whom they bear witness. Evangelical ethics, however, is not oriented toward the inner spirit or conscience but toward the transcendant God revealing himself in mighty acts—above all in the mighty act of Jesus Christ.

God-centered ethics is partly definable also by noting its differences from those orientations of life in which the center of attention is occupied by the negative counterparts of theocentrism. The acknowledgment that God saves us by his grace has as its negative counterpart the conviction that we do not save ourselves from moral and spiritual death by our works. An ethics, however, which takes the latter conviction as its starting point will differ widely and radically from one which begins

[1] It may be that Evangelical thought in our time is more appreciative of the fallible authority of the church because it has recognized in consequence of the post-Reformation development both that there is fallibility in the Scriptures and that human fallibility can substitute the Bible for the God of the Bible almost as easily as it can put the church in the place of the Lord of the church. At all events the tendency of modern Evangelical thought is to recognize the necessity and the fallibility of both these authorities and the idolatrous penchant of man to substitute any fallible authority for God.

with the former. It will be an ethics of despair rather than of hope, a negatively humanistic rather than a positively theistic ethics. And it cannot but fall into a new defensiveness, though what will now be defended will not be man's righteousness but perhaps physical life or weath or a recognizedly temporal and sinful culture. Again, the negative counterpart of the realization that God is holy is the realization that men are all profane and that they fall short of his glory in everything they do. But an ethics which starts with the realization of human ingloriousness, profaneness and sinfulness and in which men keep their eyes centered on the sin which stains all human acts will be profoundly different from the ethics of the glory of God. Evangelical ethics is God-centered, not sin-centered. When our fundamental orientation in life is that of persons who live vis à vis our own sinful selves rather than vis à vis God, the spirit of Evangelical ethics takes flight no less surely than when we live in the contemplation of our own righteousness.

It is, secondly, characteristic of Evangelical ethics that it is the mode of life which issues out of *faith in God*. Faith and God, as Luther often pointed out, belong together. And he made it equally clear that faith and ethics belong together. In Evangelical ethics faith is not a virtue which can be added to other moral excellencies. It is rather the root and ground of all man's free actions. The direction of a man's loyalty and trust gives direction to every act he performs, so that if he speaks with the tongues of men and of angels and sells all his goods to feed the poor but has not faith in God, these acts not only profit him nothing but are destructive of self and of others. The conduct of life issues out of the central faith, not as conclusions are drawn from premises but as fruit derives from trees. Men are so created that they cannot and do not live without faith. They must trust in a god, such as their own reason, or civilization, or one of the many other idols to which they look for salvation from meaningless existence. Hence the great ethical question is always the question of faith, "In what does man trust?" Moral reasoning always builds on the explicit or implicit answer given to this prior question. A mode of life that is not founded on faith in God is necessarily founded on some other faith. There is no faithless ethics. Moreover, it is clear to us in the Evangelical situation that God, the Lord of heaven and earth, the One we deal with in all our dealings, is never absent from us as we make our choices and guide our conduct in the directions given by our loyalties to idols. We can take no neutral attitude toward God. In our very acts of trust in idols we affirm our distrust of God; in our choices of good under the guidance of our loyalty to the self we reject the divine claim to our loyalty. There is no atheistic morality; it is either theistic or anti-theistic. If we do not trust God we distrust him, however much we may seek to hide this fact from ourselves by pretending to ignore him.

The recognition of this deep connection between conduct and faith is mated then with the understanding that the reformation of faith is the reformation of life and that the great work of Christ for moral beings is his work as the renewer and transformer of faith. He redeems us by reconciling us to God, by winning us out of our distrust and fear of the Holy One, by drawing us away from our despairing trust in idols and in self. Faith in God is the gift of God through Jesus Christ and with that faith all things are given, including the transformation of human conduct.

Evangelical ethics is not, of course, the result of these insights but the result of faith itself. When statements about faith are substituted for faith in God, only perverted forms of Evangelical ethics can result, for then belief is substituted for trust and loyalty. When that takes place, as has often occurred and will often occur, our real trust is directed not toward God but toward a system of truths on which we depend for salvation from sin and death. A new idol has then taken the place of the old and a new legalism supplanted the old system of demands. A related perversion of Evangelical ethics issues in antinomianism rather than in legalism. This seems to happen when faith is separated from its divine object and when the subjective condition of confidence is made the object of trust. Then we say to ourselves that we are saved by faith rather than that God alone saves us and allow ourselves to do whatever we can do with confidence rather than those things which we can do with trust in God, the Father of Jesus Christ, and in loyalty to Christ. We are sometimes encouraged in this perversion of faith-ethics by our habit of reducing our fundamental principles to a kind of shorthand. For the statement that God saves us by faith we substitute the proposition that we are saved by faith and with the aid of this device theocentric ethics may become fido-centric ethics. So also for the commandment that we ought to love God and our neighbor we often substitute the statement that love is the law of life and so both indicate and encourage the substitution of a love-centered morality for a God-centered one. But Evangelical ethics is not an ethics of faith; it is the ethics of that *faith in God* which is given by, in, and through Jesus Christ.

Such God-centered, faith-founded ethics is, in the third place, an ethics of *freedom*. Freedom is not a third and accidental attribute but belongs with God and faith as faith and God belong together. Where faith in God is present the self is free from concern for itself. It has not achieved freedom from self-concern, but has been set free by God through the gift of faith in him. It is able to accept itself as the forgiven self and as one which will continually be forgiven by God, not as though he did not take the self's sin seriously but as though he were determined to make it good and right, to redeem it from every physical and spiritual disease by whatever mild or harsh medicines and surgery are necessary. In the contemplation of Christ the mind moved by the spirit of repentance discovers at one and the same time how bound the moral self is to itself and how great was the freedom of Jesus Christ in this respect. Then, with the repentance and faith given through him, the divine possibility appears, that man can and will be free from self-concern as Christ was free.

With freedom from slavery to the self goes freedom from bondage to the physical and cultural values without which we think that we cannot live. How strict that bondage is, how heavily its chains lie on every thought and aspiration of men the whole history of our common and personal moral life indicates. Because the Jews had to cling to their culture with its values as the only reality that gave significance to their own existence they rejected Jesus Christ; and for the same reasons we who call ourselves Christians reject him over and over again. We cannot believe that if we will seek the kingdom of God and its righteousness all other things necessary to us will be given in free abundance. Do we not know what is necessary and do we not know that these things do not come to us without anxious thought? Hence we compromise the ethics of the gospel with the ethics of culture in many and devious ways. But with the gift of faith in God the possibility of freedom from this bondage arises into view as a promise that will be redeemed and is being redeemed. It does happen, not merely in visions of an eschatological future but in moments when eternity breaks into time that by faith God enables men to say, "Let goods and kindred go, this mortal life also; the body they may kill; God's truth abideth still; His Kingdom is forever." It is in such moments that the Evangelical ethics appears as a mode of life in freedom which, though impossible to man, is being made possible by God.

Another aspect of this freedom is release from bondage to the law. So long as the direct relation to God called faith does not exist or so long as the direct relation to him is one of distrust, we are necessarily under the authority of moral traditions, of churches, and states. They require us to do those things which, in their more or less fallible recognition of the nature of reality, are known to be necessary if we are to survive as men in communities. They must prohibit those deeds which arise out of our deep distrust of that reality and of one another. The direct encounter with God, the recognition on our own part of his omnipotence and goodness changes the bondage to men and their laws into a bondage to God. With that change there comes a great conversion of the power, spirit and content of the law. The law which is known to be God's, not one ascribed to him by men, has a force that compels obedience. Known, moreover, as the demand of the One who is wholly good toward us, it takes on the character of counsel while bondage turns into the freedom of sonship. And again the content of the law known as law of God undergoes a metamorphosis; what was important becomes unimportant, what was insignificant becomes great. How these things can be, Paul and the Reformers have described over and over again. But the truth of what they have said only becomes apparent to us when we find ourselves in the Evangelical situation, while everything they have said is twisted into something different when we are defensive and self-justifying.

The freedom of the Evangelical mode of life is not only a freedom *from* but also a freedom *to*. How it is a freedom to love the neighbor Luther has wonderfully described. How it sets men free to deal creatively with the social and personal situations that confront them and to respond with inventiveness and artistry to the challenges they meet needs to be set forth more fully than has yet been done in either Catholic or Reformed theologies. In the thought of the Eastern church, as partly represented by Berdyaev, something of this dimension of Evangelical morality has been suggested though in connection with a dubious metaphysics of freedom. The free creativity of a faith-in-God morality can be illustrated by the works of a Paul and of many a lesser Christian, but its analysis in theology remains incomplete. Creative morality is not bound by rule, though it knows all the rules. It does not meet the changing situations of life with the repetition of acts found good in the past, but with deeds that fit the immediate situation, recognized as a situation in the kingdom of God. Taught by faith in the creating God, it discerns beauty and glory where these had been hidden to the distrustful eye and in the Master's workshop produces moral works of art. The tragic element is doubtless always in them since they are the works of forgiven sinners in a world of sin and forgiveness. Nevertheless they are creative and new.

Finally, the Evangelical mode of life may be described as *momentary* in character. It is not a life that plans far ahead to insure the future, whether in heaven or on earth. It knows that God ties the present and the future together and that no provision for the morrow is necessary to the life which he redeems. Because the future is in the hands of Love therefore man is free to do the right thing now, that is, to love his neighbor. Because God is Lord of the present no less than of the future therefore the temporally insignificant deed may have more eternity in it than the one designed to outlast the years. Evangelical ethics does not underscore the melancholy wisdom of the world that all our pomp is to be reduced to ashes or that "the best-laid plans of mice and men gang aft a-gley." It sets this wisdom in the positive context of the affirmation that what has been done to the least of the brothers has been done unto him and that one day in the Lord's sight may be a thousand years. This "momentariness" which gets its meaning only from the presence of the eternal God who is Lord of both present and future is always offensive to our calculating human reason. Yet its apparent recklessness is deeply wise in the context of faith-knowledge.

Karl Barth has remarked that Luther wrote beautifully about Christian liberty—far too beautifully. It is easy to write too enthusiastically about the Evangelical ethics, as though the divine possibility for man had become a human possibility through the Incarnation and even through the Reformation. But it is also easy to write too sceptically about it, as though divine possibility were only a future event and as though God were not redeeming his promises and realizing his possibilities in this present world. The faith of the disciples remains smaller than a mustard seed and they remove no mountains; but it is not non-existent and sometimes they cast out demons by the power of God. The freedom to which Christ sets them free is used as the occasion for new bondage; but cribbed and confined as they are in themselves, sometimes they do free deeds and perform acts of liberation. The rule of God does not appear in their works so that men can say, "Lo, here it is." But sometimes it appears in lightning flashes that illuminate the dark scene of self-justifying, defensive human life and give evidence of the energy waiting to be received and pressing into human existence.

The ethics of the Reformation with its duality of works-righteousness and faith-righteousness, of self-righteousness and righteousness in God, of life in the world of sin and life in the world of forgiveness is a testimony to the fact that the Christian lives between the times and between the worlds. But it is only the

Evangelical element in that ethics that makes it Christian. Take that away and all that is left is an ethics of North European civilization, or of capitalism, or of democracy, or, perhaps, of socialism, or of that amorphous social religion called Prottestantism.

THE ECUMENICAL REALITY
OF THE CHURCH

Carl E. Schneider

THE Christian conception of the Church is enmeshed in the paradoxical antinomies of faith and history from which there is no escape except as the hearts and minds of men are renewed by the power of God's Holy Spirit. The history of the Christian Church begins with the gift of God's grace as revealed "in these last days" in the work and person of Jesus Christ through whom was unfolded the nature and purpose of God. The faith-experiences of the newly evolving Christian community were charged with the sacramental reality of a new Kingdom which had universal significance. Herein, however, lies the paradox of Christian life in all its varied aspects that, as spiritual realities increasingly become embraced in temporal forms, the universals of faith become the particulars of history. The normative nature of God's revelation becomes obscured by subjective elements derived from its human relations.

Within the framework of this basic tension the spiritual genius of the Protestant Reformation must continually assert itself anew. Although the Reformation does not present a full and final answer to every aspect of this question, its incisive emphasis on the spiritual quality of the New Testament proclamation leads to a keener comprehension for the radical spiritual dynamic vested in the Christian Church. In this sense it has sharpened the vision for a broader conception of the ecumenical nature of the church and will continue to lift the discussion of this subject beyond purely confessional and ecclesiastical levels.

Thus the struggle for an ecumenical concept of the church fluctuates between the spiritual (universal) interpretation which depreciates historical contingencies and the historical (particularistic) interpretation which, in violation of spiritual discernments, leads to static sociological conceptions. The interrelation of these two factors describes the ongoing process in the dialectic development of the church and lies at the center of the ecumenical problem.

In discussions of the ecumenical question it therefore becomes necessary to recognize the spiritual thrust of the New Testament; to discern the point at which and how the spiritual qualities of the primitive church were secularized in the historical development; to envisage how the universal concept of the church may be rescued from its historical restrictions. It may then become apparent that the radical renewal of the New Testament comprehension of the church may be as significant for our day as was the rediscovery of the New Testament meaning of grace and faith for the sixteenth century. From the vantage point of the Protestant Reformation, therefore, it is imperative that the spiritual quality of the New Testament legacy be constantly held in mind as the basic norm for an appraisal of the subsequent historical development.

THE NEW TESTAMENT CHURCH

The Christian Church of our day is continually being challenged to place itself under the spell of the New Testament proclamation of the kingdom of God as the dawn of a new age. The essence of the gospel is that through Christ a new redemptive order has arisen in which those who have been called by the Holy Spirit out of this world constitute the "communion of saints," the "New Israel," the fellowship of the faithful. The new household of faith was bound together by participation in the same gifts, by the testimony of a common witness, and by sharing in common the power of the resurrection unto newness of life. Thus the Church emerges into history as the gift of God's grace and the creation of his Word and assumes the mystic quality of the Body of Christ. In this sense the Church, as stated in the Apostles' Creed, is always a presupposed existing reality and the object of faith which arouses the sense of wonder in the affirmation of God's love toward man.

It is not surprising, therefore, that the New Testament, charged with the sense of spiritual reality, contains neither a formal definition nor a formative doctrine of the Church. This, in the experience of its members, represented not an empirical society but a sacramental community. In this fellowship the blessings of God were mutually shared by those who, in the common recognition of their human sinfulness and divine redemption, in the love of their Lord loved each other.

The modern quest for ecumenical unity fails at the outset unless it is initiated at the New Testament source. In the universalism of God's purpose and will, as revealed in the New Testament proclamation, we are confronted by a given unity of the Church of which Christ is the head. This unity is not based on socio-historical factors, but on spiritual gifts and ministrations (*charismata, energēmata, diakoniai*),[1] which constitute not only the marks of the Kingdom but the essential *notae ecclesiae*. The visible marks of spiritual unity are thus found in apostolic faith and life, apostolic sacraments, and in the apostolic ministry.

The ecumenical marks of the Christian Church are not assured by the formal reestablishment of its original characteristics but by the continuity of a spiritual inheritance: in the preaching and hearing of the living Word of God through

[1] I Cor. 12; especially vv. 12–13 and 4 f.

which the Spirit speaks; in the observance of the sacraments; in the ministries of service; and in a way of life. These together testify to God's love and seal man's communion with Christ—the head of the Church and the one Lord of all. In the spiritual aspiration for and in the realization of these blessings, the Lord's prayer "that they may all be one" [2] will be realized. The unifying revelation of God in the Church as the Body of Christ is not only a unique, once-for-all event but as a continuing revelation is perpetually manifest in the spiritually inspired *congregatio sanctorum* of subsequent generations.

The unity here envisaged is based on the common experience of "one Lord, one faith, one baptism, one God and Father of all" [3]—a unity which on this universal level transcends all confessional, ecclesiastical, and liturgical forms. Within this framework no variable factors of race, language, education, environment or historical situation can affect the reality of the existing oneness in Christ.

When the experiential confessing of the overlordship of Christ is supplanted by confessionalistic formulations about our Lord; when the ministry of reconciliation is cast into normative institutional and canonical forms; and when the mood of worship becomes formally ritualized, then, in the clash of faith and history, the unity of the Body of Christ is threatened. Ecumenical unity may then become lost in sociologically induced formalizations.

Evidences of such formalizations manifested themselves quite early after the resurrection. With the rise of a second and third generation and with new challenges evoked by geographical and sociological expansion, variations in beliefs, in forms of worship, and in types of ministries began to appear. A certain

[2] John 17:21.
[3] Eph. 4:5, 6.

type of "denominationalism" may be observed, for example, in the differences between the Petrine, Pauline and Johannine interpretations of the one gospel; in the distinctions between gentile and Jewish Christians with their respective legacies; in the varying traditions of the churches at Antioch, Jerusalem, and Ephesus; and in the various types of piety represented by Paul, James and John.

It remains an eloquent testimony to the ecumenical nature of the New Testament Church that the unity of the Spirit was not disturbed by such formal variations. The common fellowship, in the midst of divergent types of expression, was assured not by compromise formulas but by the unique Christ-centered nature of the evolving church.[4] Indeed, the unity of the waiting fellowship was preserved and enriched by the diversity of gifts whereby the boundless universalism of God's love and truth in Christ was apprehended in human vessels.

In its subsequent historical development, the church in ever new distress-situations was subjected to a variety of factors that, moving either toward the right or left, obscured and modified the central purity of the Catholic vision of the New Testament.[5] The rise of Montanism in the ancient church clearly indicates an effort to recapture the waning New Testament spirit. Further secularizations are manifest in the depersonalization of individual faith into rigid formalizations negotiated by a sacerdotal and hierarchal institution. Instead of spiritual experience directly creating its organic forms of expression, institutional

[4] The obvious adoption of the term *"ecclesia"* as the Septuagint translation of the Hebrew *"Qahal"* perpetuates the idea of the ultimate unity of the Church as the true Israel, the Chosen People of God, etc.

[5] The ensuing medieval deformation may not have consisted so much in the complete abrogation of the spiritual line originating in the New Testament or in the diversity of creeds and of ecclesiastical and liturgical forms which arose as in the dominance of historical relations and references which introduced legalistic emphases and obscured the New Testament premises.

formulations arose which, with normative implication, were embodied in the all-embracing synthesis of the medieval church. The objective norm of unity was supplanted by subjective considerations—which led to humanly ordered uniformity.

In this clash of faith and history—in the course of which faith was formulated into dogma, worship into rites, and the ministries of service developed into hierarchal orders—the sense of spiritual direction was lost. More and more the church became a historical institutional which, striving for religious security and thus addressing itself to concerns born of world contacts, became legalized and secularized in the process. A variety of new empirically conditioned emphases jeopardized the free movement of God's Spirit as manifest in the Church as the Body of Christ. The unity of the church, in violation of the dynamic, vital, personalized concepts of love and truth, was sought in visible norms of man's own creation. Thus the apostolic gifts of the witnessing community were increasingly devoted to the service of ecclesiasticism—a process which is difficult to follow since throughout the first fifteen hundred years of its existence the church had not seriously reflected upon its nature.

The historical limitations of the church, caught in the fateful antinomy of the temporal and the spiritual, calls for continual and consecrated effort ever anew to rediscover the sense of direction with which the New Testament began. In this sense every attempt to reinterpret the intrinsic character of the church has ecumenical significance. The history of the church is full of prophetic efforts to curb the secularisms which were disturbing its unity and to recapture the glory of its New Testament heritage. This became the peculiar task of the Protestant Reformation.

THE REDISCOVERY OF NEW TESTAMENT EMPHASES

The Reformation of the sixteenth century was born in reaction to emphases which had increasingly obscured the transcendent nature of the Church. In its historical unfoldment the Reformation, particularly in its Calvinistic and Lutheran phases, sought at various points to transcend the inherited static categories of institutionalized religion. In this sense it represents a series of creative reactions to the formalized structure of the medieval church which had obscured the mystery of Christ's living presence. In all this, the essential contribution of the Reformation was the rediscovery of the spiritual quality inhering in the New Testament conception of the Church as the fellowship of those who, in their personal experience of God's grace through Christ, constitute the congregation of the faithful. In this "New Israel" there can be no sovereignty beyond that of her Lord who alone is the author and perfecter of her faith.

Thus the Reformation represents a trenchant critique of all historically evolved intermediary agencies which, whether in the field of doctrine, organization or of cult, disturb the free spiritual function of the Christian congregation. Consistently the Reformation maintained the freedom of the Christian man which prevails in the organism of the Church in which Christ alone is Lord. The spiritual unity of the Church—whether conceived as the "universal priesthood of believers" or as consisting of those justified by faith—was grounded on the unqualified overlordship of Christ.[6] What else is this than the rediscovery of the ecumenical reality of the New Testament church?

[6] Thus Luther's dread of medieval legalism and uniformity led him to admonish those who would use his *Order of Service* not to "impose it as a law," but to "use it in Christian freedom as they may please." See "Preface" to "the German Mass and Order of Service," 1526. *Works of Martin Luther*, Ed. by Jacobs (Philadelphia, 1915), VI, 170.

This rediscovery of direction was further enlivened by the recognition that, in the effort to achieve security by strengthening the lines of historical continuity, the church had deviated from its spiritual task. Protesting against the formal secularizations that had occurred, the Reformation reaffirmed the objective significance of spiritual factors in Christian history. Not historical but spiritual continuity shapes our eternal destinies. Thus the essential unity of the church is preserved within a historical framework where spiritual concerns are the determining factors.[7]

But again, the first generation of reformers had barely passed from the scene when a rebound occurred which, increasing in momentum and continuing into our day, has brought the ecumenical question into new focus.

The post-Reformation period was characterized by the rise of rapidly changing geographical, political, racial, and ideological frontiers which all too frequently obscured the spiritual horizons. Western civilization in a characteristically empirical manner sought and found its satifactions in the particular facts and realities established by rational, technological processes. The evolutionary concept of historical development helped accentuate the relativisms that contrasted Protestant flexibility with Roman rigidity. The false concept of freedom, with uncritical esteem for the private judgment of the individual, under the guise of evangelical liberty began to fashion and dominate religious life.

Such new orientations, which emerged from the social

[7] Anticipating the critique that the Reformation movement was disturbing the unity of the Church, the "Preface" to the *Confessio Augustana* (1530) expressed the hope that difference in "the opinions and judgments of diverse parties . . . may be harmonized and brought back to the one simple truth and Christian concord . . . so that as we are subjects and soldiers of the one Christ, so also, in unity and concord we may live in the one Christian Church . . ." Philip Schaff, *The Creeds of Christendom* (4th ed., New York, 1919), III, 4 f.

dynamic of the new age, bred new evils—the evils of denominationalism. For many of the movements that now arose and
flourished in the new atmosphere became the victims of their
own rationality and succumbed to the mandates of historical
expediencies. Indeed, the persistence of sociological factors led,
at times, to the reduction of Christian communities to little more
than religious associations and societies. Although variously
grounded in the Scriptures they were often so historically conditioned in their particularistic forms of confession, worship, and
organization as to lose the sense of their spiritual calling.

One such type of secularization occurred when faith was cast
into creedal forms. It became one of the characteristics of Protestantism that the confessional standards which arose under
pressure of particular historical situations, frequently became the
test, instead of testimonies, of faith.[8] Confessional islands began
to cover the Protestant world when theologians in specific con-
flict-situations constructed their systems of thought in defense
of particular points of view. It is an unworthy triumph of his-
toricism when the faith-experience of Jesus and the authority
of the gospel are measured by the depersonalized confessional
norms of a past day.

In a similar way the New Testament conception of the ministry, rediscovered by the Reformation, became historicized by
self-assertive efforts of denominationalists to establish the canonical status of their respective ecclesiastical orders and polity
(episcopal, presbyterian, congregational, etc.) on the basis of
historical continuity.[9] It is strange to observe how, starting from

[8] When Melanchthon defined "pure doctrine" in a quasi-intellectual way as a
norm for the *notae ecclesiae,* the door was opened for the legalistic institutionalization
of the church. Thus in this early deviation from the original Reformation position a
movement was inaugurated which has plagued Protestantism to this day.

[9] Note how, in the struggle for a new church in Germany, certain denominational groups, in their high espousal of the normative significance of the *Amt* for the
unity of the church, have been accused by their fellow Lutherans of not having
properly comprehended Luther.

identical New Testament premises, such a wide diversity of ecclesiastical orders can so plausibly be defended. Somewhere along the line, under the pressure of theologico-denominational logic, the ecumenical New Testament vision of the Church has been lost.

A semblance of secularism may also be detected when Christian worship is formalized into specific and hard rites which purport to be the special and sole channels of God's eternal grace. A travesty of Christian fellowship is reflected in the rise of exclusive liturgical ghettos. The spirit of the gospel, it would seem, is violated in the ritualistic exclusion of fellow Christians from the Lord's Table and in a form of baptism which initiates the candidate not into the Church of Christ but into a particular congregation or denomination. At the same time it should be observed, of course, that not only bondage to forms but also the very freedom from forms may equally constitute a violation of the Christ-centered worship "in spirit and in truth."

These all too brief references may suffice to indicate certain spiritual incongruities which have crept into denominational practices. When an alleged loyalty to the same Lord does not result in sympathetic fellowship among those who acknowledge him, an aberration has occurred which does violence to the ecumenical spirit of the New Testament. In this sense, denominationalism, with its petty, egotistical and subjective demands, is a rejection of the universalism of Christ.

The point of these observations is not directed against the differences and variety of denominational forms which as such may be as little offensive as the diversities found in the New Testament. Far from constituting a threat to the unity of the Body of Christ, they may enhance the richness of the Protestant effort to mediate God's grace to all manner of men. Whatever particularistic emphases evolve in the ongoing history of the church, they dare not violate the unity of God's sovereign rule in man's life.

As long as the order of God is preserved in the orderings of the denominations as members of the Body of Christ, the diversity of denominational gifts glorifies the head which is Christ. On the other hand, the order of God is violated when the orderings of denominations glorify as universal norms the standards of their own historical development. The fateful bane of denominationalism lies in the failure to take the unity of the Spirit in living fellowship with Christ seriously enough to transcend particularistic norms. Dogma ever needs to be translated into faith, rites transformed into worship, and ecclesiastical orders into ministries of service.

The critique of denominationalism, it need hardly be added, is not inspired by the pragmatic design to resolve a scattered denominational line into a unified Protestant front. The challenge of our day lies rather in the need to discover anew the deeper reaching implications of the early Christian concept of the Church as the Body of Christ. Such a reorientation, in its protest against the narrow formalized order of a divided Christendom and in its radical acceptance of New Testament norms, bears the marks of what can be called an ecumenical reformation.

THE RADICAL REQUIREMENTS OF ECUMENICITY

Various factors have combined in recent years to focus attention on the need for a radical reorientation of the Christian movement. This has occurred on various levels. The sociological unification of the world and the growing sense of human solidarity have broadened the horizons of race, nation, and creed. A pragmatic impetus toward church federations and church unions is derived from the practical necessity to achieve order and efficiency in a world where tolerance and cooperation must be substituted for rivalry and competition. Disillusionment with the fragmentary nature of historical processes has awakened a new regard for spiritual factors—so that on the wide-flung frontiers of our day the church is impelled to rethink its mission in universal terms. Conditioned by the environment in which it lives, it is being challenged to place new confidence in its spiritual calling and unitedly to array itself against the world-wide secularism which threatens to engulf it.

For the last twenty-five years we have increasingly been reminded of a new spirit and of new signs of union, reunion, and unity that have arisen. In defiance of ancient tradition the new spirit has given birth to the younger churches on the foreign-mission fields; to the rise of United Churches in India, Japan, China, and Canada; and to various types of federative and organic church unions. The same spirit has sought for new orientations in the world-wide discussions on "Faith and Order" and "Life and Work" and at the ecumenical conferences from Stockholm to Amsterdam—where the unity of the Spirit in the Body of Christ was variously reaffirmed. This quest for unity has led to the distrust of a Protestantism refined by cultural sophistications and sociological commitments, and has given rise to a new vision of the one holy Universal Christian Church. In this new atmosphere the Christian churches of the world seem prepared, as never before, to take seriously the prayer of their Lord, *ut omnes unum sint*.

And yet, in the face of these insights, certain restrictive emphases persist which point to the need for a more radical rebirth of the ecumenical spirit. How difficult it is, for example, for denominations to transcend the level of federative union where particular historical legacies continue to be nurtured as embodying the essential beliefs which must be taught, learned, and held as the pure doctrine once delivered to the saints. Or, the impetus for the federation of churches and even for their union may, in some cases, be inspired by practical expediency; the demand for more efficient and effective over-all administration; the romantic desire for a common Protestant front; or by the mere quest for power. Ecumenicity on such sociological levels obviously falls short of the New Testament ideal. Such a super-church federation can not presume to ignore the theological or ecclesiastical sovereignties of its members—churches which individually may assert their loyalty to the ecumenical cause and pride themselves on their religious tolerance and yet remain smugly self-sufficient within their denominational orbits. Such sectarianism of Protestant churches is not essentially different from the ecclesiastical sectarianism of the Roman Church.

Thus the special-witness plea of particular denominations tends to stimulate a resurgence of confessionalistic emphases which do violence to the ecumenical cause. From this restrictive point of view there is no need to surrender loyalties grounded in the traditions of a bygone day. These are rather to be re-explored and consolidated into modern fortresses. The essential criticism of such a position applies not so much against what is said as against what is left unsaid and undone. For how can the denominationalistic plea for a deepening of theological understanding and for the integrity of the specific witness of a denomination be upheld if this leads to the accentuation of differences which condone and perpetuate divisions in the Body of Christ? What we deplore in such an attitude is not the loyalty to a confessional witness but the inability to break through the presumption that such a particular position embodies the final and all-inclusive deposit of the truth necessary to salvation. Denominational zeal, on this level, violates the eternal values to be preserved and compromises the cause of spiritual unity by a rationalistic underestimate of its challenge.

The hope for a more realistic and visible unity of the Church of Christ will not be fulfilled by pious affirmations which fail to break through narrowly conceived confessional boundaries. We are made free not by confessions but alone by the truth— truth which is not contained in any intellectualized pure doctrine but which radiates from the pure doctrine of the spirit. Only when so-called confessions remain hymns of a triumphant faith and do not become legalistic statements of belief will they unify and not divide the Christian Church.

A more radical comprehension of the meaning of ecumenical also seems to be necessary in view of the dubious manner in which the term is sometimes used by American denominations to refer to their own world-wide expansion. Such a denominationally restricted use of the term debases its meaning into something which violates the New Testament spirit and is contrary to its accepted usage in ecumenical discussions. Does such loose use of the term indicate the difficulty or reluctance of denominations to grasp fully the revolutionary significance of the New Testament conception of the Church as the Body of Christ? Thus again, we may be confronted by a hearty acceptance of the idea which is not matched by a correspondingly realistic fellowship of churches among themselves.

Having long spoken of unity and espoused its cause with eloquent word, we Protestants have at last arrived at a point which, in the light of the Reformation, calls for a more critical appraisal of our bondage to history and a more prophetic acceptance of the spiritual direction in which we have been called to move. The ecumenical renewal to which we are committed demands that we do not stop short of conclusions derived from the premises with which we began.

The above mentioned antinomy of history and faith which

continually projects itself can not be resolved on purely historical or rational levels. Within the sociological framework in
which the Church is inextricably woven, the radical orientation
of which we are speaking looks toward recapturing the spiritual
glow of the New Testament conception of the *ecclesia*. This is
the ecumenical hope for the future that the churches of Christendom, by the mysterious and unpredictable guidance of the Holy
Spirit, shall be led to things not yet revealed to the heart and
soul of man.

We, the children of a historical succession, whether of
Zwingli, Luther, Calvin, Knox, Wesley, or some other, cannot,
of course, ignore the forms it has produced. By psychological
and sociological necessity we proceed from the point at which
history has placed us; but at that point we shall have to decide
whether the continuing line shall be dominated by the momentum of historical continuity or whether the thrust of God's
Spirit is strong enough to open our lives to the exciting dis-
coveries of what he still may have to say unto the churches. In
this sense—not in obliterating or bypassing but in critically
passing through inherited historical forms in order thereby to
gain deeper spiritual insights—shall we become the children
of a spiritual succession that traces our lineage to Christ, the
author and perfecter of our faith. We can as little pride ourselves on having Luther, Calvin, or Wesley as our father as the
Pharisees of the Old and New Testament were justified in
claiming for themselves the fatherhood of Abraham.[10]

How will the ecumenical reality of the Church become
evident? Any formal blue-printing of the ecumenical church is
as invidious as the confessional, liturgical and ecclesiastical
formalizations of denominational theologians which threaten
to become more sectarian as they become more precise. The

[10] Mt. 3:9; Jn. 8:39.

self-righteousness vested in loyalty to forms may be as legal-istically deadening to the ecumenical church as it is to indi-vidual denominations. Not, therefore, in the direction of legal-istic formal definitions or of fixed and unified forms will the answer be found but rather in the unreserved committal to the New Testament dynamic of faith and grace. Thus the church of the New Testament has been moving through the centuries, all statutes of historical limitations to the contrary, attempting ever anew to become the one, holy, universal Christian Church.

What then are the *notae* of the ecumenical church which should be increasingly observable and realistically attainable? The answer to this question will be found not so much in the establishment of a new status as in the acceptance of a new direction and a new devotion. The spirit of the ecumenical church, which is Christ's Church and not ours, will express itself, first of all, not in the rigidity of a confession but in the joy of confessing. Churches of this spirit will no longer be anchored to particular creeds as the only adequate deposit of the truth inherited from the past, but will discover their greatest inspiration and joy in witnessing to the resurrected Lord who is "Christ the son of the living God." Whatever steadying in-fluences may yet be derived from inherited sources, these will not accentuate the normative nature of the "specific witness." The luster of such religious leaders as Calvin, Zwingli, Luther, and Wesley shall no longer dim the Light which they merely refract. We shall, then, no longer pray for a stronger confes-sionalistic witness but for a purer Christian experience of the truth which transcends all theological doctrine. In the inspira-tion of an experiential faith we shall ever anew confess the Lordship of the Christ and proclaim the judgment of God over a sinful world.

In the reaffirmation of the New Testament spirit we shall, further, testify to the Catholic unity that is not vested in any canonical order or in the authority of ecclesiastical agencies but that is sealed in the evangelical ministry of service and validated by the presence of the Spirit. In the charismatic function of the ecumenical church all vestiges of officialism will succumb to the spiritual freedom prevailing in the universal priesthood of believers. Ecclesiastical order with organizational and institutional sanctions must bow to the New Testament conception of a fellowship of the faithful established on the principle of diaconal service. The divine mystery of the Church will not be found in its ecclesiastical pretensions but in the miracle of self-effacing love and in the ministration of the Word which preaches redemption. When the simple service-direction of the New Testament Church has been rediscovered, the pride of office and status and the canons of ecclesiastical order will submit to the discipline of love which, since it is not the discipline of an institution but that of a fellowship, can alone guarantee the unity of life and truth.

The church of ecumenical vision will further find its life enriched by a worship emancipated from the thralldom of rites and ceremonies and will extend its benedictions beyond both the bondage of forms and the bondage of informality. At its heart is its spontaneous worship and not its formalized rites and ceremonies. The evangelical comprehension of the Christian fellowship will, therefore, countenance no legalistic restriction of the Table which belongs to the Lord of the Church. Indeed, the organic unity of the Church as the Body of Christ should nowhere become so apparent as in the communion of searching souls at the Lord's Table which has always been considered the innermost sanctuary of Christian worship. Here there will be no self-arrogation of rights and privileges but a humble submission to the Lord of the Church who grants his presence freely to those who desire it.

The ecumenical reality of the Church as thus conceived, although established once-for-all as a witness to Christ's presence in the world, is always being realized anew. From its earth-bound servant-form the living church continually radiates the eternal glory of Christ its Lord. The ecumenical discovery of our day points to the fact that the Church of the risen Lord is not bound to any static forms, but in new manifestations of spiritual power is continually leaving its low-vaulted past to build more stately mansions for the souls of men. The Christian Church is always in process of being born anew of the Holy Spirit; and its ecumenical reality is evidenced by the united fellowship of all confessing Christians in common witness to the one Lord of all.

Untold multitudes are today looking forward to the radical reformation of the denominationalized churches of our time and are praying for their cleansing from the historical remnants of a bygone day which obscure their common derivation and loyalties. With these hopes and prayers in our hearts, we of the Reformation tradition must penitently confess that, having started from the New Testament, we lost its sense of direction and in the wilderness and confusion of our human strivings have pitched our tents by the wayside. In repentant mood we acknowledge our guilt for the wounds and mutilations inflicted on his body. Only on the common ground of repentance will our sinful divisions break down.

The ecumenical perspective of our day takes us to a mountain peak from where, over a span of 400 years, we may see the various ways in which the Protestant churches of the world perpetuated their divisions and rivalries. But we also observe how the Spirit of God has been transforming and awakening the hearts of his stubborn children to embrace the Truth which ever anew breaks forth from his Word. The tensions between history and faith, the visible and invisible, are not to be understood in a static sense; they point to a continuing realization of the ends already envisaged in the New Testament. Ultimate unity, then, is not ecclesiastical but eschatological. The congregation of the faithful is constantly waiting for the further fulfillment of the unity found in God's grace and truth. Here alone is grounded the ecumenical reality of the Church.

THE RELEVANCE OF REFORMATION DOCTRINE IN OUR DAY

Reinhold Niebuhr

IN the history of culture and civilization the Reformation is one of the two roots of "modernity," the other root being the Renaissance. A typical modern idealist is interested in the Reformation primarily as a milestone in the story of modern man's revolt against authority. Luther's heroic defiance, "Here I stand; I can do no other; so help me God," is appreciatively reviewed in the history of thought as one of the landmarks in man's emancipation from dogmatism, as a symbol of the individual's right and capacity to challenge restrictions upon his conscience.

There is a dimension of the Reformation which fits into this estimate of its significance. But that is not the dimension which is most important in the history of faith and theology. From the standpoint of the Christian faith the most important insight and achievement is summed up in the doctrine of justification by faith and not in the doctrine of the priesthood of all believers. The reason that this is so is that the doctrine of justification contains within it the final acceptance by the Christian church of an ultimate scriptural truth, which has been persistently obscured both before and after the Reformation. That truth relates to the permanent and perpetual ambiguity of the human situation, even in the life of the church and in the virtue of the redeemed. The Reformation insisted that the righteous, as well as the obvious sinners, were not justified in God's sight by their virtues, not even if they ascribed their goodness to the grace of God. It recognized that the final reconciliation between man and God was by the mercy of God and not by any human goodness. It insisted that the divine forgiveness was not merely the initial act in God's reconciliation with man upon which human goodness could be subsequently erected; but rather that divine forgiveness was the perpetual necessity even of the redeemed and the perpetual possibility of the God who had been revealed in Christ.

It is unnecessary to record with what elemental force this insight of the gospel, particularly of the Pauline interpretation of the meaning of God's revelation in Christ broke into the church and upon the world. It resulted in the startling indictment of the church, which fancied itself the guardian of the mysteries of Christ, as being involved in the ultimate evil of anti-Christ. It shattered the carefully built up scheme of graded righteousness according to which monastic virtue could claim a greater religious security than the ordinary goodness of ordinary Christians. It brought into the open what every Christian must know in his own experience; namely, that a geuine conversion and a turning of the heart from self-will to God's will means freedom from anxiety and sin and yet not freedom from anxiety and sin. It acknowledged that there is in every confession of faith, if it is honest, an admission of doubt; "I believe Lord, help thou mine unbelief." It confessed that Christian faith triumphs over the fear of death and yet does not triumph over it, for the root of anxiety remains in the heart of even the redeemed. It realized that men may be delivered from the bondage of self and yet remain, when measured under the final judgment, selfish men. In short it insisted that the redeemed are *simul justus et peccator,* righteous and sinners at once. It applied this insight not only to the lives of individual men but also to the institutions of grace and insisted that the church, which from one perspective, is the very body of Christ, is never-theless involved, as an historical institution, in the crucifixion of Christ.

This insight of the Reformation marks a pinnacle in the history of the Christian faith. The Reformation is the point in history where everything implied in Christ's parable of the Pharisee and Publican is made applicable not merely to the particular Pharisees with whom Christ contended but with the perpetual Pharisaism of the human heart. It is the point where the community of the faithful recognize that Christ's ironic words—that he came to call not the righteous but sinners to repentance, and that the sick, rather than those who are whole, need a physician—is meant for every community of men who imagine themselves whole rather than sick, including those who have been made whole by the redemption of Christ.

The Pathos of the Cultural Struggle

We are now in a tragic period of history in which this final religious insight of the reformation is desperately needed for the spiritual health of our generation; and yet it seems com-pletely unavailable to the modern man, whether secular or Christian. It is on this final point of religious insight that the spiritual heritage of the Reformation has relevance for us. Yet it is precisely this final point which seems completely irrelevant to modern man. The truth of the gospel as recovered by the Reformation is needed precisely because our world is perishing in a conflict between various types of idealists who are so busy establishing their own righteousness that more of them have subjected their righteousness to the righteousness of God. If these idealists are ever to establish community with one another it will have to be done through a spirit of forgiveness, rooted in humility and contrition. But all the idealists are much too idealistic to recognize the ambiguity in all forms of human idealism. The very idealism which has submerged the spirituality of the Reformation has created the situation in which the truth of the gospel recovered by the Reformation is so urgently needed.

The cultural struggle of our day is usually interpreted as a conflict between communism and the spirit of democracy. Actually it is a tri-cornered struggle between Catholicism, communism, and a sadly disintegrated but yet still vigorous liberal secular society. The conflict between Catholicism and secularism is a profound one, partly because secularism does not understand the final problems of the human spirit with which the Christian faith deals; and partly because Catholicism falsely accuses the secular idealist of moral relativism and nihilism. Yet this conflict gives way to a general alliance between Catholicism and the liberal society based upon a common hatred and fear of communism. The conservative portion of the liberal society fears the communist threat to the institution of property. Catholicism fears the communist threat to the traditional societies of eastern Europe, where its intimate historic relation to a vestigial feudalism feeds the propaganda flames of communism.

There is a profound pathos in this triangular struggle. Consider the spiritual position of each one of the contestants. Catholicism, precisely because its polemical struggle with the Reformation hardened its doctrines of sanctification, is blind to the political ambiguities in which it is involved. It is always defending Christ against anti-Christ. The Pope assures the world that the struggle between the good and the evil is daily becoming more clear cut. Actually, the present struggle in the world is like all previous struggles. It is so tragic because there is truth among the cohorts of falsehood; and falsehood among the defenders of the truth. The Catholic church desperately de-

fends its "Christian" civilization, without fully recognizing
that this civilization is *in extremis* not because it is Christian
but because it has covered the untenable institutions of a de-
cadent feudalism with the sanctity of Christ. It tries to caste
Cardinal Mindzenty in the role of a pure Christian martyr but
will not admit that Hungarian feudalism was rightfully challenged by the communists and wrongly defended by the
Cardinal. The struggle against communism could be won
more easily if there were more recognition in the Catholic
church of the moral ambiguity of all political positions, including those of Catholic politics, and if the historic church were
not falsely given an absolute sanctity. "Everyone knows," declared the Pope recently, "that the Church is never actuated by
worldly motives." That is exactly what everyone does not know.
The whole history of modern secularism is partly a justified
cynicism, bred by the church's pretensions of absolute sanctity.

    The polemic of Catholicism against secularism assumes that
those who believe in God also do the will of God and that those
who do not believe in God merely follow their own interests.
Actually, those who believe in God are in danger of claiming
too easily that they are God's allies; and those who do not
believe in God do not merely follow their own interest, though
they do have a much too complacent view of their own virtue.
The liberal society, embattled against communism, believed
that a free play of all economic forces would make for justice.
This is not the case. Actually such a free play makes for the
concentration of power in a technical society. And the injustices consequent upon that concentration of power were
the cause of the proletarian communist revolt against the liberal
society. The liberal society believed that every extension of
reason and power of nature automatically made for increased
human welfare. Suddenly it was confronted by the obvious

moral ambiguity of atomic energy, potentially useful to society but immediately a great peril. The uneasy conscience of some of the atomic scientists, who meant to do good but found themselves involved in evil, was the first experience of typically modern men, relevant to the Christian interpretation of human existence. The liberal society believed that a technically integrated world would easily solve its problems in the creation of a world state. Now it finds that the Russians, whose fears were supposed to be beguiled by a world state, actually regard the conception of a world state as the propaganda tool of "western imperialists." On every hand the world of the western, secular idealists dissolves into moral ambiguity. Clericals and anti-clericals eye each other with suspicion. But both are in darkness about themselves since each knows little or nothing about the sins of the righteous, and each remains blissfully and tragically ignorant of the justified charges which the critical observer may bring against the citadel of their virtues and achievements.

Against a Catholic, semi-feudal world and a secular capitalist-democratic world the new political religion of communism has raised its banners of revolt. Communism is a religion which has corrupted the Christian vision of a Kingdom of God upon earth. It separated the part of the Christian faith contained in the prayer, "Thy kingdom come upon earth," from that part of the Christian faith—most clearly apprehended in the Reformation—in which the taint of sin on all historic achievements is recognized. It sought for a kingdom of perfect justice, a classless and universal society. It vulgarized this dream even more than did bourgeois secularism. For it thought that the abolition of the institution of property would assure a harmonious society and ultimately a sinless human nature. Thus is promised a Kingdom of God without repentance. It appealed furthermore to the pride of men by assuring the poor that all the evils in the world came from the rich, from the bourgeoisie. Its casting the proletariat into the role of a redeemed and re-deeming class in society was a vulgarization of the gospel beatitude: "Blessed are the poor."

On every point the communist creed was both nearer and farther from the Christian Gospel than the moral complacency of liberal secularism. It understood, as liberalism does not, that cultures and communities stand under judgment and may be destroyed by their sins. But it did not understand that the executors of judgment are also sinful. It knew that the poor are closer to the kingdom of God than the rich. But it did not realize that when a poor man becomes a powerful commissar he has lost his original virtue. It knew that the resentments of the victims of injustice may be the motive force of revolution. But it did not understand that there is destructive fury as well as the spirit of justice in this resentment. It knew that history does not have any natural harmonies as nature has. Yet it falsely imagined that it could establish a pure harmony of all social forces on the other side of the revolution.

The fury and fanaticism of communism is falsely ascribed to its atheism or materialism. Actually, the real peril of com-munism arises from the consistency of its self-righteousness. It is a universalist idealism, dreaming of a world community, which has become corrupted by Russian nationalism. It is a dream of an anarchistic millennium degenerated into a vexatious tyranny. It hopes for a brotherly world where every one will give according to his ability and take according to his need. In fact, it lives in a world of hate and double-dealing.

However we may criticize the horrible perversion of the original dream and whatever tears we may shed over the trans-mutation of a nice dream into a terrible nightmare, we must not fail to notice that communism has merely raised the self-delusions of idealists to a more implausible point than its Christian and secular competitors. Thus the world is locked in a partly triangular and partly simple conflict between various idealists who walk in the darkness of self-delusion. Each one sees the sins of the other but no one heeds the warning of St. Paul: "Whosoever thou art that judges, thou thyself doest the same thing."

THE CULTURAL WEAKNESS OF PROTESTANTISM

The question arises, what has become of the insights of the Reformation in this situation? Why have they not been brought to bear upon the problem of our day?

It is easy enough to understand why secular liberalism, Catholicism, and communism are bereft of the Reformation insight. They represent forms of secular and religious idealism which are historically in defiance of it. We do not equate these various forms of idealism by indicting them for a common lack of insight into the perpetual moral ambiguity in all human achievements. Catholicism, for instance, has a genuine Christian understanding of the human situation at ultimate points which both liberalism and communism lack. It knows that human virtue is by grace and not by simple human achievement. It also knows something of the continued sinfulness of all men; but it does not conceive this fact radically enough. Thus it is able to denominate some men officially as "saints" and to prescribe the conditions for higher than ordinary forms of righteousness and virtue through monastic discipline. But its real error lies in its inability to see the moral ambiguity in the "Christian" civilizations which it constructs and in the historic ecclesiastical institution which pretends to stand as guardian over its Christian values, when in reality its own pride and power are challenged, in the historical vicissitudes which bring all civilizations under judgment.

The liberal society may rightly claim the virtue of establishing human freedom against the constraints of a religiously sanctified traditional agrarian society. But the liberal society does not understand the problems of community, wrongly believing that community and justice are the inevitable by-products of freedom. Actually justice and community must be carefully contrived against the perils of human selfishness. These perils do not diminish but grow under conditions of a dynamic technical society.

The communist movement may rightly claim the virtue of challenging the moral pretensions of both the traditional-feudal and the modern liberal-capitalist world. But it was unable to do this without breeding new and more terrible illusions which lead to the final annulment of all human liberties and which create the fanatic fury of a consistent self-righteousness. The absence of the final Christian insight in these forms of idealism need not be explained. Rather it explains how each of them obscures the evil mixed with its virtues in various proportions, precisely because it does not know that evil is always mixed with good in every historic situation.

The real question is why the Reformation was unable to make its most characteristic insight more effective in the life of our culture, particularly in view of the desperate necessity of its application to the life of individuals and nations. The answer to this queston is manifold. One reason is that the human heart is so perpetually prone to self-righteousness that no historic insight can guarantee the triumph of grace over it. Protestant Christian politics is frequently as sure of its special sanctity as the Catholic variety. The Calvinist politics of our own early Massachusetts theocracy and of contemporary Holland has generated religious self-righteousness, undistinguish-able from that of Catholic politics. The Lutheran side of the Reformation, on the other hand, illustrated another difficulty. A religious position which recognizes the error and ambiguity in all political positions is easily tempted to a position of irresponsibility and neutrality in the great struggles for human justice. Such neutrality in turn always tends toward the factual support of the forces of the status quo, as Lutheran conserva-tism in Europe amply illustrates. The radical emphasis upon the doctrine of jusification by faith in the Neo-Reformation thought of the so-called dialetical theology, has been rather in-consistent in overcoming this neutrality. In its original version it weakened the spiritual resistance against Nazism by em-phasizing the moral ambiguity of all political alternatives to Nazism. Subsequently it entered the lists against Nazism to the point at which Karl Barth could give the assurance that a Czech soldier, fighting against Germany, was really a defender of the Christian faith. More recently the Barthian emphasis has tended to revert to the original position of neutrality, content to warn western Europe that there is little to choose between western capitalism and Russian communism.

These vagaries of modern radical Protestantism prove that the Reformation principle represents a final point of religious judgment upon all of life which is not easily and consistently brought into creative relationship with the necessary task of making proximate judgment in history and of preserving and extending proximate forms of justice and human virtue. The injunction and warning of our Lord, "Judge not that ye be not judged," is indispensable at the final limits of life. Yet we do have to judge and execute judgments. All proximate forms of justice in civilization and of virtue in human life depend upon our willingness to risk relative judgments. In short, Protes-

tantism failed to bring the full force of the Reformation principle to bear upon the life of cultures and civilization either
because the principle was lost in the exigencies of actual historic
struggles or because it became a principle of sheer criticism,
the purity of which was so jealously guarded, that it lamed
creative action in history. These various inadequacies in the
application of final Reformation insight, must make us cir-
cumspect in seeking to apply it freshly to the present historic
situation. For they prove that there are pitfalls to the right
and to the left in every effort to apply it. Here, as in every
other ultimate Christian insight, the rule applies: "Strait is the
gate and narrow is the way, that leadeth unto life."

The Relevance of Justification by Faith

The problem which we confront in relating the principle of
justification by faith to the twin concept of sanctification is
how we apply the ultimate religious insight about the ambiguity of all human achievements to the discriminations
which are required for the achievement of virtue in individual
life and of justice in the collective life of mankind. There are
tremendous differences between good men and bad men, between selfish and unselfish people. Some men are almost completely caught in the bondage of self-worship and others have
given their hearts to God in Christ and achieve a measure of
real sanctity. Yet in the ultimate instance "In God's sight,"
at the final religious dimension of life, the gospel is right and
the Reformation interpretation of the gospel is true: Even good
men are sinners and their wills are in contradicton to the divine
will. They are in contradiction because of the persistence of
self-interest in the life of even the redeemed. Men know this
about themselves only in hours of sincere prayer when they
face him, before whom "all hearts are open, all desires are

known and from whom so secrets are hid." When righteous
men contend against unrighteous men, when defenders of the
truth stand in conflict with liars they are of course impressed
by their righteousness. Yet what men know about themselves
only in the sincerest hours of prayer all men know about each
other. Their foibles, their jealousies, their petty vanities are the
common currency of estimates which their fellows make of
even good men. It is when the final insight of prayer is not
diffused through the ordinary self-righteous self-estimates of
men that self-righteousness turns into a monstrous evil and
becomes the instrument of fanaticism and fury.

Obviously it is not possible or desirable to wipe out the distinction between good and evil on the ordinary levels of life.
Men must not be "weary in well-doing." They must not allow
the fact that, after they have done all that they could, they
"remain unprofitable servants" tempt them to do less than all
they can. The religious insight about the sinfulness of all men
must not efface the distinctions between good and evil. The
admonition of Jesus, "Judge not that ye be not judged," and of
St. Paul, "Who art thou that judges another; we must all be
made manifest before the judgment seat of Christ," cannot be
simply obeyed in the sense that we can dispense with comparative moral judgments about ourselves and our brothers.
The ultimate truth, contained in the scriptural interpretation of
life, cannot, however, be simply dismissed any more than it can
be simply obeyed. Its dismissal leads to moralistic illusions.
Simple obedience to it leads to neutrality in all the significant
moral struggles of history. The only other possibility is that
this insight color all other insights, generate a religious reservation on all judgment which we make about each other and
create the atmosphere in which mutual forbearance and forgiveness becomes possible. The final paradox of the gospel

morality is that the highest form of goodness, namely, the goodness of forgiving love, is possible only to those who know themselves to be sinners.

If we apply this answer not only to individual life but also to the collective life of mankind, we may find a resource for the strife between the protagonists of contradictory ideals which threatens to destroy our civilization. Nations, classes, cultures and civilization do not, of course, in their collective consciousness, ever pray or experience the judgment and mercy of God as revealed in Christ. They are for that reason constitutionally self-righteous. But it is possible for the church, as that part of a culture and civilization in which the final truth about life as revealed in Christ is known, to mediate the ultimate truth as a leaven in a lump.

If we consider our own liberal society first, we must not expect it to be other than it is; a society created by middle class forces working to establish themselves against the feudal aristocracy. They required a greater degree of liberty and secured it. The liberties of the bourgeois world have virtues beyond the needs of bourgeois life. But they were not established in pure disinterestedness and are not maintained out of devotion to pure ideals. The middle class world tends not only to value liberty too highly but also to hide the interested character of its devotion. A religious criticism of its pretensions would not impart a complete moral justification for the position of its foes, whether feudal or communist. Nor need it lame the will of self-defense of such a society. A genuine leaven of religious humility would, in fact, make the liberal society more capable of spiritual self-defense. For it would destroy the self-delusions, the exaggerated emphases on freedom, the indifference toward problems of justice and community which tend to make the society unworthy and incapable of defense against its competitors. The final degradation of Reformation doctrine is to equate the Reformation emphasis upon religious liberty with the bourgeois desire for freedom from all political and moral restraints. The creative possibility of the Reformation doctrine is that it discloses to a culture that it is justified only by faith and that its achievements are morally ambiguous.

There is unfortunately only a slight opportunity to bring the Reformation doctrine to bear either upon the remnants of feudal society or upon communistic society. The former is spiritually dominated by Catholicism and the latter by a new secular political religion. It is possible, however, to challenge from a Reformation standpoint, the pretension of Catholicism that a Cardinal Mindzenty, for instance, is a pure Christian martyr who sacrificed his liberty and risked his life in a communist state for the sake of the ultimate Christian sanctities. We must not deny or obscure the common treasures of grace which we have with the Catholic version of the Christian faith. But neither must we fail to lay bare the intolerable religious sanctification of the feudal order in which Catholicism is involved in such nations as Hungary and other eastern European states, when the feudal order was preserved beyond its day precisely because Catholicism was the dominant spiritual force.

As for communism with its illusions of perfection, its belief in a redeemed and redeeming class, its confidence in perfect justice on the other side of the revolution, its inability to understand the nationalistic corruptions in its universalistic dreams, its identification of egotism with greed and its consequent inability to recognize the corruptions of the lust for power in the idealism of its elite: all these errors are so monstrous and so consistently imbedded in a total system of delusion and illusion that it is quite impossible to reach a communist believer with the truth about the human situation.

From the standpoint of the Reformation principle it is possible, however, to stand rigorously against the communist culture and yet recognize that the communist fury is merely a more consistent form of the self-righteousness which corrupts every human heart. We can recognize what is true in communism and understand it as an inevitable ideology of the proletarian revolt against a bourgeois society without capitulating to its falsehoods. For we know that truth and falsehood, good and evil are mixed in various proportions in all human achievements. We can, furthermore, recognize that the evils of communism, however monstrous, are merely extravagant forms of the pride and self-delusion to which the human heart is prone. Whether it be the tribalism of Nazism or the false universalism of communism, there are no evils in human history which are altogether unique or which derive from pure malice. Pure malice is about as rare in history as pure virtue. The evils of history are corruptons of the good; and extravagant evils are corruptions which do not recognize the mixture of good and evil in all human ambitions.

The fact that an evil, against which we must battle, is not motivated by pure malice, does not render it innocuous. We have responsibilities toward our own cultures and civilizations, which include their defense against historic foes. There is no possibility of a pure religious insight upon the ambiguities of all historic virtues, resolving the conflict between them absolutely. We are men and not God. We are rooted in particular points in the process of history; and we cannot view our duties *sub specie aeternitatis*. We can, however, preserve the religious sense of a judgment beyond our judgment. Thus a religious and moral humility may qualify our historic judgments and prevent us from aggravating the vices of our culture by over-estimating its virtues. It can also furnish the ground upon which ultimate reconciliation between ourselves and our foes must be achieved.

Thus the ultimate truth of the gospel, as discerned in the Reformation, does not contain a simple political-moral possibility upon which civilizations are constructed. Nor is it a principle of criticism which indiscriminately negates all historic achievements. It is, however, the disclosure of a dimension of life which can prevent the decay and help the renewal of civilizations and which may mitigate the fury of competitive forms of righteousness.